the POLYTECHNIC SCHOOL of VALUES

by Don Koberg and Jim Bagnall

The Polytechnic School of Values [VALUES TECH] is a portable school contained entirely within the pages of this book and any personal notebooks which may accompany it. By attending to its curriculum of lessons, workshops and laboratory experiments which are designed to reveal personal values, a reader may become more aware of the importance of developing decision-making skills and begin to gain knowledge and practice toward that end. VALUES TECH provides few answers; it simply presents the opportunity to find answers of your own. Its pages include guidance in procedure and method but it remains for each reader to benefit according to personally determined investments of time and energy.

As it is for most learning experiences, the introduction to new knowledge, skills and attitudes requires a share of "dues" to be paid. The awkwardness of the new can bring frustrations. New behavior means leaving the security of old ways behind. Dealing with life in a more conscious way requires greater effort. But the reward for all the effort is a greater appreciation of life.

The work involves establishing criteria, determining meaning, choosing, selecting and deciding between things. It includes comparing the options in life with your personal intentions for a good life and, in general, coming to grips with the value and worth of the bits and pieces of your experiences.

DEDICATION

TO JANUS, the first to be mentioned in prayer
TO JANUS, custodian of the universe
TO JANUS, opener and fastener of all things
TO JANUS, looking inward and outward from the gate

```
Library of Congress Cataloging in Publication Data
   Koberg, Don, 1930-
     Values tech : a portable school for discovering &
   developing decision-making skills and self-enhancing
   potentials.

     1. Success.  2. Decision-making.  I. Bagnall, Jim,
   joint author.  II. Title.
   BF637.S8K622      158'.1       75-19488
   ISBN 0-913232-24-6
```

© copyright 1976, William Kaufmann, Inc.

WILLIAM KAUFMANN, INC.
One First Street, Los Altos, California 94022

We extend an invitation
    to people in their teens, 20's, 30's, 40's, 50's and older
    to those on their way through school, college and university
    to those out of school who still wonder what it all meant
    to those who are working at a job and to those who are not
    to those who suspect that there's more to life than they have found so far
    to everyone — to you.

Join us in a relaxed informal environment for easy-going discussion of highly important personal matters. We'll try to help you take a closer, more objective look at yourself, your potentials, your daily life and your plans for tomorrow. There are many books that treat these subjects separately and from a "scientific" perspective. They may provide much information but offer little help in a collective practical application. Our readers will also find many important facts and methods dealing with the separate subjects of values and decision theory in this curriculum, but we have attempted to present them in a simple, usefully combined and enjoyable manner. The language used is "plain speak" to make the task of choosing directions in keeping with your potentials more comfortable and natural.

REGISTER NOW!

Are you already securely in control of your life? If so, you are a lucky member of society. But if you, like many, experience only **occasional bits of self-insight, we urge you to accept our invitation to join us at** VALUES TECH **in an attempt to deepen the intent and meaning of life.**

Western society is in the throes of major readjustments. Familiar values and behavior patterns are being reviewed and revised. In this period of fast change, many of us still seek to enrich the content of our lives; to establish harmonious rapport with nature; to develop credibility. In order to keep from stumbling across the threshold to the future, we need to develop a rich imagination and to be able to see with clear eyes. And we need to build an evaluative attitude so as to become consciously aware of the consequences of our intentions and acts.

Each passing day costs us another 24 hours of precious life. If we spend each day wisely, in a self-directed manner, we are well on our way toward achieving a happy, fulfilling personal and social life. If you have already come to grips with the necessity of planning your tomorrows, we invite you to continue with us in discovering more about how to deal with the choices in life; how to help make your own dreams come true.

the Campus DIRECTORY

VALUES TECH

An Invitation to Enroll 3	**INTRODUCTORY LEVEL**
The Pay-As-You-Go Plan 8	**The Year of Decisions** 53
Goals of the School 9	**Lesson No.1** "The Universal Life Process" ... 54
Our Creed 9	**Lesson No.2** "Let's See Now" 56
School Supplies 10	(decision-making)
Getting Acquainted 10	**Techniques: DM 1** - How to play the role of 59
Why Choose VALUES TECH ? 11	the project manager in charge of operations
Grading System 13	at both the George Gallup Corp. & the
Enrollment Form 15	Reuben H. Donnelly Corp. at the same time
Good For You 16	(establishing criteria)
Prerequisites 17	**DM 2** - How to reduce 31 flavors into one 60
Basic Tools	double dip cone (all purpose method)
Thinking and Expecting 17	**DM 2X** - United we stand (variation of DM-2) .. 61
Thinking Methods 19	**DM 3** - Rank & File (ranking criteria) 61
Inductive Thinking 20	**DM 4** - Do get ahead of yourself 63
Deductive Thinking 20	(consequences)
Analysis and Reason 21	**DM 5** - Down deep 64
Review 22	(improving criteria quality)
A Basic Text 23	**DM 6** - Osgood, et al 64
Logic 23	(better criterion statements)
How to Make Lists in a More Creative Way ...24	**DM 7** - The hard way (classic technique) 65
Entrance Exams 25	**DM 8** - Algorithmics (thinking technique) 66
Vade Mecum 25	**DM 9** - Clarence Darrow (the standard legal ... 67
Why Self-Find ? 26	guide to decision making)
Self-Inventory 27	Six tips for decision making 67
Fear 27	"Study Buddy" (a special lesson in group 68
66 You Ares 29	decision making)
Classes Begin 49	Eight guidelines to better group decisions 69
Words to the Wise 50	

4

INTERMEDIATE LEVEL
Dealing with Personal Values 71
Lesson No.1 "Who? Me?" (a lesson in ethics) ... 72
Laboratory Exercises 72
Exercise No.1 "Man-on-the-street" 72
   (expressing values)
Exercise No.2 "Trip for two" 73
   (examining values)
Exercise No.3 "60 seconds" 74
   (expressing values)
Lesson No.2 "Believe it or not" 75
   (a lesson in philosophy)
Laboratory Exercises 76
Exercise No.1 "Adjectives" 76
   (describing values)
Exercise No.2 "Reactions" 76
   (examining values)
Exercise No.3 "Man of tomorrow" 77
   (prediction as a value-revealing method)
Exercise No.4 "Monkey see" 77
   (further defining concepts)
Lesson No.3 "Oldies but Goodies" 78
   (a lesson in the classics)
Laboratory Exercises
Exercise No.1 "Dear Old Dad" 78
   (past and future values)
Exercise No.2 "Queen for a Day" 79
   (recording values)
Lesson No.4 "Values across Time"
   (a lesson in history)
Laboratory Exercises
Western mankind: a chart 84
Exercise No.1 "How It Really Was" 85
   (exploring viewpoints)
Exercise No.2 "Questions for Today" 86
   (developing beliefs)
Exercise No.3 "Guaranteed Forever" 86
   (value insurance)
Lesson No.5 "The Big Values Lesson" 87
Section V-1 Values is 87
Section V-2 Human needs 89
   "The Source of Necessity"; a chart
Section V-3 Values pyramid 94
Section V-4 Values chains 94
Section V-5 Encyclopedia of values 95
The Annual Values Tech Workshop in Values & Valuation (a special lesson) 102
Programme 103
Prayer 104
Schedule of events:
1st Day Exercises
"Truth out of Friction" (conflict of values) ... 105
"Warm up" 107
"Bloody Mary or Southern Comfort" 108
"The Price Is Right" 109
"Dichotomy" 110
"Polyglot" 110
"Peace in Our Time" 111
2nd day Exercises
"The Fine Print" (value inferences) 112
"They, The People" 114
"Boy Girl Boy Girl" 115
"Fortune Cookie" 115
"Symbol Simon" 116
"Take It Or Leave It" 117
"Yuck, Yetch, Bleah" 118
3rd day Exercises
"The Dollar Value Games" (truth worth) .. 119
Game one
Part I "Fetch and Tell" 122
   (discovering the need for criteria)
Part II "Show and Tell" 123
Part III "Wish I'd Said That" 123
   (comparing reasons for what we do)
Game two
"Pass the Bucks" (actual worth) 124
Game three
"Big Mac" (hidden value) 124
Game Four
"What Does it Mean to Have a 125
   'Helpful' place to shop?"
4th day Exercises
"Intramurals" (values in competition) ... 126
1. "Pennywise" 126
2. "Sweet tooth" 127
3. "Waste Not—Want Not" 128
4. "What's It Worth T'Ya?" 129
5. "Eros and Thanatos" 130
6. "Nonsense?" 131
Closing remarks 132

ADVANCED LEVEL
Turning values and abilities into plans 133
Lesson No.1 "There, But for the Grace 135
   of God, Go I!"
   (a lesson in goals, aims and intentions)
Laboratory Exercises
Exercise No.1 "Goal Mine" (digging for goals) 136
Exercise No.2 "Banner Year" 140
   (self-expression)
Exercise No.3 "Happy New Year" 140
   (resolutions)
Exercise No.4 "That's Not My Job, Man" ... 141
   (purposes)
Exercise No.5 "Where Does Love Fit In?" .. 141
   ((priorities)
Exercise No.6 "Give Me Strength to See ... 142
   the Light, O Lord" (abstracting intentions)
Exercise No. 7 "Said Another Way" 142
   (expressing intentions)

Exercise No.8 "A Curriculum in Consumer ... 143
  Intelligence" (planning)
Exercise No.9 "You Can Only Have One" 143
Lesson No.2 "What's In A Name?" 144
  (a lesson in criteria and objectives)
Laboratory exercises
Exercise No.1 "What It Takes" 147
  (developing criteria)
Exercise No.2 "Rules and Regulations" 148
  (developing criteria II)
Exercise No.3 "Amen" 148
  (behavior as expressions of criteria)
Exercise No.4 "Vive le Difference" 148
  (criteria finding)
Exercise No.5 "You Can Be the Architect" ... 149
  (responding to criteria)
Exercise No.6 "Boiling Down" 150
  (ranking criteria)
Exercise No.7 "Quantity & Quality" 151
  (measuring objectives)
Exercise No.8 "Polyvision" 153
  (a lesson in general studies)

Lesson No.3
Laboratory exercises
Exercise No.1 "Find a Need and Fill It" 157
  (needs & goals)
Exercise No.2 "Differences" 157
  (measuring fulfillment)
Exercise No.3 "Hard Luck" 158
  (contingencies)
Exercise No.4 "Score Cards" 159
  (evaluation)
Exercise No.5 "Consensus Made Me Do It" ... 162
  (self-decision)
Exercise No.6 "Consumer Reports" 164
  (ranking criteria II)

Lesson No.4 "Good Grades" 164
  (a special lesson in the evaluation
  of achievement for students)
Laboratory exercises
Exercise No.1 "Hop, Skip & Jump" 168
  (incremental evaluation)
Exercise No.2 "Outsight and Insight" 169
  (interpersonal evaluation)
Exercise No.3 "How to Be a Bookkeeper" 170
  (evaluative record keeping)

Exercise No.4 "What Can You Show Me?" ... 171
  (producing by-products that sell)
Lesson No.5 "Silver Bullet" 173
  (a lesson in contingency management)
Laboratory exercises
Exercise No.1 "Go Ahead, Hit Me!" 176
  (negative reinforcement)
Exercise No.2 "Booga-Booga" 177
  (blocks to achievement)
Lesson No.6 "Ad Valorem" 177
  (a lesson in consumerism)
Laboratory exercises
Exercise No.1 "How to Be a Satisfied 179
  Customer" (developing positive expectations)
Exercise No.2 "Off with the Old" 181
  (renewal)
Exercise No.3 "Have a Nice Life" 182
  (quality lifting)
Exercise No.4 "Bargain Day?" 183
  (evaluative thinking)
Exercise No.5 "Free Kittens" 185
  (hidden costs)
Lesson No.7 "Out Beyond Goals" 187
  (a lesson in planning for interdependence)
Laboratory exercises
Exercise No.1 "Hot Links" 188
  (finding interpersonal and social connections)
Exercise No.2 "Mythology" 190
  (enhancing connections)
Exercise No.3 "Your Own Dice" 192
  (increasing your chances)

"Life-Style Review" (An Annual Event for ... 194
  Advanced Students)
Session one 194
The tragedy or comedy of being myself 196
Exercises 196
Session two 206
Exercises 207
The Final Week Review: 211
  "Remodeling: A Fresh Start"
How to Avoid Getting in Your Own Way 211
Twenty-three self-enhancement methods ... 213
Commencement Exercises 226
Diploma 231
The Library 232
The School Secretary's File (index) 235
The Alumni Office (feedback) 237

VALUES TECH

Home of the Famous Universal Life Process Curriculum
("It Can Be A Valuable Experience For You")

Words of Welcome from Our President

"Welcome to **VALUES TECH**, the school where you discover what you value and learn how to value what you discover. Here you will begin to learn more about who and what you are and what you believe. We will help you learn how to make decisions and choices, especially with regard to your own desires and opportunities in life.

"Making decisions without a method for keeping things in order is like taking a trip without ever consulting a map, watching for signs along the way, or using some type of travel guide.

"Practical success involves having a reasonable knowledge of values and decision-making theory as well as skill in application. As for theory, we get that from observation and analytical research, from the whole body of knowledge representing the collective recorded experience of all our forebearers. And we derive and develop skills by our repeated attempts to apply theory to real life and by evaluating our performance to identify any improvements. Books are written, lectures are delivered and schools are founded because some of us want to guide others through the theory and practice of the ever-changing 'life process.'

"Even though you may already have lots of fun things going for you in life, you can't be sure you are moving in personally intended directions without an overall plan. A handy kit of hard-working tools for operating on the large and small decisions in life is a practical necessity for a self-controlled life. But even with such a tool kit, you can still end up using the wrong tool on the job at hand. Or, you might realize you've selected the wrong job in the first place. (Having a hammer doesn't mean we know how to use it or what to bang it on.) So our aim at the Polytechnic School of Values is to equip you with the proper tools—consciousness of your process, planning techniques, awareness of interdependencies, decision-making methods—and to help you sharpen the tools you already have—for knowing yourself and evaluating your hopes and dreams and making the best of them for yourself and those closest to you.

"Godspeed to you all."

— President Brandywine

the PAY-AS-YOU-GO plan
• • •

VALUES TECH differs from some schools, where many potential students do not even dare to apply or attend public lectures or seek advice because they fear initial high costs. Our pay-as-you-go plan works without undue hardship or anxiety. At VALUES TECH, students are charged only for benefits received. For few benefits, there is only a small charge. As the desire for benefits increases, however, the dues increase accordingly. If the student seeks great benefit, great commitment should be expected. (Beware of paying dues for nebulous benefits or immeasurable values. Caveat Emptor!)

Tuition at VALUES TECH is based on each student's requirements for achievement. In much the same way, our graduates later will receive salaries in amounts commensurate with their abilities. Should a student desire only a quick survey of the course material, the cost in time and energy will be minimal. But if a careful comparative and analytic study coupled with concentrated laboratory application is the goal, a much higher payment is required.

Participation in the curriculum at VALUES TECH can be accomplished in several ways.

A. The Classical Approach - A teacher (learning facilitator) utilizes a classroom, schedules regular meetings, and plays the role of lecturer and/or laboratory instructor. Students attend lectures (or read and discuss them in seminar groups) and perform experiments which are later discussed and evaluated.

B. The School-in-a-Book Approach - Individual readers program it for themselves and do it all by themselves, methodically progressing from the first lesson to the last in a self-regulating program motivated by a personal need or goal.

C. The Reader's Choice Approach - No fixed pattern. Sometimes-this-and-at-other-times-that approach, never pinning one's self down to any single approach, but always responding to what seems most comfortable at the time.

D. The Guidebook Approach - Readers use the text and exercises as a portable companion along the paths to the realization of their dreams. Moving first to the Curriculum Index or Library, they then check out the section pertinent to their special requirements and pick up hints for continuing their personal journeys.

E. The Bedside or Bathroom Companion Approach - VALUES TECH is used as a casual reference book or for short-term browsing, picked up and read occasionally and then begun again later at a random place. No heavy benefits are expected because no large amounts of time and energy are invested.

As you see, VALUES TECH itself remains open 24 hours a day, every day of the year. Ours is an open-end format; books, teachers and classroom/laboratories are available to everyone for round-the-clock use. Upper-class tutors are always available to help beginners discover the relationship between paying their dues and receiving benefits in a meaningful experience. Make of it what you will.

THE GOALS OF OUR SCHOOL

We take pride in the intelligence and capabilities of our graduates.

: They can make conscious decisions in an increasingly responsible manner.
: They are proceeding to give active form to their individual and personally defined ways of life based upon a more intimate knowledge of the additional options open to them.
: They are more deeply involved with living in the present as a viable link between the past and the future.
: Their actions include an awareness of how some values change over a period of time.
: They can detect and expose the true values which often lie beneath the surface of things.
: They are able to determine and achieve desired results in any endeavor of their own choosing through conscious and orderly reasoning prodedures.

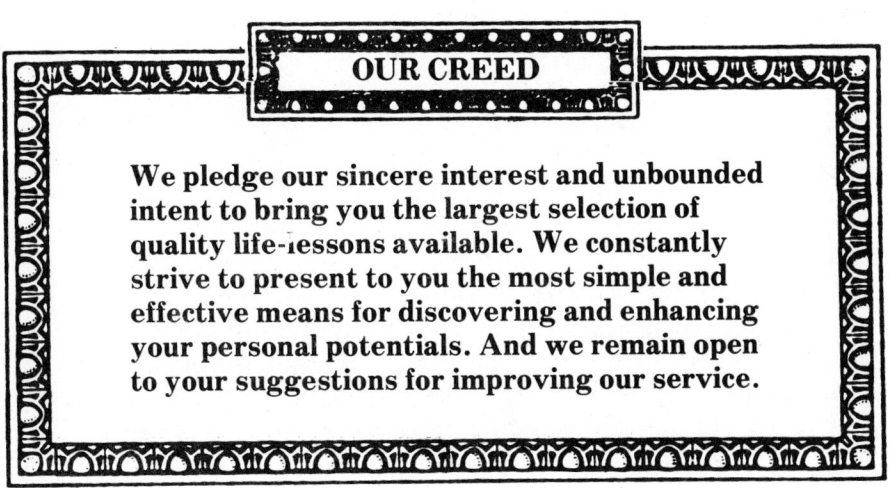

OUR CREED

We pledge our sincere interest and unbounded intent to bring you the largest selection of quality life-lessons available. We constantly strive to present to you the most simple and effective means for discovering and enhancing your personal potentials. And we remain open to your suggestions for improving our service.

SCHOOL SUPPLIES

Before classes and exercises begin, visit your local bookstore or stationery store and equip yourselves for the work ahead. Since you have already acquired this "textbook," your only remaining requirements are to obtain a notebook, some writing tools, and a few assorted drawing aids. The notebook [a 2- or 3-ring binder with filler paper will do] should be the sort that is easy to use and allows your laboratory notes to be added to, categorized, rearranged, edited or occasionally removed. Notebooks come in several sizes and degrees of "comfortable" thickness, weight, portability and cost. Select the one you think will be best for the job. [Don't personalize the notebook immediately. Wait until you get the feel of the school and the lessons, and what you then select to put on the covers of your notebook will better express what it contains.] Next find a comfortable writing tool [or tools], perhaps a good fountain pen [something hard to find today], or a special pencil or pen you like the feel of and that you can write with legibly. The tool should help make your writing easier and never block your efforts, so watch out for points that break or pens that go dry or bleed through to other pages because they tend to lessen the quality of what you do.

Finally, pick up a few soft pencils, some crayons or color pens, rubber stamps, stencils, stickers or whatever else strikes your fancy for illustrating, decorating and enhancing the written stuff in the notebook so that it will increasingly become fun to work with and to share with others.

GETTING ACQUAINTED

Our earlier book, THE UNIVERSAL TRAVELER, is a "soft-systems guide to creativity, problem-solving and the process of reaching goals." In it we showed that design or creative problem solving is "a process of making dreams come true." We will review and summarize this process briefly later. In this book, we are primarily concerned with the ways of applying that process to the problem of clarifying our individual choices in this complex, option-glutted world. At a time when planetary, national and urban goals are up for grabs, getting to know more about ourselves is a highly desirable goal. This book's main objective, then is to get you better acquainted with the many selves within you and to help you make your various self-components work together toward a unified end. It is sort of a "Sears and Roebuck Wish Book" of the choices open in life, accompanied by a guide to self-measurement (so that selections made will have a good chance of being a proper fit). Above all, it is designed to help you help yourself and also to provide a link between human values (what you believe) and chosen directions (where you expect to go). Life planning is a tricky business. To do it wisely calls for knowledge of the spectrum of options available to us, a deep awareness of self, and recognition of the needs of others. And it requires a working knowledge of the processes of decision making, problem solving and goal achieving.

The VALUES TECH curriculum will help you make better decisions toward the attainment of more responsible and enjoyable personal and social goals. Your coursework is subdivided into lessons and events which are grouped into four major sections:

the CURRICULUM

1 **Prerequisites and Entrance Exams.** Orientation to the school and to thinking, reasoning and self-assessment techniques

2 **Introductory Level.** Basic theory and practical exercises involving making decisions and exploring human values.

3 **Intermediate Level.** Discovering personal beliefs and the values which support decisions

4 **Advanced Level.** Making plans, giving physical form to intentions and working toward self-idealizing ends

All day long, decisions, decisions, decisions. Decision-making never ends:

What to say about this? How to handle that? Where to go to buy this thing? Who to ask for help? Which one to select? Whether to spend, save or invest? Who to vote for in November? When to ask for a favor? What to do about the fast-changing times? about sex? about human relations? politics? pollution? inflation? How can we make our feelings and needs known to "them," the other decision makers who influence consumer prices, nuclear power, domestic and foreign policy?

Questions, Problems, Decisions:

Simple and complex, close to home and far-away, pressing situations and long-range desires. Every day, in countless ways, we are all faced with making up our minds. Early in life most of us learn how easy it is to delegate decision-making responsibilities, and we also discover how easy it is to make decisions for someone else. Here is the way we reason it out: If we allow Mom, Dad, a big sister, teacher or friend to decide things for us, we can never be caught making a mistake or error of judgment. We never have to explain "why" or "how" to anyone because the responsibility is off us and on someone else's shoulders.

Paradoxically, it is equally clear that when we become the decision-maker for others and tell them what to do or when to do it, it becomes their responsibility to follow our advice to the letter if they decide to act upon our judgment. This lack of having to be responsible really simplifies things: there is always someone else to blame for our mistakes in selection. The process works so well that by the time we are sixteen we can hardly move without

WHY CHOOSE VALUES TECH?

```
BIO    ELECTRONIC ENGINEERING
BIO
BIO    EL   303-01    SIGNAL TRANS
BIO    EL   307-01    ELECTR DEVICE
BIO    EL   308-01  * ELECTRON CIRC
BIO    EL   308-11    ELECTRON CIRC
BIO    EL   309-01    ELECTRON CIRC
BIO    EL   319-01    LOGIC/SWITCH
BIO    EL   321-01    ELECTRONICS
BIO    EL   321-02    ELECTRONICS
BIO    EL   343-11    SIG TRANSLAB
BIO    EL   343-12    SIG TRANSLAB
BIO    EL   347-11    ELECTRON DEV
BIO    EL   348-11    ELECTRON CIRC
BIO    EL   348-12    ELECTRON CIRC
BIO    EL   349-11    ELECTRON CIRC
                                    LAB
HISTORY                             LAB
                                    LAB
HIST 102-01    HIST CIVILIZ         LAB
HIST 202-01    U S HISTORY          LAB
HIST 204-01    ERICAN DEMO   PROBS
                ERICAN DEMO  FIELDS
ELEM FRENCH     ERICAN DEMO  FIELDS
                WLD AFFAIR   THY
                WLD AFFAIR   PROJ
                WLD AFFAIR   PROJ
CAL FRT GROW    WLD AFFAIR   AD SEM
CAL FRT GROW    WLD AFFAIR
CAL FRT GROW    DEMOCRACY
                UES IN US    APPL
                CIAL PROBS P APPL
                R REVOL      APPL
MANS IMPACT     T ASIA       APPL
PHYSICAL GEOG  SIAN HIST     APPL
GLOBAL GEOG    OR PROJ       STUDY
ECONOMIC GEOG  RGRAD SEM     ODELS
ECONOMIC GEOG  ADV TOPIX
ECONOMIC GEOG                THES
AREA GEOGRAPHY               THES

                TION
                TION
PHYS GEOLOGY    WLD NUTR  TRNCS
PHYS GEOLOGY    UTRITION  TRNCS
PHYS GEOL LAB   FR SPEC   TRNCS
```

11

"Checking around" for peer validation. We have already become programmed to rely on others to take charge of the choices in our lives. And we are satisfied with that. Or are we? Not for long; inevitably, we get fed up with being told what to do and how to do it. We decide to break loose, rebel, choose for ourselves, establish independence, only to discover that old habits and reliance upon others are stronger bonds than we dreamed possible. Taking charge of just one decision is often tough stuff; it puts us out in the open, makes us vulnerable to criticism, requires explanations. But worst of all is the sudden realization that deciding in favor of one thing rules out the alternative choice . . . while all the while we wanted to have both.

The ability to make a choice requires relying on facts we are not always eager to accept. Making up our minds entails "taking a stand"; "standing firm" implies "standards"; "standards" require consistent arguments for similar situations. The costs are more than we bargained for, and we are often forced to give up and go back to being dependent on others to make our decisions for us.

The pattern repeats itself over and over again as we get nagging urges to assert ourselves. But time and again we retreat due to lack of knowledge, low self-esteem, faltering courage or just plain lack of stamina. Why try to hack it? Will we ever win anyway? The more involved we become, the less control we seem to be able to exercise. And the older we get, the more aware of life we become and the more alternatives there are from which to choose. It's a first-class dilemma: The more decisions we struggle through, the more we seem to be faced with choices.

The popular solution is to forget it and to simply take out a lifetime subscription to *Time Magazine* or *TV Guide* for guidance in our choices. But the more desirable plan is to "figure it out" for ourself, to discover a viable process for simplifying our decisions by identifying our purposes.

At VALUES TECH we are less concerned with removing all of life's uncertainties than we are with finding ways for improving our ability to deal with uncertainty and to choose reasonably and wisely from among life's alternatives. Our focus is on the point of balance; that fulcrum which supports the satisfaction of needs, abilities and desires on one side and the realistic assessment of experience on the other.

PROCESS IS OUR MOST IMPORTANT PRODUCT

It is something of a paradox to encourage a conscious knowledge or awareness of the balance between product and process because we are asking you to concentrate on an infinitely small point (much like trying to concentrate on the net instead of the players while watching a tennis match). This consciousness of the point of balance should not, however, restrain your attention from flashing back and forth to see how each side is doing. Our purpose is to facilitate the discovery and development of skills and attitudes which will allow you to become more engaged participants in the match between your dreams and your existence . . . between arriving at a goal and having a relevant trip . . . between product and process. By exposing the many options available in life, and by your own self-examination of how your personal values are formed in relation to some of those options, we will help you build a bridge between theory and practice . . . between what you may dream and the realization of those intentions.

GRADING SYSTEM

Evaluation techniques at VALUES TECH are similar to those employed at most educational institutions; still, there are certain distinct differences.

The unique part of our system is that the students are held responsible for keeping their own grade records. However, at various check points (the beginning of each instructional level), students and faculty get together to pool their observations of past performances in order to plan an approach to the work that follows.

Evaluation of your own performance is the most important part of this process. Use it to discover what you have accomplished along the way (by-products of the process) in terms of what you intended to accomplish, which tactics (techniques, methods, behavior, etc.) were reinforcing and which weren't, and how your future intentions will be altered by that experience.

IF YOU ARE FOLLOWING THIS CURRICULUM ON YOUR OWN, YOU WILL HAVE TO RELY ON A FRIEND TO TAKE THE PART OF THE TEACHER . . . OUTSIDE EVALUATION IS VERY IMPORTANT.

IF YOU ARE PLANNING TO FOLLOW OUR ADVICE AND KEEP AN EVALUATIVE NOTEBOOK OF YOUR PERSONAL EXPERIENCES AT VALUES TECH, WE SUGGEST THAT YOU PREPARE THE FOLLOWING INFORMATION FOR YOUR OWN USE:

A. Your personal intentions or purposes in attending this school. This will help you to measure your progress in terms of how well and how much you are satisfying your own desires. It should only take three to five minutes. Do it now!

B. The school's intents and purposes. This will help you decide whether or not you wish to participate in our overall program or whether you wish to concentrate your energies on particular parts of the program. It will also help you see the curriculum context into which your own goals must be integrated. Go back a few pages and review our goals. Do it now!

C. What you agree that others should be able to expect from you. This is your understanding of your responsibility to society, friends, parents, etc. In sort of a "Do unto others as you would have them do unto you" sense, decide now on an "expected level" of performance quality . . . your expected standards for acceptability. What levels of achievement do you expect? You'll have to estimate this so take care as to being too easy or ambitious. Do it now!

D. Previous commitments. This will guide you in making reasonable plans for how much you expect to receive here. If at the moment there is only a small place for VALUES TECH in your life, you should expect only small benefits. How much can you afford to give?

E. What will you allow to get in your way?
Illness? What kind?
Death? Whose?
Accidents? What sort?
Lack of resources? How much? For what?
Friends needing help? What levels of need?
Unexpected offers? What kind?
Change of plans? Such as?

F. What you think you will be doing here. This will help you gain a better perspective of the kinds of activities you may be asked to judge.

You can be assured your "evaluation" is always up to date if you know where you stand with respect to the foregoing matters. If you want to know how well you are doing or how far you have progressed in terms of these six factors, the comments you have made to yourself (in your journal) will be helpful. Perhaps you might wish to use a standard academic grading system to guide your comments . . . or to devise one of your own.

Standard Academic System:

A (Excellent, Superior, Outstanding) Doing extremely well. Improvements will be high degrees of refinement.

B (Above Average) Doing very well. Improvements will be toward higher refinements of the expected outcomes.

C (Average, Normal) Doing well. Meeting acceptable level of expectations. Improvements will be to work toward refinement in quantity or quality.

D (Below Average) Doing less than expected in quantity or quality; something is wrong. Improvements will be to reach the acceptable level of expectations.

W (Withdrawn) Given up. Working in other directions.

F (Failure) Doing far below the expected level of acceptance. Improvements are to renew purposes, seek better assistance, change goals, lower standards to achievable incremental levels. increase efforts, etc. (Actually the term "failure" is a theoretical term since we rarely learn much from our successes).

VALUES TECH ENROLLMENT FORM

Given names _____ Desired names? _____

Address _____ Address of your dreams? _____

_____ _____

_____ _____

Age _____ Height _____ Sex _____ Weight _____

Statement regarding how and why you think your answers to the above might affect your beliefs and daily behavior _____

_____

_____

_____

Mother? _____

Sister[s]? _____

_____

Friend/Lover? _____

_____

Father? _____

_____

Brother[s]? _____

_____

Husband/Wife? _____

Sketch or photo of yourself

How do you think the beliefs of those close to you affect your own beliefs and/or behavior?

_____

_____

Occupation[s]? _____

_____

Desired occupation[s]? [what you'd like most in the world to do] _____

_____

Why? _____

Which special behavioral traits, practical skills or attitudes do you expect to be changed or developed by participation in the VALUES TECH program? _____

_____

_____

How much energy do you expect to be able to devote to your participation in the program?

_____

What things would you be willing to risk to realize your dreams? ☐ friendship? ☐ love? ☐ years of your life? ☐ relaxation? ☐ marriage? ☐ honesty? ☐ health? ☐ money?

GOOD FOR YOU

If you filled out the Enrollment Form, you have undoubtedly decided to take a closer look at how you might begin to save time, money and other personal energy potentials as a step toward building a better you. And although you may end up paying a little more effort by "participating" in this curriculum than you would by just "reading" the text, the additional investment will reap worthwhile dividends...

In an exceptionally practical book of personal success methods, HOW TO GET CONTROL OF YOUR TIME AND YOUR LIFE, author Alan Lakein says, "You can drift, dream or drown, or you can decide." You have already taken the first step toward becoming a more self-directed person by reading this far. Here are some additional reasons for allowing the VALUES TECH Universal Life Process to help you learn more about who you are, what you believe, how to make even better decisions and, ultimately, how to take charge of your own life:

Your life is your most precious asset. It consists of minutes, hours and years. How you spend your most valuable resource deserves to be a top priority.

The Universal Life Process discussions and methods are designed to simplify and shorten self-finding and life-organizing tasks.

You want your life to have high quality as well as to be full of varied, interesting and enjoyable experiences.

VALUES TECH covers a broad spectrum of life issues.

You want to develop insight in order to simplify dealing with decisions.

The Universal methods are easy to apply; they can open doors to many of life's dilemmas painlessly.

You deal more creatively with your world when you can organize the jumble of daily experiences.

The systematic and process-oriented approach to problem solving found in our Universal methodology underscores creative and orderly behavior.

You can look into your own future and take charge of its contents when you get involved with the Universal Life Process on a conscious level.

The Universal Life Process is truly universal; it allows applications to present problems as well as to future projections. It can help you realize your aspirations, just as it can illuminate the choices open to you.

Some basic tools you'll need to deal with the curriculum of studies at Values Tech

PREREQUISITES

 NOTE!

The following section is a refresher course or brief summary of some basic elements of conscious thinking. Although we include it now as a reminder of its essential role in the curriculum which follows, those who are anxious to begin might pass it by and return at a later time if a need for review is felt.

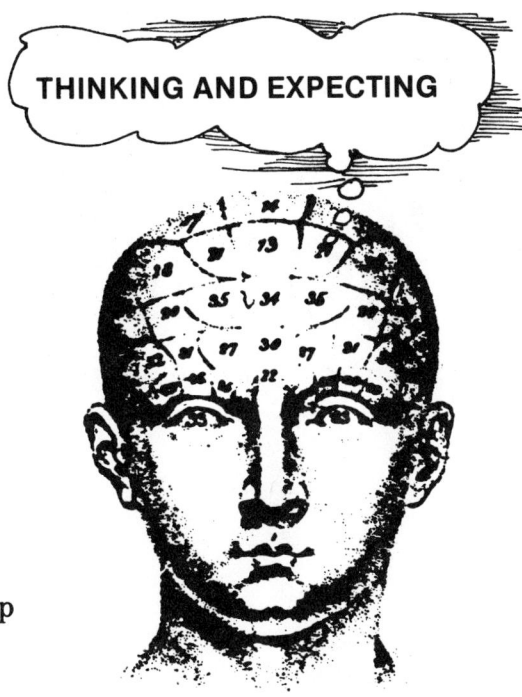

This section is about thinking and reasoning, about the many different methods people use to make sense of their lives. We begin with the assumption that everyone has the same general and ultimate goals: to operate under one's own steam and cognizance, with complete public approval, while working toward achieving a *meaningful* and *satisfying* life. Basic individual differences center around how each of us translates those terms ("meaningful" and "satisfying") and how we use our separate and unique potentials to arrive at our very personal translations.

It's hard to find two people who "think alike" who haven't also spent years practicing that skill together. Marriage is the prime example. Children growing up together also learn the technique. Usually, however, we have our own thinking peculiarities; our own individual "style" of thinking.

Our physical bodies act as discrete sensory mechanisms, picking up selected bits of information from all that is available in the surrounding environment. In other words, the human animal, whether awake or at rest, is a "receiving" instrument which sorts out and retains some of the vibrations and messages from the environment outside of itself.

Why don't we consciously take in all (instead of just some) of the cosmic and earthly vibrations from outside? The answer is simple: We can't deal with them all at once. We must be selective. Furthermore we don't expect them to be there; we aren't aware of them. And because we are concentrating on specific things, we often limit our acceptance to those special things alone.

What do we do with those bits of information we decide to receive? We translate them and compare them with the stuff that's already on file in our memory (memory is what we call the information storage cells in the brain). Then we store that new information along with what we already have for future reference. The process involves "thinking" and "evaluating" . . . turning our feelings into knowledge . . . objectifying sensory responses.

Because of repetition, the number of operations involved and all the different ways we could handle them, there is a tendency to make "mistakes" in the thinking-evaluating process. These "mistakes" are often merely the differences between the physical reality of available outside information and our personal translation and storage of that information. "Clear thinking" is the attempt to lessen the "mistakes" or differences between physical reality and our perceptions of it.

Giving knowledgeable or cognitive form to our sensory impressions would seem to be a standard operation. But it isn't, because we all do it slightly differently. Having to deal with every experience as a totally new event would be difficult, slow work, as it is with new-born infants. So depending upon our special point of view (wherever we stand), we gradually develop "expectations" or pre-cognitions to expedite the thinking tasks. For instance, we may discover it is easier to have all new experience pretranslated, compared and ready for storage even before an event occurs in order to save time and energy. However, keeping open to new information is important and we should expend the energy required to see things freshly each time.

Each of us is a mixture of both open- and closed-mindedness, and we deal with our perceptions and expectations accordingly. Some of us make few big "mistakes"; in other words, some of us sense most things consistently close to reality. Others of us are solidly blocked by preconceptions, precognitions and prejudice. The extent to which we are able to clearly and wisely "perceive" our world is a result of both our perceptual process and our personality.

PERCEPTION & EXPECTATIONS

We draw our conclusions from what appears to us to exist out there (perception) and from what we previously imagined existed out there (expectation); in other words, from appearances and predetermined images. If we want to get better at drawing conclusions, the first step will be to find ways to sharpen perceptual and "forecasting" abilities (for aligning our mental images of events with reality).

SOME WAYS TO DEVELOP PERCEPTUAL ACCURACY

Get as much sensory information as you can for each event in your life. Don't "wait" for stimuli. Reach out with your senses and grab all you can get. In doing so trust your environment as much as reason and safety will allow: Have faith that the information in your environment is good and yours for the taking.

Free your curiosity:

Let your senses roam freely over all surfaces and in all the corners and insides of things. Be conscious of sights, sounds, tastes, temperatures, textures and odors. (Read AWARENESS by John O. Stevens, Real People Press, Box F, Moab, Utah 84532)

Build a "many-windowed house":

Don't allow your point of view to become "rigid". Arrange your life so that you can view things from many positions, not just from one "best" standing place. Learn to "dance" with life, not merely sit on the sideline.

AND SOME METHODS FOR DEVELOPING REALITY-BASED EXPECTATIONS

Teach your senses to think:

Link as many questions to your sensory experiences as you can. Don't believe your own eyes until you are sure they are seeing reality.

Since knowing comes after sensing, we often make the error of thinking that we can stop sensing (being sensitive) once we think we know something instead of realizing that knowledge must be constantly renewed by sense information in order to remain alive and valid.

Throw out the "experts-know-it-all" fallacy:

Develop a strong respect for the natural process of change. Learn to anticipate the metamorphosis of things as opposed to having a fixed, static viewpoint. Realize that yesterday's information is not necessarily true for today.

Expect the unexpected:

Make it a practice to wait to hear both (or all) sides of the case before you make up your mind.

Play "judge" [not just prosecutor or defender]:

Fill in the specifics of general conclusions. Don't be satisfied with "Blanket" answers.

Become interested in details:

ಜಾ THINKING METHODS: INDUCTION & DEDUCTION ಳೆ

Thinking is a process which begins as a response to environmental stimulus and proceeds evaluatively to a conclusion (or to alternate ends). We begin the process by attempting to describe (with words or actions) what it is that we have felt with our senses. Just as the *kinds* of thinking include both the sensory or feeling kind and the expecting or knowing kind, so it is with the *methods* of thinking: some are sensing, some are knowing. The kind of thinking toward which we tend (whether we are predominantly sense-oriented (perceptive) or predominantly expectation-oriented (predictive-knowing) should normally determine our preference for either inductive or deductive thinking methods.

INDUCTIVE THINKING METHODS are favored by the sensitive. They are characterized by direct sensory observation and perceptual record-keeping. The basic inductive process includes living with something or some situation for a period of time, observing and carefully noting how it operates and then drawing a conclusion from the experience. Since this is an observation method, the amount of knowledge, skill and objectivity the observer applies will affect the credibility and quality of the conclusion.

The act of waiting for an elevator in a tall building can provide an illustration of such a typical inductive-thinking sequence. We push the button and watch the lighted number or rotating arrow progress toward our floor. By observation we then assume that the cab will either stop for us or not depending on how many floors it has stopped at along the way, how fast it appears to be traveling, how many people we note using adjacent elevators, etc. Our conclusion is the sum of all the "observed" evidence, and if our observations were correct, our answer was not dissappointing.

SOME INDUCTIVE THINKING METHODS COMMONLY USED ARE:

Bird-Dogging. Persistent chase after sensory stimuli and underlying clues to situations; digging many holes to find evidence and digging some holes deeper than others. Closing off escapes; narrowing down to a conclusion from lots of processed information.

Incubating. "Mulling it over"; observing first and then carrying the observations into another environmental context, where the change of surrounding allows relaxation and new viewpoint possibilities . . . resulting in a conclusion.

Transfixing. Giving complete mind and body attention to the subject being observed; concentration to the point of empathy.

Subverting. Manipulating the subject under observation to the degree that allows it to be sensed from many points of view. Often this means examination to the point of destruction, as in experimental engineering models, and dissections and chemical or physical analysis in biological reasearch, etc.

DEDUCTIVE THINKING METHODS are preferred by the systematic, mind-over-matter predictive group. These methods bring previous experience to bear on present and future situations. The deductive process includes using the rules of logic and the organization or construction of a "case" based on a single premise or pyramid of premises. The final conclusion is an outgrowth of successively conclusive steps.

Again using the elevator example, let's see how deductive thinkers might deal with this situation. First of all, they would not be as concerned with the sensory clues of the moment as they would be with applying previous conclusions regarding elevator traffic patterns. They might conclude, for instance, that since it is lunch time and since cars are usually jammed at this hour, the cab might well pass them by. Or they might conclude that since "down" cars tend to be packed while "up" cars are empty, it might make sense to first go up to insure finding room on a down-going cab.

SOME DEDUCTIVE THINKING METHODS FOR YOUR EXAMINATION:

Interlacing. Relating many things at once and cutting across many points of view so as not to build premises while wearing blinders.

Pattern Making. Finding connections and determining relationships; ordering the parts of situations so as to simplify dealing with many parts.

Teaching. Facilitating the potential for discovering essential premises by trusting the situation (student) and by priming it (her/him) to produce ever more relevant and truth-revealing clues to its identity.

Systematics. Sequential, step-by-step procedural approach. Matching proper methodology to overall strategy required by specific situations.

Following. Taking the lead from someone, something; choosing some special clue and riding on its tail to a consclusive finish. Building onto or tagging onto.

Analogy-Whizzing. Simile finding and searching for paraphrases or other ways of saying and "seeing" established associations.

Pragmatics. Determining to base an entire case on one shaky footing; allowing a few considerations to outshadow others for unclear reasons.

All thinking and reasoning methods branch into multiple variations of the same two INDUCTIVE AND DEDUCTIVE themes. Some are quite simple and some are cursory while others are extremely complex and comprehensive. And conclusions which are drawn from conscious choice of a thinking method tend to follow suit: that is to say, they can be off-hand and suggestive "guesses" or highly documented, credible testimonials (or any degree between the two).

ANALYSIS and REASON

Although information comes to us in isolated bits, intellectual survival requires us to classify it into manageable groups. We normally do this at the instant those "bits" are received as outside stimuli. Immediately this information all gets analyzed, classed, grouped and filed "in its proper place." Even though we learn through experience that this leads to mistakes, misfilings, loss of informational content and occasional prejudice, we nevertheless often go through the process very quickly, especially when information starts coming at us from all directions or in large amounts as it does when we are trying to learn something new in a classroom or laboratory.

Because survival often depends on fast thinking, we tend not to consider those isolated bits of information but, instead, to work with them in groups, sets, classes, and types. Reasoned thinking involves isolating patterns, not too dissimilar to the way a gypsy finds patterns in the bottom of a teacup: instead of focusing on the separate and random tea leaves, she organizes the apparent chaos at the bottom of the cup into a total meaning. And because it takes lots of practice to become skillful at pattern and set-making, we associate pattern-making skills with higher intelligence and the process of "growing up." The older we get, the more patterns we are expected to find and the more individual items we are expected to include in each group we form . . . as may be seen in this typical example:

A child senses a dog in its environment and classifies the sensation into one or more of the following groups:
1. Dogs.   2. Noisemakers.   3. Dangers.   4. Protectors.
5. Toys.   6. Playmates

An adult sensing the same dog might classify the sensation into a combination of at least several of the following groups:
1. Dogs.   2. Animals.   3. Pets.   4. Noisemakers
5. Dangers.   6. Protectors.   7. Playmates.   8. Sidewalk polluters.   9. Garden menacers.   10. Neighbors' possessions.
11. Alter ego expressions.   12. Devices for communicating with others.   13. Status symbols.   14. Economic dependents.
15. Law offenders, etc.

Just as we learn to use the classification technique for dealing with the variety of stimuli in everyday living situations, we also begin to use it in a conscious way for improving our reasoning abilities. The trick of course is to consciously establish some sequential relationship or connection between those things or actions in our world which we classify as being "natural" (or elemental) and those things or actions which we classify as "interrelating"; i.e., to determine "reasons" for things, events or situations by determining how those things, events or situations interrelate. When we make such connections and develop a sequence of relationships, we are, in effect, establishing a pattern . . . an organized "reason" which grows out of our attempt to organize apparently unrelated information.

REVIEW Let's review the entire process to this point:

1. We begin inductively, deriving some preliminary inferences from our sensory observations.

2. Next we proceed to deductively classify those preliminary inferences into sets or groups and we give names to those groups.

3. **Then** we determine the basis of our groups: which of them are elemental or "natural" and which of them deal with relationships or connections.

4. Finally, we form some sequence of linkages using the interrelationship groups to connect or "activate" the elemental groups.

The result is the product of our reasoning ability.

ILLUSTRATION

1. Many stimuli are grouped into images

2. which become classified into groups and named

3. and determined as to whether they are "elemental" or "relationship"

4. which allows us to form a connecting pattern between them

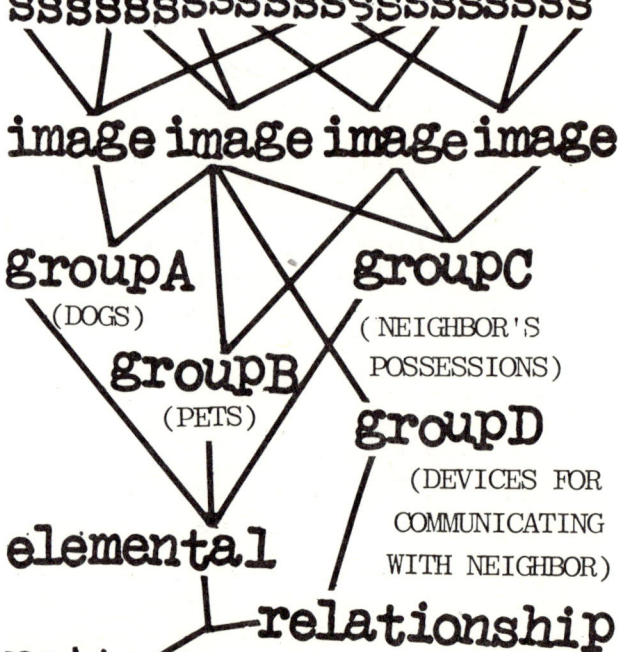

A BASIC TENET

Nothing happens independently in our world. Making patterns by the dozens can be greatly simplified by merely applying the age-old truism: EVERYTHING IS RELATED TO EVERYTHING ELSE; ANYTHING IS A PART OF EVERYTHING. All things are the result of influences and movements. The more consciously we can apply energy toward learning to reason in a natural way, the closer we will come to being able to deal with the world as it truly is.

Learning to *differentiate between things* (finding the separate and similar characteristics of things) and learning to *determine relationships between things* are keys to developing better reasoning abilities. Together they allow us to utilize broader and more complete classifications and to choose from more of the potential patterns of interrelationships in life.

LOGIC: A SURVEY FOR BEGINNERS

Forming groups and classes is not the only way of viewing the reasoning process. Another time-honored viewpoint for this process is LOGIC.

Like Grouping, Logical Thinking is also a form of link making in this case involving the building of a chain of linkages between three (3) statements. When the first two statements are expressed as measurable facts, then the third, final, conclusive statement derived from them can also be implied to be fact. The three statements (A, B, & C) taken together are called a "syllogism," and within each syllogism there exist six possible statement couples (A=B & B=A, C=A & A=C, C=B & B=C) or potential relationships for reaching a conclusion.

There are various kinds of linkages, they may be very *close* and highly reliable, *inferred* and not totally reliable, or *false* and unreliable. We can begin to figure out which is which by challenging each statement in a methodical way to locate weaknesses in the links. That's all there is to basic logical reasoning. For advanced logicians, there exist precise textbooks which delve into diagrammatic relationships, fallacy detecting, strategies and ambiguities. For the simplest of these, try WFF 'N PROOF: The Game of Modern Logic by E. Allen, Box 71-BA, New Haven, Conn. 06501 or the game book THINKING STRAIGHT by Monroe C. Beardsley, Prentice-Hall, Inc. (1956).

Logic is at least as old as Aristotle, who worked out the syllogism combinations. However, logic is not an end or a conclusion but merely a process for deducing reasoned conclusions. It increases in complexity to yield increasingly exacting conclusions. Familiarity with its rules can bring us closer to analytic-reasoning reality.

HOW TO MAKE LISTS IN A MORE CREATIVE WAY

A list is a group of items representing various kinds, types, ways, means, components, parts, etc. for describing a subject heading. The previous sentence contains a brief list describing the subject called "list." The extent, variety, imaginative quality and open-mindedness of our lists is limited by the time we have available, our background and our knowledge, the psychological blocks we face and above all by our degree of awareness or consciousness of what it is that we are attempting to do.

One of the chief prerequisites of freedom is to become more conscious and/or deal more positively with the alternatives in life. Having knowledge of our possibilities coupled with skill in deciding which possibility best suits our purpose is the basis for the creative application of freedom. At VALUES TECH we aim for both aspects. And to get you started in the making of lists of your alternatives in a more creative way, we suggest using a tool devised by Alex Osborn (as related in his book *Applied Imagination*). The tool is Brainstorming.

rules

The "rules" for Brainstorming are all-important and might be paraphrased as follows:

1. Defer Judgment

To keep from throwing away potentially good items, it will be necessary to save decision-making for a later stage. Don't allow concern for right or wrong, good or bad, expensive or inexpensive or what others may think to get in your way. At this stage they are all blocks to creativity.

2. Quantity

In order to generate many alternatives, you're going to have to include everything and anything you can think of that might even be remotely connected to the subject being listed. Put it all down.

3. Be Free

To be able to obey rules 1 and 2, you must relax and give yourself the authority to be a free-wheeler and to record everything that crosses your mind in relation to the subject. Look through many sets of eyes. Try to include all points of view.

4. Tag-on

The number of alternatives can always be increased by making more out of what you already have; changed endings, combined thoughts, additions.

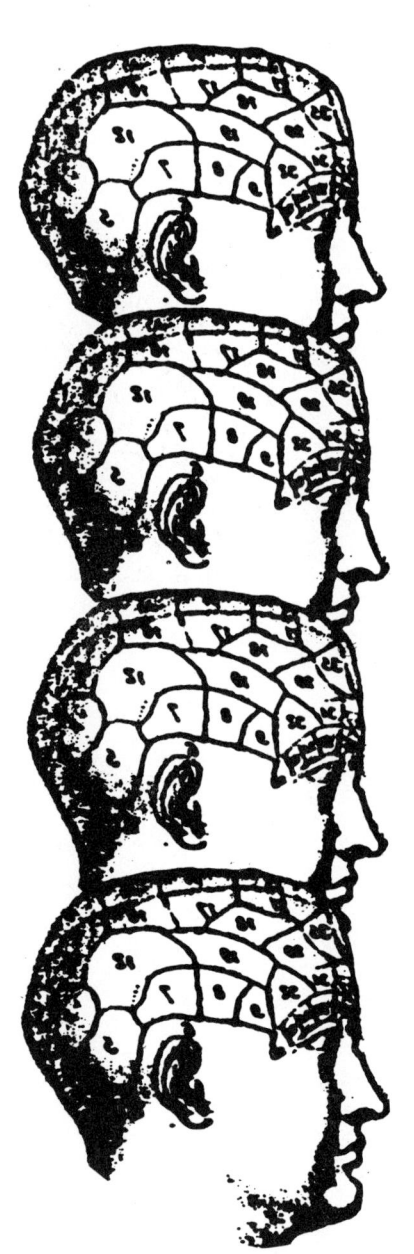

VALUES TECH is a "how to think" school, not a "what to think" school. Consequently, the thinking *process* is stressed, while the *products* of thought often are treated casually. Active students will learn both to concern themselves with process *and* product. They take away with them the knowledge, skills and attitudes of process involvement, which makes them capable of dealing with almost any situation that confronts them. They also learn to freely express what they think and why; i.e. to discover and clearly identify the thinking procedures.

The difference between process and product is not always evident to beginning students. It takes time to realize that if you only strive to learn "what," that's all you get; but when you come to learn "how," you get much more: the process and all the "whats" (products) it can produce.

The curriculum of VALUES TECH is designed to help you find stacks of "what-you-believe" products while you are working your way through the exercises of the value-revealing process. But to help make your work as self-oriented and meaningful as possible we present the following "self-examination" as a basis for helping you to write your own personal study guide or companion to the textbook.

ENTRANCE EXAMS

VADE MECUM
(A Priceless Companion)

Not so long ago, many schools prepared incoming students by supplying them with a study and information guidebook. In it were tips dealing with upperclass pranks; books to read; the best people to ask for help in a pinch; where the various buildings on campus were located; names; what the climate was like and what to wear; how to behave and other useful information. The books were called Vade Mecums (Go with Me!). Some schools still prepare such guides for their students.

A similar kind of book could help you progress through our curriculum. But the big difference between VALUES TECH and other schools is that at VALUES TECH each student must write his own. We provide only the outline.

Your Entrance Exam, therefore, takes you through the process of beginning such a "book of yourself." Remember, too, that it is also a book *for* yourself. Put as much in it about yourself as it can hold: your various and sometimes conflicting beliefs; changes in your beliefs due to new information and the acquisition of new skills; your goals; changing objectives; evolving life plans; all your schemes and dreams.

Call it your personal Vade Mecum, and think of it as a "priceless companion." The subject of the book will sooner or later become your best friend—the one you can least be without in a pinch—*yourself!* Make your Vade Mecum an on-going exercise. During your stay at VALUES TECH it will only just get started, and because it is a record of your life experience, it will only be complete at your death. Having a place to collect and value the things you discover about yourself is what is most important. You will therefore need a notebook or journal to write this personal record (**You may decide to start by making your personal comments in the margins of this book. There's lots of room provided.**) Or you may simply decide to add pages to your notebooks for other studies.

WHY SELF-FIND?

We strive to know ourselves better because:

1. We do not want to become unconscious victims of our own reactions. For example, being unwanted as a child could condemn one to a life of striving to be wanted or of indifference to interpersonal relations. But being aware of the basis for one's own feelings may help control such unproductive or unhappy reactions and improve one's outlook on life's satisfactions.

2. We feel isolated from the world. Self-awareness is prerequisite to making intelligent connections, so we search for ways to understand the meaning of things and to relate to those things.

3. We wish to use all of what we've got going. We don't want to ignore any of our potential. Everyone desires to find work best suited to their resources.

4. We desire to be "self-controlled" rather than "other-controlled." When we know ourselves, it is easier to get to know others and thus we can become more effective in achieving satisfaction for our human needs.

5. We want to stay within reason in balancing the achievement of our dreams and the dues we can expect to pay for dreaming. If we don't know our needs and limitations, we cannot assess the costs and benefits and construct a balance sheet. We have to know who we are before we can make workable plans for transcending or exceeding current limitations.

6. He who knows nothing, loves nothing. To know one's self is to love one's self. To value one's self, we must first know the attributes which shape the value. Love and knowledge must be concurrent. It's impossible to have true self-love and respect without the insight that allows for depth of understanding.

Knowing who we are helps us better to evaluate what others tell us we should be. When parents, teachers, friends or intimates attempt to influence our lives, we can deal with their suggestions in a tolerant and constructive way.

7. Knowing ourselves helps us determine our values which give form and expression to our needs through a series of urges, wants, desires, intentions and goals. Success in self-finding makes consequences part of the intentions, not regrettable situations after the fact.

8. It's natural to know. Natural systems all strive for balance through internal stability, cohesion of components and controlled response to change. And we are individual natural systems.

9. Being tuned-in to ourselves can save headaches and wasted time. We want to remain open to our own possibilities even though such openness invites anxiety. Getting involved with ourselves is going to take time; and we usually have an abundance of time for everything else but ourselves. To start the habit of attending to ourselves first requires exploding some conservative anxieties:

Fear of becoming selfish — Being concerned about self does not imply selfishness. We can't very well help anyone else until we learn to help ourselves.

Fear of weakness — Introspection does not imply insanity or weakness. Self-improvement can only come from critical evaluation. It will never come from praise alone (which may produce only a level of consistency, not development).

Fear of ignorance — The fact that we imagine we know little about ourselves doesn't make it true. Subconsciously, we know a great deal about ourselves, and this knowledge must be brought to the surface to be useful.

Fear of instability — Questioning what we've done in the past and being candid with our motives does not contradict previous goals. When we evaluate our behavior and plans, we look for values received as well as costs charged. Education can be a valuable asset.

Fear of meaninglessness — A self-examination can never be complete so long as we remain alive. However, this doesn't mean that a thing which has no foreseeable end is valueless. Remember, the process can be more rewarding than the product. What is the ultimate product of life?

In life we think of ourselves as students for different reasons. And we go to "school" to learn how to think and reason, how to plan and study, to discover where much of the world's information is kept and how to use it. But the greatest benefit of going to school is in the finding of "ourselves." We learn about systems and experiments and how others have solved problems in the past. We learn philosophies and formulae, theories and methodologies and where to go to find the processes and rules for dealing with our futures. But most of all, we search to find the intrarelationship of our many inner selves: the key to who we really are. In that search for self, we may find the going as tough as any other part of the general curriculum of life. Sitting around passively waiting for self-discovery to happen gets us nowhere. Action is usually the best course to discovery . . . including the uncovering of our own inner selves.

The longer we remain students of life, the more it becomes clear that we are all made up of many sub-persons: we are like assemblies where more than one of our inner selves may rise simultaneously to propose different things. We see that each member of our species has uniquely different ends and therefore utilizes different means and behaviors for achieving those ends. We conclude that mankind is not a "thing" but something beyond the concept of things: that man has a spiritual self-quality . . . another name for the sum of those many separate selves found to exist inside every one of us.

To get to know ourselves takes plans or strategies; some of which might be simple, some complex, but all quite demanding.

Here are some hints and facts regarding the keeping of a Self-Inventory:

1. **Relax.** Get into a receptive attitude. Turn off your other demands. Accept yourself as you would a stranger, with both positive feelings and reservations, trying to discover what makes this stranger (you) behave the way he/she does. Start fresh and act as if none of the programming which is you could stop you from self-inspection. Breath deeply in tempo with your pulse . . . **four beats in . . . four beats out. Loosen up.** Stop thinking that you know who you are and start sensing the different selves within you.

2. **Help yourself.** Become aware of the parts of you that may be "hiding out." Feel the process of doing what you're doing, flow with your selves, hear their arguments, sense their needs. Neither support nor reject any of them. Realize they are all separate and important in themselves, just as you are another important self—a combination of them all. Be tolerant of the separateness inside you just as you know you want to be tolerant and supportive of the separateness outside you.

3. **Don't try to manipulate** your inner selves. There is no real humanity or love in the selfish manipulation of others. Free yourselves to become yourself. (Free others from your control to help them to become themselves as well.) Finding your whole self is **really a matter of seeking out your many separate selves.** It's not a search for one but a search for making a oneness out of many: what you conceive your selves to be (both overstated and different), your projected self-image, the self others have helped you become, your limits and potentials and how they might be nurtured to include new and renewed selves.

4. **Avoid negative criticism.** You are here to discover and to examine things: evaluate them later!

5. **Don't worry about being someone other than yourself.** You are already many selves within a single totality. When only one part of you is recognized at a time, it will surely appear as if you are patterning yourself after another person. No one of your selves is sufficient to control the rest, although one may be stronger and more easily seen than others.

6. **It is necessary to begin self-search in vague and broad terms** even though seemingly unrelated material and meaningless stuff may be accumulated in the process. Later on you will be able to digest the material and distill it to the essentials. Don't spend a great deal of time on any one of the many selves within you. Instead first work to expose as many selves as possible. Later on you can come back to look at the important ones in detail. Each component is only important insofar as it relates to the whole.

7. **Write down as much as you can** because this material will help you evaluate your selves; it is a further means of self-expression, and it provides practice in concentration and self-motivation.

8. **Try to keep an open mind.** Since you will only see what you want to see, make certain you don't stand in your own way. Self-clarification experiences require motivation and methodology.

You can increase your chances for getting to the heart of your self by applying methods and placing yourself in a position of advantage. It will require concentration.

9. Try to become mentally disengaged from the self-components inside you and realize you are no one of them; you are all of them. If one part of you is disagreeable, it does not mean that you are totally disagreeable. If one part of you is beautiful, it doesn't mean that you are totally beautiful. You are a composite; something more than any single good or bad component part. Laughing at one of the selves within you is fair sport. But to let one of your selves get you down is simply a waste of your time.

You will find two self groups within you. Within each of these groups, variations and numbers of different selves can be wide and many. The *basic* group (sometimes called the "id" group) represents your physical characteristics and emotional responses. These are the animal creature-human species selves within you. Controlled by your conscious mentality, this group behaves according to orders from above (brain). When your mind is not active, these selves behave on their own, often doing things you would never consciously allow them to do.

The higher controlling group (sometimes called the "ego" group) represents your mentality and brain content. They make your choices and tell your basic selves how to act. These are your planning and thinking selves which are sometimes at war among themselves because they have given conflicting orders to the basic group. Within this group, you will occasionally find some leaders (super ego) who tend to keep the others in line.

The real "you" is the spirit which hovers above both major groups of selves although you are separate from them and have no form or body in yourself. Normally, you are either awed by the awkwardness or grace of the groups within you, or you are satisfied by their teamwork. When you are conscious of both *basic* and *controlling* selves (including the super ego leaders), a peaceful harmony and balance is maintained. But when you ignore either group, anxieties arise which upset the entire house.

66 you ares

Sixty-six "self-find" methods follow. The first twenty-one are designed to yield information regarding your given, assigned or otherwise non-self-determined characteristics. The last forty-four are designed to help you discover your values, beliefs, attitudes or concepts. One method (Histogram) is a transition and should be attempted in some form or other by all participants.

In dealing with the following methods, you may wish to choose only those which feel most comfortable. Write down all you can about the ones you do choose. When friends get into the act, be sure to take note, especially of the references to your personality traits. And try to keep similar things together in groups so they'll be easier to deal with later on.

Working on the problem of finding out about yourself is like working on a jig-saw puzzle without knowing what the picture will be. There are many clues. Some of them add up to parts of the picture . . . sometimes leading here . . . sometimes there . . . at times conflicting with parts you were sure were correct just a moment or a day before. If you demand a complete and clear picture in the end, your task will be frustrated over and over again. Relax. Enjoy the process of your search.

NOTE! When you see type face like this it is a signal for you to take action. An opportunity to participate is being offered.

1. Nice circle

you are...

what your friends and acquaintances consider to be your attractions and redeeming qualities

Form a circle with as many friends as you can (maybe at a party or after a meeting). Ask everyone to take turns saying one nice thing at a time about each member of the circle. Write down what's said about you and paste it or rewrite it in your journal.

2. The Best Teacher

you are...

the sum of the effects of the most influential people you have had as friends or teachers, the books you have read, the films you have seen, the trips you have taken.

Using the five titles: friends, teachers, books, films and travel, make lists of those elements of your experience which are most memorable. Try to remember why they impressed you and how you have incorporated their influence into your behavior.

3. Net worth

you are...

the statement you might have to make to take out a loan at a bank or to begin an association with a financial consultant.

This will give you a reading on your financial stability and responsibility. (Security might also be measured here.) After answering each question, make a written statement regarding what you think is "implied" by your answer. For example:

Age? 23 - At that age someone is probably anxious to participate in life; a young adult; excitable; a generalist; active; competitive; etc.

Age?
Marital Status?
No. of Dependents?
Yrs. at Present Address?
Yrs. at Present Job?
Telephone in own name?

```
Education?
Travel Experience?
Income (annual or monthly)?
   Salary?  Inheritance? Dividends?  etc.?
Expenses (annual or monthly)?
   Rent? food? clothes? payments?  enter-
     tainment?
Savings? Cash?  Insurance?
Investments?
   House?  car?  equipment?  furniture?  etc.?
Solvency Test:
           Cash + Accounts Receivable (other
           valuables and debts owed to you)
           + other marketable resources
Net worth = _____
             Current liabilities
```

you are···

4. Paper dolls

your wardrobe and how it fits on your (photographed) body to form an image.

```
Have a full-length photo taken by a camera-buff
friend.  Stand up straight, face forward, arms
slightly separated from the body.  Wear under-
wear only, no socks or shoes.  (Nude is o.k.,
too.)  Have the photo enlarged until your image
is about 12" high.  Then mount it on stiff card-
board and cut it out with a sharp X-Acto knife
or razor blade.  Using white or colored paper,
make the replicas of the essentials of your ward-
robe.  It's easy to do if the paper is semi-
transparent and you can trace the proper sizes
right over the photo of yourself.  Make sure to
leave tabs to fold over and hold the clothes
onto the photo.  Color the clothes with pencils
or "flow pens."  Then "try on" all your normal
outfits...occasionally making notes of what's
going through your mind.  It helps to talk it
over with a friend so that you can "hear your-
self think."  Hang it all up nearby so that you
can see it often in the next few weeks.  This
is more fun as a group project; costs for pho-
tography can be shared and members can help one
another with cut and paste skills.
```

you are···

5. Family tree

the lineage or heritage found in the interrelationship of families making up your genealogical chart.

```
Make a chart of your family tree with you and
your sisters and brothers (if any) placed at
the top.  Connect your names with your parents,
aunts and uncles.  And then branch them out to
your grandparents, great aunts and great uncles,
etc., as far as you can go.  Try to get and list
some information about each name in order to get
a better picture of how you came to be the way
you are.
```

6. Family names and given names

you are...

the names and titles assigned to you at birth (or earned in life)

Find out what all of your names mean. The library has references to help out here. But first, write down what <u>you</u> think they mean. Do you believe that your names have some influence on how you behave? Do you try to live up to your names?

7. Nicknames

you are...

the names people have given you.

List all the nicknames you've ever had...Sissy, Bubba, Sonny, Junior, Smiley, Ace, Tiger, Butch, Buster, Sport, Dimples, Blue Eyes, etc. How'd you earn those names? Do you secretly love or hate to be called by them? Which ones stuck? Why?

8. Mirror, mirror

you are...

your vital signs and physical characteristics.

This exercise takes you on a body tour. In a comfortable room, stand nude in front of a full-length mirror and take the grand tour of your own body and organs. Keep your notebook handy to record all you find. A close friend can really be helpful here, too, to take notes for you and to help you see the hard to see places. Begin with a drawn outline of yourself to serve as a map and guide to the various parts. Starting from the hair, scalp, skin, ears, nose, teeth, chin, etc., move all the way down to your toes. Don't rush. Take it easy and be careful. The tour may take over an hour. (For more on this technique see <u>The Well-Body Book</u> and other "self-help" medical guides.)

9. Home tour

you are...

your physical environments of the past and present.

Beginning with where you live now and mentally going back through your history, attempt to recreate the feeling of the different environments in which you have lived. Were they open, friendly, dark, damp, city-related or nature-related, noisy, clean, etc.? Try to describe them in physical terms. Then try to see a relationship between your current environment and those of your past. Are you continuing on the same line or are you reacting? Are you complementing or balancing where you've lived before?

10. Astrologer

you are...

your natal horoscope.

Get a good astrological consultant or an astrological book (SUN SIGNS by Linda Goodman is a start) to help you discover all you can about your birth sign. Knowing more about the specifics of the planetary relations at the time of birth will make it easier to deal with the consequences of the cosmic forces active at that time. (Don't brush this method aside until you've tried it.) Write down the outstanding characteristics of your sign and its symbols.

you are...

11. Graphologist

your handwriting and drawing analysis.

Your writing reveals quite a lot about your personality over and above your mood at the time of writing. Have a professional graphologist analyze a reasonably large sample of your handwriting and/or drawing. (The Police Dept. may help you locate one in your area. Also several self-analysis books on graphology are available.)

you are...

12. Temperamentalist

your basic emotional expressions.

Where do you fit in the scale of "temperament" types? Draw a circle to represent your total temperament and then divide it into pie-shaped wedges which indicate how much of each "type" you are.
Electric (dynamic-optimistic)
Magnetic (static-dependable)
Acid (active-impatient)
Alkali (passive-lazy)
Mental (intellectual--non-physical)
Vital (physical-solubrious)
Have some friends help out on this one.

you are...

13. Laboratory of human engineering

your aptitudes and developed skills.

Physical and mental aptitudes can be measured by tests of a variety of kinds which include:
1. Personality - behavioral expressions
2. Graphoria - clerical ability
3. Ideaphoria - creative imagery
4. Structural visualization - ability to think in 3-D
5. Inductive reasoning - turning scattered facts into clear patterns
6. Analytical reasoning - turning patterns into component parts
7. Finger dexterity - manual skills
8. Tweezer dexterity - ability to manipulate small tools
9. Observation - ability to take notice
10. Design memory - ability to recall working interrelationships

11. Tonal memory - ability to recall sounds
12. Pitch discrimination - ability to differentiate between musical tones
13. Rhythmic ability - keeping time
14. Timbre discrimination - ability to differentiate between pitch and octave
15. Number memory - recall of numbers
16. Proportional appraisal - ability to discern size relationships
17. Silograms - language learning
18. Foresight - ability to predict from given facts
19. Color acuity

Plus
the kinesthetic sense
the sense of duration
the sense of size constancy
the sense of extension, etc.
Many testing services exist to serve you. They are often free at colleges and universities.

14. What little girls (and boys) are made of

you are...
what you eat.

During a typical two-day period, keep track of everything that goes into your stomach. Then use a reference (FOOD IS MORE THAN SOMETHING TO EAT available free from Nutrition, Pueblo, CO 81009 or THE COMPOSITION OF FOODS from the U.S. Gov't. Printing Office) to calculate how you rate in terms of meeting the minimum daily requirements and the four basic food groups. (Calorie intake can also be established.) You might eventually aim at trying to find a relationship between how much energy you need to do various kinds of work. But for now, just see how close your eating habits compare with average national nutritional needs.

15. The numbers game

you are...
the numbers assigned to you in life.

Make a list of all your numbers...
social security
employee number
driver's license
license plates
house and apartment number
zip code
area code and phone number
draft number
student number
credit card numbers
membership numbers

What do they mean to you? How do others (such as the police, the postal service, the Internal Revenue Service, etc.) use your numbers instead of your name to serve you? Do some numbers or combinations seem to appear more than others?

you are...
16. Movie star

the way you act in front of the camera, or film, video tape, photographs and sound tape.

Find or rent a camera, movie camera, tape recorder or video tape recorder (all college audio-visual service departments have them) and have someone "shoot" you while delivering an imaginary talk or while doing some everyday thing...like conversing with friends, washing your face and brushing your teeth, etc. Then sit down with the results and discuss your hidden talents (traits heretofore unseen) with some friends.

you are...
17. "As You Like It"

how you behave as one or more of the "seven ages" as described by Shakespeare in his popular play.

"And one man in his time plays many parts,
His acts being seven ages. At first the infant,
Mewling and puking in the nurse's arms.
And then the whining school-boy, with his satchel
And shining morning face, creeping like snail
Unwillingly to school. And then the lover,
Sighing like furnace, with a woeful ballad
Made to his mistress' eyebrow. Then a soldier,
Full of strange oaths and bearded like the pard,
Jealous in honour, sudden and quick in quarrel,
Seeking the bubble reputation
Even in the cannon's mouth. And then the justice,
In fair round belly with good capon lin'd,
With eyes severe and beard of formal cut,
Full of wise saws and modern instances;
And so he plays his part. The sixth age shifts
Into the lean and slipper'd pantaloon,
With spectacles on nose and pouch on side,
His youthful hose, well sav'd, a world too wide
For his shrunk shank; and his big manly voice
Turning again toward childish treble, pipes
And whistles in his sound. Last scene of all,
That ends this strange eventful history,
Is second childishness and mere oblivion,
Sans teeth, sans eyes, sans taste, sans every
Thing."   *As You Like It, Act II Scene 7*

you are...
18. 48 hours

how you decide to spend your time.

Without changing anything intentionally, try to keep a fairly accurate hourly record of what you do for the next 48 hours. Make it as typical as you can...just all those things that you might normally do in a period of 2 days. Then categorize your actions, noting what you do most, what next most, etc. This will give you a fairly clear picture of your current priorities as being put into action. How you spent your time is how you spent your life in the last analysis.

19. Barney Oldfield ## you are...

how you drive your airplane, bike, scooter, skate-board, etc.

Is it true that the alter-ego takes charge the minute we "get behind the wheel"? Probably not! But perhaps you can get to know one of your selves better by getting two or more friends to help out on this one. Ask those who have driven with you more than a few times to tell you about your personality differences when you're "on the road." Is there really an assertive-aggressive tyrant inside there? Or is there a submissive, cautious lamb snuggling inside you? What do you find? Write down the comments.

20. Ups and Downs ## you are...

the highs and lows and critical days in a chart of your personal BIORHYTHMS.

BIORHYTHMS are the name given to those biological rhythmic sequences which some people believe run concurrently through our experiences. They say that the three "curves", which can be plotted on a median line from your date of birth onward, each express a unique body-mind rhythm: a 23-day physical cycle relates to strength and endurance, a 28-day emotional cycle (moon-menstruation related) and a 33-day intellectual cycle. When curves are "up" (above the median), you are up. When they are down, you are low or "recharging". When they cross the median, there is a critical time of change or transition. When they cross in pairs, it's "double critical", etc. What's your chart look like? How do the ups, downs and crossings relate to your life? Take a look!

21. Dr. Freud ## you are...

the types of dreams you usually have.

Most of us have dreams - usually occurring as we are in the hypnotic-prone alpha brain wave stage of going into deep sleep or coming out of it. At that time we re-envision or reconstruct bits of past experience or anxiety in our minds. Some of it we remember. Some we do not. Get a "dream book" and take a handful of your recent dreams through it to see if some hidden selves can't be revealed. Try Freud's <u>The Interpretation of Dreams</u>, Fromm's <u>The Forgotten Language</u>, etc.

HISTOGRAM (to be done by all) ## you are...

the chart showing relationships between your time, your accomplishments and your disappointments.

On a large piece of paper or in several pages of your journal, or on a blank wall which will take tacks and tape well, draw (or tape) a horizontal line representing all the years of your life. (Go on and guess at how many you think you've got left.) Put your birthdate at the left end. Divide the line into decades and subdivide decades into years by marking on the tape or by using vertical lines. Then use symbols and notes to mark keypoints in your life: graduation, marriage, the year you broke your leg and were forced to relax for six months, etc. Draw, pin, paste or write everything you think relevant on your personal histogram to indicate changes in directions, high points, discoveries, disasters, influences, dreams. Use this chart as a general reference to the history of you.

you are...

1. Ten Commandments

what you consider the value of the laws of humanity to be (how do you rank the Ten Commandments from the Old Testament?)

Write down the Ten Commandments. Then rank them according to how much you think they fit into your own modern interpersonal or human relations. Check back over your recent behavior to see if you really act in accordance with your ranked preferences. Then write down some comments about why you approve or disapprove of your behavior in those terms.

you are...

2. Humble pie

your concepts of the worst things you've ever done in your life.

Confess all of the major remembered "sins" (remissions, misdeeds, counter-beliefs) in your life and try to rank them according to their degree of "evil". Why did you think doing what you did was so bad? Do you still think the same way?

you are...

3. All riled up

your reactions to being provoked.

Using the following list of "touchy" subjects, write down your immediate responses in terms of what you'd do about them if you could. Later when you have cooled down and are more objective, try to find a nickname for the sort of person who'd act the way you proposed to act; such as "hothead", "softy", etc.

<u>Subjects</u>
The press is caught falsifying information
Technology produces motherless child
Voting is restricted to property owners only
The neighbors have parties every night
Bureaucrats give themselves a pay raise
Father teaches son to shoot stray cats

you are...

4. How could they?

your reactions to group values outside of your own.

Imagine that as you are walking down the street, someone hands you a pamphlet which favors a "cause" 180° counter to what you believe. What would you do? Not accept it?

Take it back? Throw it away? Read it later and analyze the differences? Record your probable reactions. Then analyze your behavior to determine the sort of person you think you are by behaving that way.

5. Irate citizen
you are...
your reactions to being victimized by those you help to support.

Suppose the city water dept. tore up the street in front of your driveway, blocking your car (in the garage) and then left it that way for the entire Christmas season. How would you respond to City Hall? By letter or phone call? Soft, mild-mannered, low key? fiery? irrational? assertive? angry? or not at all. (Analyze your behavior as above.)

6. Captain caption
you are...
the captions you'd write for photos and cartoon situations.

Cut a group of situational photos or cartoons out of the newspaper or a magazine, being careful to leave out all titles or captions. Then add captions of your own to each one by "putting words into the mouths of the subjects" depicted. Next try to analyze what sort of cartoonist or writer it would take to have written such things in the first place. Are you a Cobb or a Capp? What sort of subject and imagery do you prefer?

7. Critic
you are...
your analysis of stories and plots.

After watching a TV drama, write an outline of the plot and give reasons for why you think things turned out the way they did and why the actors behaved the way they did. Classify the players into personality types. Then compare yourself with the various players and try deciding if you'd also behave that way in real life if similar situations occurred.

8. Color test
you are...
what you believe about interracial situations.

Write a list of 10 "test questions" which might be used to determine someone else's prejudice or intolerance. While the list is in progress, note the problems you have in setting up situations and in choosing characters to portray the roles of "top dog" and "underdog". Write down what you discover about your own values in this regard (and then throw the questions away...they were only a means to an end).

you are…
what you're for and what you're against.

What 5 things are you most against in this world? Are the things that you are most "for" the opposites of your antagonisms? Do conflicts exist between your wants and dislikes? What sort of person is it who would want what you want or be against what you're against?

you are…
what you get trapped into saying.

You can trick yourself into saying things you mean but wouldn't have said otherwise by merely asking "why?" after every answer to the question, "What do you want to be when you grow up?" (Try it. We're certain you'll get to some "hidden truths" before you reach the 10th "why?")

you are…
what you discover from adversity.

Successes do little to educate. They give few clues as to what to do differently next time. But failures of any degree provide a training ground for improvement and development (or learning). What do you believe are the worst disasters to have happened to you in your life? What did you learn from them? Are you still behaving according to what you learned from them? If not, why not?

you are…
your response to the fantasy of the genie in the lamp of Alladin.

What three wishes would you make and what are your reasons for wishing them? Try writing down some of the throes you go through while attempting to outthink the inevitable need for a fourth wish.

you are…
what you'd write in a daily newspaper column devoted to your own behavior.

Imagine a newspaper which was exclusively your own, devoting all its news to news about you. What would you, as the star reporter, write in columns entitled:

Lost & Found
For Sale
Wanted to Buy
Sports
Editorials
Travel News
Drama News
Cartoons
Police Reports
Vital Statistics
Society News

9. Pro and con

10. You tricked me!

11. Saturday's Child

12. Three wishes

13. Star reporter

14. Does it matter? **you are...**
what you imagine in terms of long-term importances.

> Taking items at random off the front page of today's newspaper, imagine and write down an outline of what you think the consequences of each of them might be both six months and ten years from now. Afterwards, review what you have predicted, and note whether your concerns were for people, the environment, money, resources, etc.

15. The perils of Pauline **you are...**
how you respond to matters of extreme urgency.

> Are you an activist? a weeper? resilient? beyond restraint?
> How would you react to the thought of:
> ...being locked in a meat freezer which closed down for weekends on a Friday night?
> ...seeing your most intimate friend tortured by "the enemy"?
> ...being told to "get lost" by the one you love?
> ...losing your eyesight?
> ...being lost at sea?
> Write down what you think you'd do.

16. My ten titles **you are...**
the various roles you play in life.

> Make a list of the ten titles which seem to describe your various positions in life (student, daughter, chauffeur, etc.). Rank them according to how influential they have been in making you what you are today. According to what you included in your list and how you ranked them, you should discover something about what you believe relative to your job, your school, your marriage, your parents, etc.

17. My God **you are...**
the religion you choose to follow.

> What are the tenets of the formal or personalized religion you declare your own? Write them down in an abbreviated version which covers only essentials. Compare your actual behavior with what is deemed good behavior according to your religion. Then decide if you are hypocritical, a true believer, a sinner, or if you use religion as a "false front" for social or other reasons.

18. Seriously now **you are...**
what tends to amuse you.

> Consider the jokes you tell, the comics you read, the comedies you see, the things which "broke you up" today or yesterday. What are the kinds of things which tend to get you laughing? Begin a journal page entitled, "Things Which Crack Me Up," and fill it with the funny things you remember in your life. After every entry, write down a reason for why you believe it to be humorous.

you are...

19. Too much

your responses to stress and overly taxing conditions.

People who analyze systems often intentionally use the device of overload to discover weaknesses. The method is to make the system try to do more than it is physically capable of accomplishing so that components which tend to fail first are deemed the weakest and can be strengthened. When the system is made operational again, it is much stronger for its ordeal. Suppose you, as a system, were overloaded by:
...the death of someone close to you
...too many responsibilities at the same time
...too much work to do in too short a time
...hunger on a life raft in mid-ocean
...having too many questions to answer in a police "grilling"

How do you think you'd react? Close your eyes, relax and imagine these predicaments one at a time. In between each bad dream, stop to write down which of your component selves seems to break down first.

you are...

20. "What do you say to a naked person?"

your reactions to nudity (*seeing* a nude body).

How would you react if you stepped into a public elevator, the doors closed and you found yourself locked in for a 20-floor journey with a nude person of the opposite sex? Record the sequence of behavioral events you might experience. What do you think, do or say first? What next? etc. What do your answers tell you about how you feel regarding nudity? Interpersonal relations? Prudity? Open-mindedness? Lust? Compassion? Human interest? etc.

you are...

21. Let's all take a dip!

your reactions to nudity (*being* a nude body)

How would you react to finding yourself at a house party where "everyone" decided to go skinny-dipping in the pool? Again, what would be the order of the various stages of your total behavior in this situation? Why? Does your behavior suggest a particular kind of personality type...prude, open-minded, accepting but squeamish, secure, etc.? Do you have a physical "defect" which you prefer to keep concealed?

you are...

22. Take a letter

the choices you make in writing a letter.

Write two letters: one to Mom, Dad or a close friend and another to someone you admire from afar: a matinee idol, someone you'd very much like to meet, someone you'd like to leave with a good impression of you. Have someone else look at both letters and give you a reaction as to how they look and sound. Record all the reactions, even your own (especially when they refer to personality traits). Did you think about changing the paper and writing style in one of the two letters?

23. Circle of friends

you are...
the people who surround you.

Those you choose to be around tend to have a definite influence over your behavior (as well as being expressions of what you yourself believe). Your intimate partners and your close and casual acquaintances reinforce and enhance what you believe. List the names of approximately eight people who make up your circle of friends. Follow each name with a one or two word personality description (example: Sam Lovelady--cheerful, mysterious) and make an attempt to see how these people reinforce or complement your own matching selves.

24. Card carrying member

you are...
the cards you carry in your handbag or wallet.

Take out all the "cards" you normally carry with you and lay them face up on a table. One by one, try to recall why you carry them, how often you use them, what you think it means to be the possessor of each one, in terms of security, efficiency, status, etc.

25. Problem solver

you are...
the manner in which you solve problems.

How do you rate yourself as a problem solver? (Choose as many as you deem appropriate.)

logical	systematic
insightful	orderly
habit-breaker	tradition-bound
open-minded	close-minded
deductive	inductive
experience-based	consequences-oriented
preconceived	asks for help
gives up fast	persistent
nervous	secure
confident	research-oriented
conceptual	choosy
evaluative	clumsy
irresponsible	accountable
spontaneous	studied

26. The fragrant breath of springtime

you are...
the lovesong a close friend might write about you.

The text of a popular song of yesteryear entitled "All the Things You Are" deals with poetic analogy and metaphor between lovers. If a similar song were to be written about you, what would it say? Here's your chance. Ask your dearest friend to write such a song, and you can later encircle and extract the "key words" while still retaining the whole as a precious keepsake. (Tell the friend not to worry so much about the music and to concentrate on the words...which don't have to rhyme.)

27. Party time

you are...
the social gatherings you enjoy the most.

What kinds of parties do you attend? List all of the varieties: "dinner," "just drinks," "come on over for coffee," "have a swim," "come as you are," "slumber" parties, "heavy booze blast," "cards and games," etc...Which ones appeal to you most? Try to number them in order of preference. Maybe you like some parts of a party and not other parts. Take the top three favorites and try to explain why they please you the most, trying to see which of your inner selves is having the most fun and how it's being accomplished.

28. Big needs and little urges

you are...

your own specially proportioned quantities of basic human needs.

The many selves within you are really no more than formal expressions of your particular system of responses to the spectrum of human needs. Try writing down the things which you feel you need most (at least 5 to 10 things). Then try ranking them by seeing which ones you could most easily do without and which you could least do without until they have all been cross-compared.

29. Time capsule

you are...

what you'd leave to posterity to represent your existence on our planet.

"Looking through the contents of a 2'x2'x2' stainless steel box, the people of the 21st Century review all the clues you have left for them to reconstruct your life thus far." What have you included in the box? Why?

30. My personal drawer

you are...

the special box, drawer or closet which contains the bits and pieces of memorabilia of your life so far.

Take inventory of all the stuff you normally save or collect to remind you of your past: ticket stubs, skate keys, greeting cards, love letters, badges, knives, old posters, etc. After cleaning house of things which have lost their meaning, try to establish why you keep the things that remain. Sentimental? Money oriented (saving them for a flea market killing)? Reminds you of things you no longer allow yourself to do?

31. First of the month

you are...

the things you spend your money on and the order in which you pay your bills.

What bills did you pay this month? If you have a checkbook, look back over the stubs or entries to see what you paid, to whom and in what order you paid them. Did your savings come first, last, or not at all? What did you put off 'til the end? Why? What criteria did you use to decide on how to dole out the payments...love? threats of jail or loss? appreciation? Personal priorities seem to be easy to see when money is involved.

32. Teleological phenomenologist

you are...

your philosophical classification.

At your bookstore, pick up a one-page plastic "Quick Chart" on the subject of philosophy. Then check into all the definitions and try to pick out those classifications which seem to describe your own approach to life. Write down the summary statements which accompany the fitting titles.

33. Red dragon
you are...
the images and symbols that others form about you.

At a party or over coffee, get some friends to tell you which varieties of the following you remind them of. (You might offer to tell them about what they remind you of as payment.) Don't forget to find out "why".

which color? which country?
which type of weather? which kind of food?
which type of music? which famous person?
which part of the body? which book or movie?
which species of pet? which kind of vehicle?

34. Matinee idol
you are...
the great people you like to dream of being associated with.

Patrick Henry was reported to be independent, subversive, very gentle, self-aggrandizing, a soaring idealist, etc. Marilyn Monroe was known to be sensitive, insecure, caring about the opinions of others, caught between being private and assertive, etc. Who are your idols and which of their traits do you admire and try to emulate the most?

35. True face
you are...
the portrait mask you make of yourself or that others make of you.

Offer to draw a life-size, full-face portrait mask of a friend if he or she will draw one of you. But beforehand, in secret, try drawing your own portrait mask. Then, later on, compare your version and your friend's version of yourself. (Make sure to account for your different drawing abilities and limitations.) Place both drawings near to your own face as you look into a mirror, and spend some time musing over the differences between how you saw the real thing and how the friend saw it. Record your thoughts when they involve personality traits.

35. Semantic differential
you are...
your personality graph as you might plot it between the personality extremes.

In their book, THE MEASUREMENT OF MEANING, Osgood, Suci & Tannenbaum devised a simple way to write a personalized description of something...by plotting points between the extremes of the various attributes of the thing. Write out as many attribute extremes as you can think of. Leave ten spaces between each pair and then plot where you imagine yourself to be in the whole list.

	5	0	5	
smart				stupid
powerful				inadequate
nice				mean
likeable				hateful
good-looking				unattractive

Ex: (above)

etc

you are…

38. I'd die first

what you live to achieve and what you'd die to protect.

List the important things which you believe you might die to protect. If you can find nothing, try deciding what you would like to live to achieve if, for instance, you could be granted a reprieve from a fatal disease?

you are…

37. Tee shirt tatoo

the names, pictures and sayings you choose as adornments for your body.

Which buttons, badges, patches or special tee shirts do you own? Where and when do you wear them? What slogans or pictures would you like to wear if you could find them? Why?

you are…

39. Age-changer

the "dirty" or "colorful" language you allow yourself to use.

Did you ever notice how street slang seems to make kids sound more grown-up and adults seem more childish? Make a list of your full slang vocabulary and follow each word with your personalized "dictionary" of meanings and usages. Then try to note why you use these words and what you seem to feel when you hear others using them.

you are…

40. "This is your life!"

the 30-minute TV show which starred Ralph Edwards and exposed the "best" parts of some famous subjects' lives.

This is your chance to write an outline of your very own THIS IS YOUR LIFE show. Who would you invite to come and tell the TV audience what they could about you? an old grammar school teacher? an old playmate? an old friend? relatives? former boss? What do you think they'd say? Write it down.

41. In propria persona

you are...

the various things you select from the wide array available to most of us.

Which sports do you prefer? Why?
Which games do you play? Why?
Which TV shows do you watch? Why?
Which pets do you choose? Why?
Which neighborhood did you select? Why?
Where do you eat lunch? Why?
Where did you spend your vacation? Why?
Which electives did you choose in college? Why?
Which magazines do you subscribe to? Why?
What hangs on your walls? Why?

The result will be a large and varied potpourri of values and criteria.

42. Qualifications

you are...

your knowledge and skills in summary.

What are all the important things you know about and can do?
Do you know about cooking? sewing? How to speak out in a group? How to take care of yourself when alone? How to ski? What to do when the baby cries? How to sail? Make the biggest list you can and subdivide it into SKILLS and KNOWLEDGE...the things you can do and the things you know about. Be realistic. You don't have to include basic skills like being able to ride a bicycle...unless you happen to do them very well.

43. Definitions

you are...

the way in which you define words and situations which arise in your life.

Your descriptions of things express your definitions (values, concepts, beliefs) of those things. Try defining things apparently not related to yourself and then quickly switch over to you. For example:

Define these words: house
                         home
                         pet
                         bathroom
then switch over to: your body
                         your skin
                         your teeth
                         your hands
                         your fingernails
                         your health
                         your stamina
                         your hair

When the going gets tough, stop and go back to things outside yourself again for awhile.

you are...

the statement you'd submit to a contest asking for your personal philosophy in a nutshell.

If you could wrap up all your current values into one composite statement (100 words or less), what sort of expression would result? (It might not be a bad idea actually to use the product of this method as a reminder to concentrate on what you deem important in life.)

44. One hundred words or less

HOW TO USE THE INFORMATION GATHERED THUS FAR

The ultimate purpose of VALUES TECH is to facilitate your self-discovery and to encourage you to use the many available tools for self-improvement. Your Vade Mecum Self-Inventory becomes a foundation for building up to those ends.

If you have taken the Entrance Exams seriously, you now have pages and pages of important but apparently unrelated bits and pieces and are probably wondering what to make of them. In order to understand the importance better, it may now be helpful to look to the curriculum ahead. In subsequent lessons and laboratories, we will ask you to become even more familiar with yourselves by discovering more of your personal concepts or attitudes. Each lesson is intended to be a part of an overall values-revealing program, and you will find that the effect is cumulative. As you continue to reveal your beliefs and develop new concepts of life, you will be better able to deal with what you have already discovered by allowing patterns of related facts to form as naturally as possible. Later on, in the final week of class, you will be asked to reconsider your self-assessment in terms of direct and conscious self-improvement. We now ask that you analyze the information gathered thus far in the following way:

1. Don't take any single part too seriously. (Even when taken dead seriously, the most popular of all the psychological personality tests administered by institutions is only approximately 50% accurate.)

2. Do look for repetitions and patterns. Try to detect self-characteristics which tend to reappear often, kinds of behavior you are prone to repeat. One-time quirks probably do not give an accurate description of you, so forget them. They were things you "tried on" for awhile and found unpleasant or unrewarding.

3. Do build a "model" of yourself. Allow the various self components to express themselves according to their predominance in your overall behavioral and physical expression. The "model" can take many forms. It can be three-dimensional and contain physical representations of your characteristics with name tags, colors, etc. It can be a two-dimensional graph or chart which interrelates all your parts in a matrix or "flow-diagram" sort of arrangement. It can be realistic and self-explanatory or abstract, requiring long-winded verbal explanations. It can be anything which sums up in your mind the important aspects of your many self-components. Since a model is a form of analogy, it can take an endless number of expressions. (Your workbook or journal is a model of your study process.) For some, the self-model will be three dimensional; for others it may be a box with personal expressions in it and on it; still others may use a tack board to express themselves.

The model will function to allow an objective understanding of your separateness from your own components; it will demonstrate that you cannot be what you also control; that you actually are a spirit and a concept outside of your behavior and physical appearance. It will also serve as a summary test ground, providing a place to organize and synthesize the diverse bits of information you gather along the way. This model need not be misconstrued as a test of your craftsmanship or graphic ability (although that skill characteristic would be revealed by doing it.) If you are a person with "ten thumbs," mark that observation in your journal and either select a non-manual approach to model-making or decide to get better at using your hands by attempting to build something.

Do keep your model with you as you progress through the curriculum. When you detect a change in a belief, make the change in the model. Having a model for its own sake is of little value, but keeping it as a working testground for self-development and improvement increases its value with each use. **have fun!** (If it's not pleasurable, you will have trouble retaining interest in it as a project.)

NOTE! More Ways

Many tests have been invented to help physicians, statisticians and psychologists determine the same type of information being sought in these exercises. If you have access to a testing service (college and university counselling centers usually provide the full range), you might get assistance from a counselor in taking some professionally administered test.

We recommend the following tests:

1. Myers-Briggs Type Indicator Test
    (available from Educational Testing Service, Princeton, NJ)

3. Shostrom Personal Orientation Inventory
    (available from Educational and Industrial Testing Service, Box 7234, San Diego, CA 92107)

3. Rokeach Value Survey
    (available from Halgren Tests, 873 Persimmon Ave., Sunnyvale, CA 94087)

4. Eysenck Personality Inventory
    (available from Educational and Industrial Testing Service, Box 7234, San Diego, CA 92107)

5. California Psychological Inventory (Gough)
    (available from Consulting Psychologists Press, Inc., Palo Alto, CA.)

6. The Study of Values Test (Allport, Vernon, Lindzey)
    (available from Houghton Mifflin Co., Educational Div., 111 Tremont St., Boston, Mass. 02107)

7. The Luscher Color Test (Short Version)
    Pocket Books, NY

8. Minnesota Multiphasic Personality Inventory
    (available from the University of Minnesota Press, Minneapolis, Minn.)

WORDS TO THE WISE # WORDS to the WISE

[Periodic Messages from the Counseling Office]

The Counseling Staff at VALUES TECH is here to help you survive the typically hectic and confused time which accompanies discovering and change. Confusion and difficulty normally accompany any learning experience ... because learning is a time of beginning new ways of doing things ... putting aside old and comfortable behaviors. People who are making intentional changes in their lives for purposes of self-improvement need all the help they can get. For that reason, we occasionally offer helpful hints and tips for smoothing out the rough spots of the scholastic excursion. Here are a few basic hints to help you in your first days in class.

A STUDY TIP !

We suggest that each student develop consciousness of his/her abilities to relax, concentrate and imagine and to begin to work on intentional improvement of those skills.

Relaxation is the key to acceptance. The best way to study is to do it in a relaxed state. While there is no doubt that responses can be conditioned by using fear or stress-laden tactics, such conditioning is not easy, pleasant or natural. So relax! Drop your defenses. Trust yourself to respond to real dangers if they should appear, but spend your time trying to learn, instead of worrying that you won't or can't learn.

Rest often. Try to make every activity, even running, as restful as possible. Then stop to consider what you have done and the consequences of what you might do. Size things up to simplify the task of trusting yourself. A relaxed, evaluative way of life forms the basis for all natural goals. Try to see that conscious relaxation is a positive act whereas laziness represents avoidance of intention.

Imagination is the form-giver of learning. It is the way we turn abstractions into familiar reality. The task of taking in new information is far more difficult without a functioning imagination.

Concentration is the proven method for study. This requires focusing skills, It's as if the mind were being trained to act as a camera lens which could control its depth-of-field, blurring out all extraneous information, and focusing on what is most important to interrelate at a particular time.

NATURAL BARRIERS TO LEARNING

THE NATURAL BARRIERS TO LEARNING WILL ALWAYS BE WORKING AGAINST YOU. THEREFORE YOUR FIRST LINE OF DEFENSE IS TO BE AWARE OF THEIR PRESENCE.

NATURAL BARRIER No. 1 — FEAR

We fear that which comprises an anti-goal or anti-need . . . not being loved, not being treated respectfully, not being intelligent, etc. Fears center around these "negative" aspects in life.

NATURAL BARRIER No.2 — POWER

A little knowledge can turn us into fools. Knowledge is power, and its force is immediately felt. We must exert caution and respect for new power as we receive it so that we do not use it unwisely.

NATURAL BARRIER No.3 — FATIGUE

Physical and mental activity wears us down quickly. Rest is a much-needed part of every student's life. To overdo is a sign of imbalance and will eventually curtail your activities through illness or disease.

NATURAL BARRIER No.4 — OVER-EMOTION [IMBALANCE]

Questioning what we read is necessary to remain open minded. But often we merely disagree with (instead of question) what we observe in our world which is not an intellectual mode but just an emotional reaction. For a constructive disagreement we will need to back up our natural reaction with an open-minded question.

NATURAL BARRIER No.5 — OVER-OBJECTIVITY [IMBALANCE]

Learning tends toward an increase in objectification and a decrease in sensitivity — to know more and to feel less. To retain the whole human potential, we must strive to strike a balance between the two.

NATURAL BARRIER No.6 — DIVERSION

The fact that we exist in a sea of stimulus with dozens of elements sending out alluring vibrations to our senses makes it difficult to stay on any one track. To realize our intentions we must often use "blinders" to much of the information, deemed unrelated, which surrounds us.

REASONABLE THINKING

Humanized thinking is just reasonable thinking . . . the reasonable man suspects that perhaps he is wrong and is therefore always right. — adapted from Lin Yu Tang, The Importance of Living.

Four Precepts of Reasonable Thinking

1. Never accept as absolutely true that which you do not clearly know to be true.

2. *Subdivide statements into components as needed in order to deal with them better.*
3. *Begin with the simple; progress toward the difficult.*
4. *Be comprehensive and complete.*
— *adapted from Descartes*

A Basic way to deal with reality, is to separate its parts into things which are to be saved for further use and things which are to be discarded.
—adapted from the Social System by Parsons

"Newspapers ought to be divided into four [4] parts: Truths, Probabilities, Guesses & Lies."
— attributed to Thomas Jefferson

"Reason must rule the appetite in a way which derives its power from the laws of nature."
— adapted from C.S. Lewis'
The Abolition of Man

To think into and through any situation with clarity, freshness and without prejudice, it is necessary to return to the unbounded wisdom of the child, who, although limited in knowledge, grants himself complete freedom to obtain it.
— Caption from the June 1946 calendar of
The Polytechnic School of Values
Art Department

One of the hardest parts of reasonable thinking begins with the terribly difficult job of turning feeling into words. Free thinking builds on top of a free vocabulary.
— Motto seen under a glass paper weight in the office of the Associate Dean

At best, thinking, reasoning and making decisions are inexact sciences. We can do our best. We can improve our skills, gain more knowledge, open up our "receivers," become highly proficient at manipulating certain methods. But in the end, after all is done, we still have only one conclusion . . . "it all depends."
— *President T.B. Brandywine*

It all depends

The Year of Decisions

THE UNIVERSAL LIFE PROCESS
[The Foundation of the Polytechnic School of Values]

Any process can be frustrating without the conscious knowledge of "what to do next" and "how to go about it." Conscious adherence to a plan for reaching conclusions along with the persistence required for moving through a sequence of interrelated steps is basic to the intelligently organized pursuit of any goal.

At VALUES TECH we believe that the intellectual problem-solving process is a **seven stage** universally applicable procedure which is summarized as follows:

Acceptance

Stage one — Problem solving begins with your O.K.: a willingness on your part to do something about a situation which you find unsatisfactory. Your degree of involvement and your determination to "see it through" depend on this initial self-investment period. If you want to become a creative problem solver, you'll need to get good at "giving in" to the process of solving your problems. That's the only practical way to get to know them well enough to be able to control their outcome. It is possible to make it all the way to the end of the process before realizing that a low level acceptance has resulted in an unsatisfactory result. Complex or drawn-out problems may require a manifold re-investment of our time and self before resolution is ever in sight which means that the acceptance stage carries over into all of the subsequent stages of the process.

Analysis

Stage Two — Much of the work of problem-solving is done acquiring information about the problematic situation. This is the crucial stage of gaining "insight" and of finding out how the problem and its components relate to other things and interrelate among themselves. Analysis can of course be a time-consuming task (as in the case of complex, or lengthy problem areas) or it can be instantaneous and based on experience alone as in the case of our everyday problem situations requiring quick conclusions.

Definition

Stage Three — Following analysis some statement of overall conceptual content must be derived out of the new knowledge gained. In this stage, we determine the criteria to be used in determining all future actions in the course of this particular problem. And knowing more we can now make a re-statement of overall intention or purpose (clarified goal) which gives meaning to the separate criteria including what we expect to achieve (objectives) in order to satisfy the problem condition (reach our goal). This stage forms the connecting link between the foregoing analysis stage (taking apart) and the forthcoming "synthesis" (putting together) stages. Our stated "definition" will become our direction or decision-making "rulebook" for all sub-problems within the problem.

Ideation

Stage Four — Next it's the free-wheeling judgment-deferring stage of discovering the alternative means to achieve our known and stated objectives. We must free ourself from a choiceless condition and expand our potential by building a list of varied ways for resolving the defined problem situation. This requires an open-mind and realization that judgment, although important, will come in the next stage; not now!

Stage Five — After generating a reasonably varied list of alternative choices or means to our definitively stated goal we can proceed to make some judgments. By comparing and relating newly-found ideas (and their consequences) with the defined goal and its accompanying objectives, the wide list of choices is narrowed to a few "best bet" alternatives which are considered as being "most likely to succeed" . . . and a final combination or single approach is selected.

Stage Six — In this near to final stage, physical form is given to the chosen alternative. At last it is possible to do something responsible and intelligently physical about the problem situation. Depending upon our knowledge, our skills and our attitudes and intentions, the task of carrying out the chosen "idea" can be quick and easy or long and difficult. Subproblems are more likely to appear now than at any earlier stage . . . each requiring a separate tour of the total process just experienced.

Stage Seven — Comparing our achievements with our initial intentions and determining ways to improve our behavior or performance through increased knowledge, developed skills and more relevant attitudes is a final and necessary stage in the process of creative problem-solving. We look backward so that we might move forward with less confusion and greater enjoyment. When evaluative thinking becomes part of the living process, life smooths out; there are no endings and there are no beginnings . . . things transition into one another.

Our systematic "tool" is adaptable for all purposes. It is truly "universal" . . . a guiding hand to help us cope more consciously and thus more intentionally creatively with life's problematic situations. Where there is a need for more accountability the process provides an outline. If efficiency is desired, the process can help us to "stay on the track." Further work in the VALUES TECH curriculum should provide ample opportunity to become more familiar with this seven-step procedure or sequence of problem-solving events. Work becomes much more meaningful when the tools are understood.

But meaningful work is also a function of various points of view. The fable of young George Washington and the cherry tree illustrates this fact. Given a new hatchet and having no purpose other than to try it out got George into deep trouble. In devising the personally meaningful but socially unacceptable intention of testing his "tool" on the family's favorite tree, young George created far more problems than he solved. The tool was good; it was just not applied to an acceptable, socially supportive task.

Selection

Implementation

Evaluation

Choosing from a restaurant menu [via THE UNIVERSAL LIFE PROCESS]

1. **[Acceptance]** Determine to become an intelligent meal selector whenever faced with the many options offered on a restaurant menu.

2. **[Analysis]** Size up the situation: Yourself [your physical, psychological needs and limitations, your desires, your cash resources, current weight, amount of food already eaten that day, etc.; Your Dining Companion[s] [their influence over your choice]; the Environment [time allowed for dining, the occasion, the culinary quality, etc.].

3. **[Definition]** Draw some conclusions. Derive the "essence" of the situation. Determine the desired outcome and consequences.

4. **[Ideation]** Consider the options; including any combinations and alternatives which are not included in the menu but which may still be possible.

5. **[Idea-Selection]** Decide. Compare your defined outcomes and desires [3] with the options available [4] and choose the one[s] most likely to fill your needs.

6. **[Implementation]** Order your meal with the assurance that your decision is the best you can make at the time. Enjoy the results of your decision.

7. **[Evaluation]** Consider ways to improve your performance as a meal selector. Enhance your appreciation of eating and choosing your meals as the process unfolds.

A CREATIVE PERSON IS

- **Accepting** — Open-minded, adventurous, free-wheeling, unafraid, relaxed, brave, adaptable, anxious.
- **Analytic** — Curious, skeptical, questioning, divergent, subversive, perceptive, conscious & aware, sensitive, discontented.
- **Definitive** — Insightful, purposive, strong-willed, conceptual, concentrative, independent.
- **Idea-Prone** — A generator of alternatives, concerned with choice, variety conscious, inventive, original.
- **Selective** — Decisive, assertive, courageous, discerning, self-assured.
- **Implemental** — Self-motivated, persistent, active, dedicated, willing to work, resourceful, enthusiastic, manipulative, constructive.
- **Evaluative** — Concerned with improvement, comparative, judgmental, critical.

Decisions

LET'S SEE NOW …[A Lesson in Decision Making]

When "reasonable" thinking matures into systematic thinking, conclusions which were previously the result of observation or habit become the products of intelligent choice. At that point decision making takes on the characteristics of both science (uncovering relationships) and art (expressing relationships).

From the inductive-deductive thinking types discussed previously, three types of decisions emerge. Like the thinking-type sources from which they generate, these three decision-types stem from either the intuitive, sensory, perceptual (inductive) or the intentional, knowing, expectant (deductive) types of thought process. And similarly, we have named the decision-making types according to the techniques they represent.

THE THREE TYPES OF DECISIONS ARE:

1. Responsive — intuitive-inductive, impulsive, sensory, perceptual, reactive, subjective
2. Habitual — intuitive-deductive, compulsive, knowing, expectant, injective
3. Systematic — intentional, productive, propulsive, organized, evaluative, objective

Responsive Decisions

In the basic survival aspects of living, responsive decisions are the type most often used. They are our spontaneous and inductive reactions to daily sensory stimuli. In a single day, we generally make dozens of responsive decisions. For example:

We may choose to bike down Main Street instead of Elm because the latter affords a few more moments of sun. Or we may push the vending-machine button for "Choco-Drink" instead of milk on a whim to taste something sweet after being seduced by the full-color photo of a chocolate milk shake on the machine display panel. Such "impulse" choices are useful in simplifying life: they quickly satisfy needs and are useful in managing minor decisions while allowing ourselves to remain alert to possibly larger ones. (Market experts thrive on such spontaneous activity; they use it to manipulate consumer response.) Responsive behavior is best balanced by a questioning consequential concern.

Habitual Decisions

Habitual decisions are based on self-established or socially-sanctioned patterns. (Like responsive decision-making, habitual decisions are also used to simplify life and to quickly satisfy our needs.) Habits sustain our stability by "fending off" the often painful transitions caused by change. Habitual decisions are made out of relating deductive "foregone conclusions" and are dependent on forces exerted by pre-determined habit patterns and on our personal ability to either resist or yield to such forces.

Here is a sampling of habitual type decisions: We might choose to take the No.12 bus to work ("because it never stops between major intersections"). We always take elevator No.1 ("because our employees take No.2"). At the movies we choose the 10th row ("because that's where the upholstered seats begin"). During stressful periods we have a peanut butter sandwich and glass of milk for lunch ("because that's what Mom gave us as a protein booster when times were tough"). We scorn "Newsweek" ("because our friends read "U.S. News and World Report"), etc.

Systematic Decisions

Systematic decisions represent the third decision type. This process follows the same or similar problem-solving steps outlined in the Universal Life Process in Lesson Number One. Because "everyday" decision making centers around responsive and/or habitual choice, we don't get much practice at being intentional. Instead we tend to save our systematic decisions for choices with what we believe will have long-lasting consequences. We could, however, increase our self-control and assertiveness significantly by making more of our decisions in a systematic way. All it takes is a "conscious" effort. If for instance, we were to make systematic decisions daily, we would soon become skillful at it and better able to chart our future and to insure personal participation in our own progress

Comparing Decision making with Problem solving

In principle, making a decision in a systematic way is no different from solving a problem in a creative way. They are somewhat synonymous processes. The comparison chart (below) shows the direct relationship between systematic decision making and creative problem solving.

Creative Problem-Solving Process		Systematic Decision-Making Process
Accept problem	1	accept need to make a choice
analyze situation	2	determine variables and factor interrelationships
define over-all purpose and objectives to be reached or satisfied	3	define criteria, values and required level of reliability
ideate, find alternative means for resolving underlying cause	4	consider alternate means of fulfilling criteria
synthesize alternatives. Select one which best fulfills definition(s)	5	measure consequences of means & select one which fulfills criteria best
implement	6	decide
evaluate consequences	7	evaluate consequences

These stages for both processes can be combined and are elaborated upon as follows:

1. Accept the problematic decision-making situation.

2. Determine the variable factors and emotional influences involved. Identify which components make up the sub-issues of the situation.

3. Establish an order of preferences and thus rank the deciding "criteria" which will define the choices to be made. Determine the decision-maker's values and set up standards or the expected degree of reliability. Decide overall unifying meaning.

4. Consider feasible number of alternative means to the determined end.

5. Compare and measure the consequences of the alternatives with their proposed benefits. Eliminate all but the most favorable.

6. Act on your decision, and

7. Look back to determine value received compared to energy expended and to note progress at becoming a better decision maker and problem-solver.

Aside from using a conscious and orderly approach, good decisions are made by applying well-chosen methods, having clear definitions and comprehensive analysis of variables, as well as consideration of ample alternatives and making complete comparisons of alternatives and criteria. It's a lot to think about to make a responsible decision, but that's what it takes. (And then of course it's just as simple as following the chart.)

WORDS to the WISE

It's always wise to tailor the method to the job. Don't drag yourself down by using a tool that's too heavy for the job or so light that it never seems to make a dent in the work.

The ultimate goal of any problem-solving or decision-making task is to get closer to our overall intentions. This has been variously called "optimizing benefits," "maximizing objectives," "realizing values," etc., all of which adds up to the same thing: the satisfaction of important needs.

Deciding between alternatives requires self-confidence and learning how to ask your own questions and finding answers to those questions. It also requires the ability to size things up, to distinguish between things and to classify and group them as well as to break them apart into their basic components. Decision making means picking the one from the many, but it also means not picking the others. An insecure person may find this to be a psychologically "tight" situation. Stating a preference is much easier than choosing between things. Deciding takes confidence and maturity.

A group of systematic techniques which are useful in organizing a strategy for choice follows. The simpler techniques are useful for both easy and complex situations. However, you need not reserve the more complex methods only for complicated choices, since it is often the unsophisticated choices which backfire most in life. All of these methods may be adapted to meet your personal or special problems.

How to play the roles of the project manager in charge of operations at both the George Gallup Corp. and the Reuben H. Donnelly Corp. at the same time.

Technique No. DM-1
an indirect approach to establishing criteria

This is the easiest method of all; it is just a matter of convincing yourself you can do it. (You might think of it as a form of "mind-control" or self-hypnotism.) It works like this: The Gallup poll gathers many individual opinions on a specific question. Since opinions are cheap in our society, the poll taker has a relatively easy time getting a large response. Now you, too, can simulate a Gallup pollster. Stop worrying about having to make a decision. Instead concentrate on getting together all your opinions or preferences. When you've gathered a long list of opinions on the subject in question, change roles and move on to the next stage; imagine yourself an "impartial judge" at the Reuben H. Donnelly Corporation (which selects winners for numerous contests and competitive promotions). Using the "preferred" list of opinions you acquired as a pollster to serve as your judgment criteria, compare your list with the alternatives from which you must choose. You will thus become better able to make a clear decision as to which "preference" wins the "sweepstakes." In short: decide in two stages: develop criteria and then compare criteria to choices. It's simpler that way!

Technique No. DM-2
a Basic method for selecting from a wide field

How to reduce "31" flavors to one double-dip cone

There's a lot of psychology tied up in ice cream counter behavior. Baskin & Robbins, Howard Johnson's and other multi-flavor ice cream makers "drive folks crazy" with all those choices. But people seem to love to stand in front of the large selection and thrill to their indecision. Choosing two flavors for a double-dipper means rejecting twenty-nine others. It's exasperating, but fun. Some try improving the odds (two people working together gain an advantage by sharing four instead of two flavors); others enjoy persistence reinforcement (they always get the same thing regardless of the wide choice); some test their liberal natures with "freedom teasing" (they never get the same flavor twice as proof of their open-mindedness), etc.

Here's the systematic way to select your ice cream cone [or dinner guests, vacation spot, doctor, or make whatever other "important" decision you may have]

DEVELOP personal intentions or purposes ... Then

1. Divide alternatives into sets, groups or classes by finding out what they have in common, such as

A. colors
B. fruit flavors
C. non-fruit flavors
D. richness
E. additives
F. names
G. previously experienced by you or recommended by friends

2. Subdivide the classes into more specific groups, such as

A. reds, yellows, browns, etc.
B. natural fruits, processed and sweetened fruits, etc.
C. chocolates, vanillas, spices, herbs, oils, etc.
D.E. nuts, candies, glazed fruits, marshmallows, etc.
F. classical, regional, personal, political, religious, etc.
G. very messy to eat, melts fast, granny loved it, dad's favorite, etc.

3. Circle your preferences. Narrow the field as much as possible without eliminating favorites.

4. Reduce the list further by considering external limits and personal needs such as near repetitions, the need for flavor and color balance and harmony, weight gain or dental sensitivity problems, caloric content, sugar content, personal curiosity, self-assertiveness, etc.

5. Select the best bets from those which remain.

6. Enjoy your decision.

*At first glance it might appear ridiculous to go through all of these systematic operations for such a relatively unimportant task. But when systematic thinking and decision-making skills are developed the process can be applied to problems of all levels of importance and/or complexity.

United we stand

Our original motivation for classifying, grouping and sub-dividing groups was to determine the mutual exclusiveness of elements within a choice situation. However, the actual truth of the matter is that nothing stands alone. The variables in every situation are interdependent, and any conclusion we draw or any choice we make automatically enhances and calls attention to but one or a few groups while subjugating and diminishing the others. Separating bits and pieces from the whole simply allows us to study them; it's something we do in order to get closer to things and to be able to concentrate on them. If we make our choices without considering the interrelationships between groups and sub-groups we miss out on an important area of analysis.

This method "refines" the previous one by adding step 4(a) which reads:

4(a). Rank and weigh all groups and sub-groups according to the multiple points of view revealed to be involved in their interrelationships.

Technique No. DM-2X
a variation of No. DM-2

Rank and File

Trying to assign an order of importance to groups and sub-groups can be confusing. To do it well with relatively few anxieties, it's best to start out slow and work up to more complex manipulations.

First of all, ranking things is a matter of comparing them to one another as well as to a set of criteria. By comparing how "useful" two things are, we can stipulate that we prefer one thing to another because one of them meets our standards (of usefulness) better than the other; i.e., it fulfills the "usefulness" criteria best. If "economy" were to be the standard of evaluation, a low-cost, long-lasting item would normally be preferred to a higher-priced, glamour model. And if we were forced to choose between more than one low-cost, long-lasting item, we'd have to break our economy standards down into separate parts, such as cost of maintenance, life of service, energy expended, size, guarantee, etc., using progressively basic standards to determine relative importances.

To visualize comparable components, place two identical lists side by side.

Example: In trying to decide how to rank ten items of criteria (standards) for choosing a pocket calculator, the items are placed in two identical columns:

Technique No. DM-3
a method for ranking things

```
       initial cost  |  |  |  initial cost
    life of service  |  |  |  life of service
       energy spent  |  |  |  energy spent
       size of item  |  |  |  size of item
  maintenance costs  |  |  |  maintenance costs
    operating costs  |  |  |  operating costs
frequency of repairs |  |  |  frequency of repairs
    time saved by use|  |  |  time saved by use
        adaptability |  |  |  adaptability
         flexibility |  |  |  flexibility
```

* Each item in the two identical columns is compared with every other item in the columns. The person (or group) performing the

Extra Credit

The Fool-Proof Coin Trick

It is reported that Sigmund Freud used the following 'coin-tossing' technique to help his patients reveal their personal values:

When faced with a tough decision between two apparently 'equal' choices, try assigning each of the options to the faces of a coin and flip it to determine which of the two will be chosen. The big difference here is that the decision is not final. If you aren't satisfied with the way the coin lands, go on and turn it over . . . thereby using your unexpected disappointment as the clue you needed to make the decision..

ranking operation asks a consistent question regarding the relative merits of each pair of items; as: "Which one of the two items would be a more important consideration in terms of overall performance?" or "which item is the more crucial to the sales of the product?" etc. When one item is chosen to be more important than the other, it gets a check ✓. After all pairs are subjected to the same test question, the check marks are tallied to determine the ranked order of items in the column. If items are considered equal, they would both get checked.

Note: the math formula for revealing the number of combinations which must be interrelated is

$$C = \frac{n(n-1)}{2} = \frac{10(10-1)}{2} = \frac{90}{2} = 45$$

where C=number of combinations and n=number of criteria).

Another way to achieve the same thing is to put both lists into a "matrix" or x-y relationship:

	1. initial cost	2. life of service	3. energy spent	4. size of item	5. maintenance costs	6. operating costs	7. frequency of repairs	8. time saved by use	9. adaptability	10. flexibility
initial cost 1.										
life of service 2.										
energy spent 3.										
size of item 4.										
maintenance costs 5.										
operating costs 6.										
frequency of repairs 7.										
time saved by use 8.										
adaptability 9.										
flexibility 10.										

Since the diagonal of the matrix will represent a one to one relationship (each item related to itself), it can be eliminated. And since all decisions are symmetrically "twice listed," only half of the matrix need be compared (although the other half can be used to double check your decisions).

As items are compared, the one of the two which is preferred is noted by having its number placed in the intersecting square found by extending both items until they meet. In the end, the sums of numbers determine the ranking of preferences; the one most preferred is first, and so on. Variations include subdividing squares so that they contain not only the preference number but also degrees and types of interrelation between the two being compared and to others in the matrix. When preferences are tied, a runoff is in order.

Still another variation is the "pyramid" or single-list matrix. In this variation, the list of variables is also numbered, and after each decision is made, the number of the preferred variable is again placed in the connecting cell of the two items being compared. Ranking is accomplished in the same way as before by counting the number of times each item is peferred and by a renumbering of the list after the fact.

Try your skill at filling in this one using the same preference techniques used in the basic two column list. Which do you think is more important . . . No.1 or No.2? Place the preferred number in the appropriate cell.

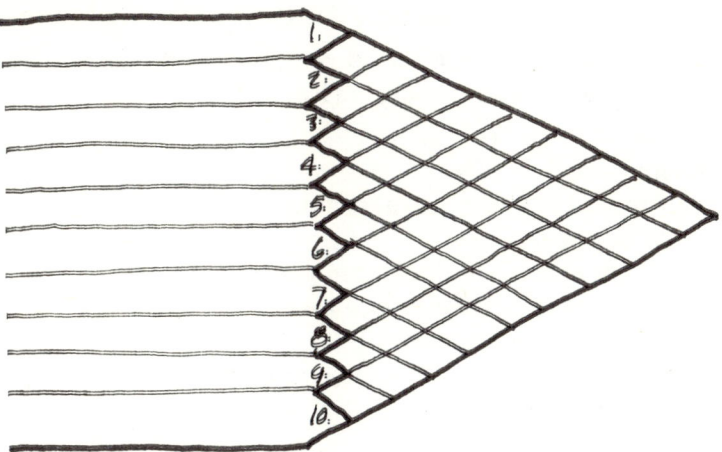

The number of times that the numbers appear in the matrix cells again determines their degree of importance to you.

Here are some things that make decision-ranking difficult:

. . . if we have too many items from which to choose, it may take more time than it's worth to rank them in hierarchical order. Scanning and simple grouping can help, allowing us to work with criteria groups instead of individual pieces.

. . . if we have a perceptual problem and just plain can't see the value of one thing over another because it is hidden from us by reason of lack of education or experience or because we may be concentrating on other things.

. . . if we inadvertently list some things more than once, by including them in more than one group (thus giving them more value than they deserve).

DO Get ahead of yourself!

Looking into the future is not one of the things we do best. Nevertheless, systematic techniques involve just that. Being systematic helps us to make the best-possible-outcome actually happen instead of allowing it to remain just a dream. So far we've seen how helpful it is to classify things into sets, groups, types and batches of "similarities." We also considered a series of techniques for ranking information variables according to personal preferences. Now let's look at a way of calculating profits and losses by adopting a "business" point of view toward making decisions.

Whether or not a product sales venture is economically feasible is determined by estimating unit costs in order to predict total costs. Future business profits will depend on accurate estimations of

Extra Credit

WATCH OUT MADISON AVENUE

You decide which fast-food franchise is Number One.

1. List at least six criteria for excellence in operating a fast-food franchise in the space provided at the top of the matrix below.

2. If you assign a factor of 1 [one] to the first criterion, try to assign a factor of relative worth to all the other criteria; i.e. if criterion two is only half as important as the first then it will have a factor of .5 and if criterion three is twice as important as the first, its factor will be 2, etc.

3. Next rate each franchise according to your criteria on a 0 to 10 [poor to excellent] basis, multiply by the factor and insert your decision in the appropriate box. Example: If Franchise Number 3 was rated average [5] on criteria number 1 [factor 1], the number 5 [5 x 1] would be placed in the box which connects Franchise Three and Criterion One.

4. Add up your rating to determine your order of preference. If the answer is different from the way you normally consider selecting quick meals, is it possible that one or more all-important criterion has been left out?

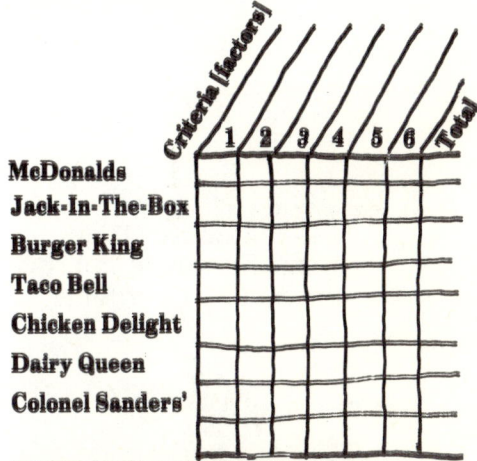

Technique No. DM-4
A method for measuring consequences before they occur

miller

how much to buy, when to sell, when prices will rise, etc. When estimates are "off," all sorts of uncomfortable things occur: money may have to be borrowed; work crews may have to be laid off; there may be a loss of sales; even bankruptcy. But when the estimates are "on," things hum along without too many unpleasant "surprises." It is the estimator's job to smooth out the kinks and to minimize unexpected consequences. Here's how it works:

1. List all decision-making criteria which are to be used as standards for success.

2. Try to determine the nature of all the necessary decisions required for success.
(As many as you need for your desired level of reliability)

3. Estimate the anticipated result of each possibility by checking its effect on these general criteria:

a. cost
b. time loss
c. ultimate use of natural resources
d. social acceptance
e. enhancement of long-term goals
f. energy conservation or waste
g. satisfaction of needs
h. environmental pollution or improvement
i. emotional impact
j. educational content
k. other

If only one negative consequence is changed into a positive result, the investment in time and energy will probably be well spent. Sub-problems should also be considered: hidden costs? increasing material costs? devaluation of the dollar? increased shipping costs?
etc.

Technique No. DM-5
A terrific way to improve the quality of criteria

Technique No. DM-6
Another way to improve criterion stating

Down deep

Being overly casual as to how you rank preferences and number variables may lead to unreliable consequences, especially in weighty situations. So if consequences are really touchy, you may want to penetrate the surface treatment of mere preference-listing in order to understand the "basis" of preference. The key to revealing foundations is bare-faced honesty, and the secret lies in self-questioning. For instance, by alternating between asking yourself "why?" and noting your response you soon get down to basic facts. If you give up too soon, however, without demanding straight answers, you'll never probe very deep. Self-discipline works for some; letting someone else do the asking works for others. They still will vary. However, once you have articulated your underlying values and rules, you can proceed to state your preferences with the assurance of personal consistency.

Osgood, et al

In their revolutionary book, THE MEASUREMENT OF MEANING, Osgood, Suci and Tannenbaum introduce a device for clarifying meanings called "the semantic differential." This tool makes it possible for you to clearly state your descriptive concepts and decision criteria in performance terms. Here is how it works:

1st First put into conceptual terms what it is that must be decided. Put your feeling into knowables . . . words.

2nd Second, break the words down into separate concepts . . . separate parts of the total meaning.

3rd Third, build a list of polar-adjectives (two words which describe opposing extremes such as sharing/selfish, brave/cowardly, truthful/dishonest, etc.) which meet the following rules:

a) They should be directly relevant to the separate concepts. For instance, for the term ice cream (sweet/tart) is o.k., but (tall/short) is irrelevant.

b) Only one of the two terms should have good or bad connotations. For the subject "hands" (dirty/clean) is o.k., but (tough/clean) should be avoided since both may have relatively good connotations.

c) The list should contain adjectives relating to the subject's value, intensity and behavior as broad areas of measurement potential.

4th Fourth, place each pair of polar-adjectives on a seven to ten-step linear scale with a neutral origin centered between the two extremes: such as

truthful 5 | | | | 0 | | | | 5 dishonest

5th Fifth, organize the concepts and polar-adjectives into related groups.

6th Sixth, decisions are then made by selecting a preferred point between the two extremes and by placing a mark on that spot.

Examples:

truthful 5✓ | | | | 0 | | | | 5 dishonest
 . . . very truthful; not dishonest at all

truthful 5 | | | | 0✓ | | | 5 dishonest
 . . . undecided; sometimes either, sometimes both

truthful 5 | | | | 0 |✓ | | 5 dishonest
 . . . a bit more dishonest than truthful

When a series of decisions relating to the subject are seen collectively a more comprehensive decision can be derived for the overall subject.

7th Seventh, remake the initial criteria statements based on the newly-gained information from the adjective descriptives.

Our control over the decisions we make is limited by many factors: human needs, past performances, energy effects, technological developments, social relations, climatic considerations, etc. The more we can increase our understanding of those limits, the more control we can expect to exert over our decisions.

The hard way

Experience comes with living. The older we get, the smarter we expect to become. Unfortunately, it doesn't always work out that

Technique No DM-7
the all-time classic method

way. We may never allow an experience which could totally change our lives to happen.

Most of us base our decision-making strategies on the reinforcements derived from our previous experience. We proceed through life, painstakingly gaining experience and building up an intuitive feeling for things on the basis of remembering the results of one decision after another. If the reinforcements are positive, we take one step forward toward making other similar choices; if reinforcements are negative, we withdraw.

If we were to use this technique in a systematic, methodical way, we would find ourself needing to try out all of the choices of each and every decision situation, one-by-one, and having to set up evaluative criteria by which to objectively rate our tests. In the ice-cream cone example it would mean trying out all of the 465 double-dip "31" Flavors combinations and testing each against a previously determined and yet ever-changing set of criteria.

It's the long, hard way to determine which one is "best," out of many but it's the only sure way to know we've tried 'em all. The trouble with this method is that most of us don't have the time or energy to try out everything available. Still it's important to realize that "the hard way" is always available when extreme comprehensiveness is required.

Technique No. DM-8
The convergent abstraction method

Algorithmics

"Logical" decision making consists of reducing all the facts of a situation into a series of verbal equations which can be integrated into a conclusion (Mathematical symbols and equations are sometimes employed to determine results in an even more abstract way.) Basically the method follows this outline:

Things which are similar are organized into groups: Ascertain which parts are similar and group them together. Then make statements which relate to and describe the individual groups, such as, "Ice cream is hard when cold and my teeth are sensitive to cold."

Find the most significant relationship between the statements describing the various groups. (This is sometimes called the "key variable" or "essence of the situation.") Make deductive statements to describe that significant effect; i.e., "My teeth should not be subjected to cold, hard foods."

Once the total situation has been reduced to interrelated pattern statements, we usually find that we are dealing with values and concepts rather than with isolated facts and unrelated conclusions. Via the "if such and such, then so and so" method of rational thought, we can then make an overall conclusion: "I better not eat any 'fresh from the freezer' ice cream until my teeth are less sensitive."

Clarence Darrow

There are many laws and many interpretations of the law in every society. A holding in one legal case tends to set a precedent for later cases. The law calls this <u>stare decisis</u> (Latin: to stand by what has been decided). In preparing a case for court, an attorney researches all applicable law relevant to the issue at hand. When a previous ruling which supports the desired outcome is discovered to be "on all fours" with the case, it is used as the basis for building a logical argument leading to a judicial decision. Thus precedence sets the foundation for advocacy.

Technique No. DM-9
Legal guide for decision making

Systematic decision making is a process of optimizing benefits. Through it, we work toward the ultimate goal of getting the most out of life. Out of it, values find expression.

The elements of nature obey the laws of nature; we can apply the principles of life to the elements of living. Essential to any choice is the application of criteria [expressed by emotion, values, life style, personality, intentions, desires, needs, drives, etc.] to determine the amount of energy we are willing to expend.

To be sure that choices coincide with intentions requires consciousness and knowledge. Knowledge is acquired by compiling and relating important alternatives and consequences. Having a wide-awake consciousness of the environmental forces which might affect or effect conclusions facilitates the task.

Security flows from the ability to predict reliable results. But the scope of reliability ranges from "totally unreliable" through "maybe" to "extremely reliable." The degree of anticipated reliability determines the amount of effort that you should expect to be charged in order to achieve it.

Although it can produce reliable and accountable results systematic decision making should not be utilized exclusively; responsive and habitual choices are also valuable skills to develop. For most daily routine, systematic decision making would be a waste of time. Consequently, it is necessary to analyze conditions

67

quickly and make good judgments in any given situation. Sometimes ends are important while means are not; at other times means are important when ends are not. But since both assume importance at some time, a general awareness of both can save time in the long haul. As noted earlier, it is important to select the tools most appropriate to the size or complexity of the job to be done.

Back in 1892, Oscar Wilde commented, "It is only shallow people who do not judge by appearances. The mystery of the world is in the visible, not the invisible." This is strong reinforcement for those who are sensory oriented, but it's of no use whatsoever to those who merely look without questioning. Unless sensory data is organized and analyzed into generally relatable abstractions its meaning remains shallow.

Rational, systematic decision-making is an activity of the mind. It offers a practical approach for coming to grips with confusion. It's primarily an objective process, but subjective emotions are also important. If we try to eliminate emotion from decision-making an unnatural imbalance results. Don't try to be "objective" at the cost of eliminating all emotional content from the decision-making process. Intelligent choice implies a balance of fact and emotion. We must not only deal with what can be seen and known, but we must also learn to objectify emotions by turning them into words, acts and other "measurables."

Because it's easier [and therefore natural] to move away from potential stress we tend to turn our backs on accountability and work. But our intellect [an equally natural element] can function to help us to maintain the balance needed to remain actively involved in life's choices.

The FOUR ENEMIES of intelligent choice are:

ENEMY No.1 - Evasion of responsibility
ENEMY No.2 - Avoidance of the facts
ENEMY No.3 - Aversion to organization
ENEMY No.4 - Denial of emotion

the FOUR ALLIES of intelligent choice are:
ALLY No.1   Systematic Process-Consciousness
ALLY No.2   Knowledge of Alternatives and Consequences
ALLY No.3   Skill in Using Decision-Making Techniques
ALLY No.4   Open-Mindedness; Willingness to Change

GROUP DECISIONS

If the job is too large or too consequential to tackle alone, you may want to try

THE STUDY BUDDY CONCEPT

(An Extra Lesson in Group Decision Making)

Complex social problems call for group decision. It makes sense for those who share common interests to team up and make the big decisions together. However, experience indicates that group decisions can sometimes be even more prejudicial and unreliable than the individual efforts. Two cases in point are "Twelve Angry Men" and "The Oxbow Incident", classic films discussed in many psychology and education classes.

In "Twelve Angry Men" a group of biased jurors are prepared to convict an innocent man of murder. Their minds have been

swayed by previous (prejudicial) experiences and a "well-presented" case of circumstantial evidence. In order to teach the moral lesssson of the perils of prejudice the author adds one open-minded juror to act as conscience for the group. In a dramatic and uplifting ending, this juror breaks the spell of injustice by exposing the hypocrisy and prejudice. As the story ends, the classroom audience invariably vows to cleanse itself of laziness and prejudice and to make all important future decisions based on a reasonable examination of the facts.

In "The Oxbow Incident" a posse of vengeful ranchers search out what appears to be the band of cowboys who rustled their beef. The cowboys are innocent, but the ranchers have rigid preconceptions regarding their guilt. It's a shocking tale, ending with the innocents being hanged and the ranchers finding out too late that their cattle and the dead "rustlers" weren't related. This time the film ends in tragedy . . . there is no open-minded "juror" to purge the ranchers of evil. We are left with a feeling of helplessness. Under the circumstances there doesn't seem to be anything that anyone could have done to save the cowboys. We begin to wonder what decision we might have made if placed in a similar situation. Perhaps only later is a moral decision made to be more tolerant and open-minded in our own group actions and decisions.

In both examples, the group did more harm than any individual could possibly have done. When people convene to make decisions, group dynamics produce strange results. Kurt Lewin, Irving Janis, Jay Hall and other social psychologists have conducted experiments which show that a systematic group decision process can yield results far superior to those produced by an individual. Conversely, their studies reveal that non-systematic group decisions can yield results inferior to those produced by a single independent decision-maker. The conclusion is that if people are going to decide issues in groups, they had better be systematic.

The reason for this is easy to understand. When semi-strangers gather to decide issues, they bring with them all of their personal and interpersonal conflicts. They may be disoriented, inattentive and insecure. They may feel threatened by others. Some are anxious until a responsible leader emerges. In short, new groups don't act like groups at all; they still behave as individuals waiting for a group spirit to form and a systematic format to be established.

On-going groups, on the other hand, have their own problems. Here the chain-of-command or "pecking order" determines input. Such groups develop subtle prejudices toward competing groups and to members within their own ranks who advocate change. They attempt to preserve the status quo at the expense of self-renewal. Eventually most such organizations rigidify and die.

Systematic decision making and a commitment to group renewal can change all that. There is no reason why groups should be less effective than the individuals who banded together to maximize their mutual ability in the first place.

Here's how to help your group produce valuable decisions

Creative group decision-making can be accomplished by following

Extra Credit

Back in the Sixties there was a rumor going around claiming the popular artist Andy Warhol was running an ad in the Classified section of the New York Times. The ad supposedly made an offering similar to the following: Warhol will add his signature to and thus make an original work of art out of any artifact anyone wanted to bring to him for the purpose of increasing its appreciable value . . . for a fee. This purportedly was another of Warhol's legendary schemes to help people become more aware of the value of the pieces of the process of life. If they could not appreciate in a full sense what they thought was valuable, then he would give them the "authority" to appreciate those things by turning them into "works of art" before their very eyes. Whether true or not, the message comes through clearly. Do we really need someone else to tell us it's O.K. to appreciate what we imagine to be important or beautiful or valuable?

Kirby J. Hensley, a simple but brainy minister in California did a similar thing with his Universal Life Church concepts. By eliminating all requirements for credentials, he ordains brother and sister "ministers" by mail, free of charge, and en masse at rock concerts and other public events. He thereby gives many people the "authority" they may feel to have needed to begin acting out the "good lives" they would not lead otherwise. If you suddenly had the "authority" to solemnify a wedding ceremony, what do you think you'd say? How would you handle the situation? If you had the "authority" to administer over a funeral proceeding, what form would you allow it to take? If you were the one who had to deliver the "sermon" at your church service, what do you think the "authority" of your position would allow you to say that you might not say otherwise?

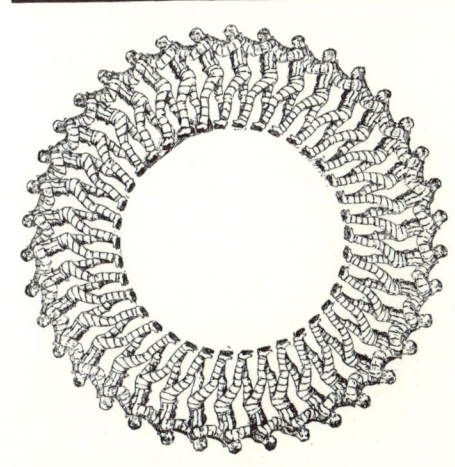

the process outlined below.

1. If the group functions efficiently, it will get more done. All members of your group should have a clear understanding of procedure. A procedural Sergeant-at-Arms should guard against prolonged detours from a mutually chosen course of action.

2. Benign leadership is a must. A good leader should engender enthusiasm and encourage participation. This requires a balanced, self-confident person who appreciates the relationship between goals, process, results and accountability. Ideally, a leader should be an impartial moderator who helps the group to function efficiently in a mutually supportive way. The undesirable leader is officious, tyrannical and manipulative. Both approaches can accomplish similar ends. One is simply far more socially redeeming than the other

3. There is no need for a team if it only produces a hurried consensus; a public opinion poll would work as well. The attempt to arrive at a fast consensus without evaluation of separate individual viewpoints fosters a tyrannical attitude: "Don't bother me with the facts; I've got my mind made up." Prior to group discussion, it is even a good idea to let each member submit an anonymous written opinion.

4. Potentially hot issues should not be avoided. To squelch conflict makes group decision a farce, and sharing points of view is one of the primary benefits of coming together.

5. Before a final vote, the group should have agreed upon the criteria to be satisfied by the decision. If the goal is unclear, the task is irrelevant.

6. Decisiveness is fostered when decision-making groups regularly identify their purposes and potentials:

... why they meet at all
... what general goals they work toward
... what individual areas of expertise are available
... what strengths they collectively represent
... what potential weaknesses are to be avoided
... what tools and outside help are available
... what the various roles of the members are

And the group must constantly reinforce the open-minded attitude necessary to formulate well-analyzed conclusions. Without these prerequisites, group members are merely an audience listening to speakers and settling for the conclusion of a few.

7. The secret ballot should be used as often as possible because:

... it encourages all to participate by giving each a confidential vote
... it emphasizes individual participation
... it reduces authoritarian behavior in leaders
... it encourages speakers to address the entire group instead of power figures only.

8. Groups are better able than individuals to consider the consequences of alternatives before reaching a decision. Groups can sub-divide, present segmental reports, experiment and compare data in ways not usually available to the individual.

END OF INTRODUCTORY LEVEL

Dealing with Personal Values

Participants who have completed the Introductory level lessons to their satisfaction may proceed to the Intermediate Level which provides lessons and exercises designed to reveal personal beliefs and values.

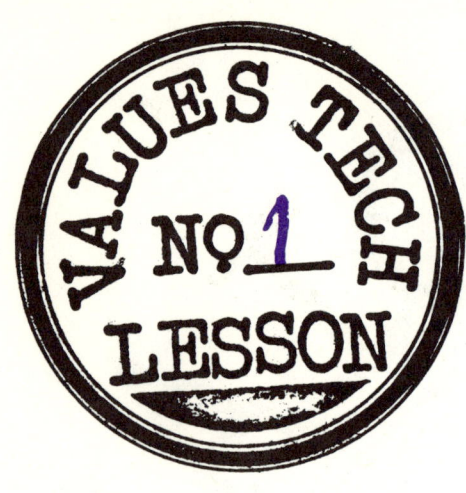

Who? Me? [A Lesson in Ethics]

Decision-making is a manipulative activity.

We manipulate elements when we choose the one and reject all others, and eventually this manipulation involves larger systems; nothing moves or gets moved without everything else feeling it in some way.

"No man is an island." An act by one member of society invariably affects all others. So when people make choices without regard for others, irresponsibility rears its ugly head. Choice implies responsibility; this is basic to all decision making. Even the act of selection among alternatives is a decision to accept responsibility. Responsibility is a social-environmental concept; a link between the intentions of the individual and the survival of society. Being responsible is an intentional act, whereas irresponsibility may simply be due to unconsciousness or ignorance. To accept responsibility means accepting accountability; it suggests we are willing to back up our actions with reasons.

Truly responsible people habitually check to see how their self-controlled lives fit into the universal scheme of things.

When we make an independent choice, we expose our beliefs, whereas indecisiveness implies lack of conviction. When a person "knows what he wants," it's a fair bet this person has worked out some personal beliefs in a conscious way. We say we are capable of "standing on our own two feet," and we respect that kind of purposive behavior. People who are aware of their values (know what they believe) do things intentionally; they are constructive at least unto themselves. Great institutions arise when decisive people "take a stand" on a particular issue. Unfortunately, purposive behavior isn't always beneficial, as witness all the classical and romantic suicides and murders, from Socrates drinking the poison hemlock in ancient Greece to the Kennedy assassinations of our own time, which were performed by "responsible" people, too. The threat behind "the impossible dream" is that we all have the potential power to re-direct the immediate course of history by virtue of our responsible or irresponsible behavior in acting out our intentions and purposes. It is this realization that prompts us to clarify personal beliefs and to harmonize our own values within the entire system.

Lab Exercise for 1

Man-on-the-Street [Expressing Values]

(Realizing the need for personal values and responsible behavior)

Suppose you are downtown shopping. It's lunch hour, and you've got to hurry in order to grab a sandwich and also buy a pair of tennis shoes. As you rush past a small crowd, a roving reporter pushes a microphone up to your mouth. "I'm a street reporter for the Daily Puzzle, and we'd like your opinion on the subject of capital punishment."

Surprised, confused, embarassed and dumbfounded...in that order...you might respond, "I don't think it's right, but I guess we've got to do something about crime." In the hours that follow, would you think a lot about capital punishment? Sure you would. By the time your spontaneous words and unexpected photo appeared in the paper the next day, would you be ready to explain to your friends just how you really feel about capital punishment? Probably. (At least a lot better than the explanation you gave to the reporter.)

Of course, we can't expect to always be prepared to express intelligent opinions on every subject a roving reporter might ask. Nevertheless, the possibility of public disclosure can be useful as a tool for forcing us to clarify vague beliefs.

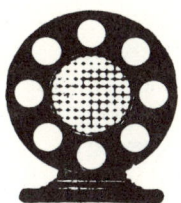

How would you respond to these typical "man-on-the-street" questions? Imagine that you have only a few minutes to answer each one. Don't watch the clock, however; just try to feel out the time a reporter might allow before cutting you off and moving on to the next person.

1. What do you think is the best way to enjoy life?
2. Should the government take over television?
3. How would you like to spend your retirement?
4. How does your answer to Question No. 1 relate to the "fair" distribution and use of world resources?
5. What does nationalized TV have to do with presidential elections?
6. Should older people receive more benefits than others?

Along with your answers, record some comments about how well you think you performed under pressure and what that might mean. Discuss your performance with someone else (if possible) to get a reading on how your beliefs and the extent of your knowledge regarding these subjects compares with others.

Lab Exercise for LESSON 1

Exercise No. 2

Trip for Two [Examining Values]

Suppose that your favorite daydream has just materialized: by signing that toothpaste company entry blank at the drug store, you've just won a one-month, all-expense-paid vacation for two to any place in the world. Take one minute for answering each of the following questions:

Who'll be your partner on this trip?

Where will you go?

What month of the year?

What'll you have when the trip is over?

How will you be better or worse off for your adventure?

Spend two or three minutes explaining each answer in writing so that you are able to see your thoughts.

60 Seconds [Expressing Values]

Suppose you are the lucky one-millionth subscriber to cable TV, and the company has awarded you the grand prize: the use of the staff and production facilities of station KPTV to produce your own one-minute prime-time major network TV spot announcement. Cash Value: $100,000.00 (winner may not receive cash in lieu of TV time or sell or trade the award).

A) What would your message be?

   Would it further society's needs as well as your own?

B) Spend half an hour alone or in a group actually designing the 60-second videotape; record all that you discover about yourself in terms of what you consider to be important. Those things reflect your values.

HOMEWORK

Before going on to the next lesson, participants may desire to discover more about their beliefs and values regarding the subject matter of the current lesson.

You can broaden your knowledge of your beliefs; you can heighten your value-revealing skills and you can deepen your understanding of this subject by attempting to design other lab exercises or experiences of your own. The criteria we used to write the foregoing warm-up exercises were:

Will the exercise cause values and beliefs to be expressed?

Is it feasible? Can the exercise be experienced in a reasonably short period of time with a reasonably small amount of energy expended?

Is the experience somewhat familiar, i.e., does it contain some tie with previous experiences so that fear of the totally new and unknown will not block accepting it?

Does the exercise contain immediate reinforcing values?

What additional exercises can you design to reveal your attitudes regarding the subject just completed?

Believe It Or Not [A Lesson of Philosophy]

One sure-fire way to appreciate the need for conscious personal values and responsible behavior is to be asked leading questions. It is embarrassing when we are unprepared to explain our reasons, and it points out that values and credibility go hand in hand. If we can't say what we believe, we won't earn much believability.

Still, it would be a waste of time to articulate reasons for every little decision. Doing so could require all our energies . . . and for what? To avoid embarrassment? Even for that, we could easily learn to live with some embarrassment if it meant saving energy (most of us do that anyway).

The generally intelligent way to make decisions is to develop a personal philosophy of life. An overall view of things provides a basis of reasoning which will cover most situations. Then later on, when all of the separate reasons we give for specific situations are examined as a whole, the consistency provided by a general philosophy will give unity and credibility to them all.

It's not so hard to build a personal philosophy of life. It requires a decision to limit one's self to a certain set of rules. And like almost everything else, it can be a two-edged sword. On the one hand, it helps us keep things in order and to deal with events more positively; on the other hand, too rigid a form of habitual behavior can keep us from experiencing new viewpoints.

Most personal philosophies deal with life's purposes in broad terms, "Fun-loving and honest," "Civic-minded and sympathetic," "Adventurous and carefree," and so on are typical examples. Here are seven basic and general frames of reference for defining life's purpose:

1. We can define life's purpose in physical terms: Example: "Life is approximately 75 years of enjoyment, hard work and confusion."

2. We can define life's purpose in terms of behavior: Example: "Living life to the fullest, enjoying every experience is what it's all about."

3. We can define life's purpose in terms of interrelationships: Example: "Life is just one problem after another in the big game of survival."

4. We can define life's purpose with analogy, simile or metaphor: Example: "Life is like a good beef stew; it's only meaningful when it's got lots of different components and when it's hot and spicy."

75

5. We can define life's purpose in terms of experience or history: Example: "It's a dog-eat-dog rat race where hard work seldom pays off."

6. We can define life's purpose in the structural terms of force interactions: Example: "Life is a paradox of change within a desire to remain unchanged."

7. We can define life in fatalistic terms: Example: "Life is what happens while we're making plans to do something about it."

But personal philosophies don't have to remain as abstract as these examples have been. They can get far more definitive and specific and measurable. Consider two examples:

In the first assume you know what you believe in general. Suppose, for instance, that you say you believe in "honesty." Once conscious of that belief, you can use it to test every new decision which is concerned with "honesty." Your individual responses will either clarify or negate the initial belief, which, in turn, either reinforces or ignores the stated philosophy.

In the second example, assume you're not too sure of what you believe. When you begin that way, you can use your responses to each specific decision in life as a guide toward a conscious determination of what overall things you do actually believe.

Once more, "consciousness" is the key. It takes intent and purpose to "know" something. Desires have to be turned into actions. But once something is known, it becomes a basic belief. And the sum of our basic beliefs is our overall philosophy; the basis for determining selections and judging value in all new experience.

"Adjectives" [describing values]

Leaf through an abridged, paperback dictionary and make a list of many of the adjectives you find there. You might take as long as an hour on this. Check off each one that seems to fit your behavior.

Get two friends to read your list and make a check next to each adjective they think describes you. In the week that follows, try to consciously evaluate two or three of your decisions by comparing the criteria you used to make the decisions with your behavioral description as perceived by your friends. (Whether their description fits or not, you will probably be more conscious of your beliefs and behavior in the future. But if their description of you does coincide with your behavior, you have uncovered still another clue to a deeper self-knowledge.)

"Reactions" [examining values]

Imagine a TV news reporter talking to a female consumer in a supermarket. As the consumer puts four five-pound bags of sugar into her cart she says, "I don't believe in hoarding or inflation, but you've got to protect your family." Moments later the conflicts in her statement emerge in the thoughts of many viewers, but the show has progressed to other matters, and there's no opportunity to question what she said.

But now there is plenty of time to consider what she said. If you've got a tape-recorder handy, record your feelings about what the lady said, what you think she means, and how you might act in a similar situation. (If a recorder's not available, write down your feelings as in a casual letter to a friend.) Later on, share your results with someone while you try to decide if you really agree with all, some or none of the consumer values you have stated. Add the results of your evaluation to the "philosophy of life" section of your journal or Vade Mecum.

Man of Tomorrow [prediction as a values-revealing method]

What we do and what we say we'd like to do are often very different things. Both can reveal what we believe. The degree of separation between the two is a function of will power or strength of purpose. But let's put reality aside for a moment and take a look at our dream world where true values might be exposed by examining intentions instead of the hidden needs encased in past behavior.

Draw a picture of yourself as you imagine you'll look five to ten years from now according to your fondest dreams. A stick figure will do, but try to include most of the following in your drawing:

    What would you like to be wearing?

    What would you like to be doing?

    What would you like to be saying?

    Where would you like to be? mountains or seashore? city or country? inside or outside?

    What things would you like to have surrounding you? other people? recreational equipment? work tools? transportation? house? plants?

Write a sentence or two (to accompany the drawing) which supplies meaning to the separate "dream" components.

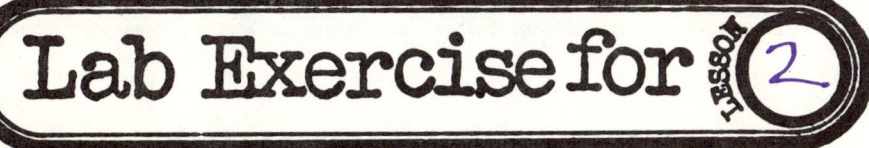

Monkey See [further defining concepts]

A former VALUES TECH student wrote the following statement in a mid-term self-evaluation paper:

"One of my current concepts is that all things are interrelated and interdependent! This leads me to conclude that everyone has the same basic needs.

Individuality is determined by each person's specific proportion of those universal common needs; i.e., we all have different amounts of the same set of needs. Also, this helps me realize that everything is anything and anything is everything. I am you. We are a rock. No matter where you push, everything else moves somewhere. Except for law and education, there are no separations. The names which we assign to things are only fantasies for bits and pieces of everything which is the same."

This statement prompted a discussion which lasted for an entire class period but which resulted in a deeper understanding of what was meant.

For the next ten minutes write down some of your own current beliefs; then see if you can't find someone with enough time to discuss them with you. After the discussion, your beliefs will perhaps grow and change into a different, more profound form.

OLDIES, BUT GOODIES (A Lesson in the Classics)

Sometimes it seems as if the ancient Greek, Roman and Chinese philosophers "said it all" before us, and we merely run around in circles inventing new ways to translate the already stated universal truths. Every time we think we have made some progress, we discover we have arrived at the same point of understanding achieved by Plato, Aristotle, Cicero or Confucius.

The past is not merely our heritage; it is rich in guidelines for tomorrow. To think of it as a separate entity is academic and does not take into consideration its inherent value as a part of the total continuum of history which includes both "then" and "now" as well as "yet to come." Until we make the tie, in mind and behavior, between "new-fangled" and "old-fangled," we remain on the exasperating course of repetition and rediscovery of things.

In the humanities, where we find the prized thinking of recorded history, "words to live by" flow freely . . . a stream of ideas for finding ways to live meaningful lives. From Lao-Tse to Chairman Mao and Aristotle to Martin Luther King there are endless variations on the basic human themes just waiting to guide us in the search for what we believe.

Dear Old Dad (past and future values)

Time is a continuum, not a disconnected segment of existence. The present is a link between the past and the future. We participate in the continuum by functioning as three generational "pivot points"; we all learn something from our parents and we may teach something to our children. In that way we become a conscious part of the dynamic chain of historical events.

If you want to get more actively involved with history, try this:

1. Write down three things that you recall your mother or father having done well or valued highly. (Perhaps you were "lectured" for falling short of those skills or standards yourself.)

2. Select one of your parents' achievements or values that is most valid today and which you think you'd like the most to emulate and pass on to others.

3. Find some ways to develop a greater appreciation of that thing by getting involved in its "process". As you discover its aspects and meanings, try to translate them into personally relevant terms.

4. Let your behavior reflect your interest: Talk about it. Share it with friends. Teach others (especially the young) about it. Find some classic quotations which relate to it. Write about it. Incorporate it into your life so that others might learn it by observing you.

Lab Exercise for LESSON 3

Exercise No. 2

"Queen for A Day" [recording values]

Yesterday is today when tomorrow comes.

Old tintypes and daguerreotypes often present eye-opening reminders that folks of an earlier time were in many respects the same as us. When we see a photo album documenting the entire lifetime of one person, for instance, we begin to realize that Man, like many other natural elements, sprouts, blooms and withers as a small separate process which is but part of a bigger, continuous process. After following (in photographs) one person through life from a baby to an adult, we come to recognize that person's "look" and traits. We learn to pick him or her out of a crowd. Toward the end of the album we can almost predict the photos which come on succeeding pages.

Now, try this experiment:

1. Construct or review a photo album of yourself. Maybe the photos are scattered and will need to be retrieved from relatives and friends. Or maybe your parents have a collection you can borrow intact. If no photographs exist, perhaps you can get an old neighbor or friend of the family to describe how you looked and acted at various stages of life. (Outside help is always a good way of checking up on the accuracy of your own memory.)

2. When you have a reasonably complete series of photographs (or descriptions) lined up chronologically and you are able to see the growth line which connects them, you should be able to start making predictions. (NOTE! Some participants may wish to add the photos to the HISTOGRAM they constructed during the ENTRANCE EXAMS.)

As you work on this project, remember that some things in
your life are inevitably going to happen. But some things
are pretty much up to you to determine if they will happen
or not. Don't lose sight of the fact that stories
similar to yours have been told many times; that each
of them could be described at any point during their
process as the result of forces acting on them which are
both similar to and uniquely different from yours.
Because of those "similar" forces (natural growth and
aging), you can certainly look forward to getting
progressively older, slower, grayer, weaker, bent over
and inactive after "peaking out" (perhaps more than once)
with periods of great activity and sensory awareness.
And because of the "different" forces (philosophical,
environmental, educational and social), you can begin to
look ahead to future values; to what you will be doing;
to where you will be living and to how you will expect
society to affect all that...all by virtue of the
selections you make and the intentions you have in your
life.

VALUES ACROSS TIME [A Lesson in History]

In previous lessons, we have seen that value-shaping forces begin to emerge when people gather together in groups. These forces are far more complex than most of us realize, and to unravel such intertwined networks of self and social needs initially appears impossible.

It is just that seemingly impossible task of making sense of the patterns of society which is the historian's job. First, historians fit together small factual and artifactual bits to form small patterns. Then they arrange the smaller patterns into larger pictures of human values and behavior at various points along a time continuum. Looking backward and forward, historians therefore use the expressed values and behavior of a society to clarify the interrelationships between time periods. The knowledge, skills, tools and attitudes of a society combined with their expressed actions then become distilled into generalizations that represent each time period. Via such generalizations (which grow from accumulated detail), blocks of time have been characterized as "Early Christian," "The Dark Ages," "Renaissance," "Victorian," "The Roaring Twenties," "The Fabulous Fifties," etc. We use these titles to recall the many interrelated components which comprised the total process of an era.

History is an important tool for education because it involves the recording and comparative analysis of details, as well as its production of summaries, conclusions and other total views. The study of history allows us to begin to grasp overviews as summations of a vast complex array of details and causations, to see details as pieces of larger patterns. It is important for us to see the relationship between the whole picture and the underlying causes and details; otherwise we are left with a superficial, one-sided view of things. In other words, having an historical point of view implies analysis and evaluation of the bits and pieces as well as the whole. It's not enough to deal with the products of life as if they were devoid of the processes which determined their form.

To illustrate, look at these two examples:

Suppose you found an Indian arrowhead in your backyard. Since you are working toward developing a balanced appreciation for both process and product, you might do some research to discover the causes and forces leading up to the making, use, discard (or loss) and eventual burial of that arrowhead in your part of the country. The result of your research would be greater awareness of the interrelationship of cultures across time and of your own culture. Analysis of the values which produced the arrowhead could lead to a better understanding of your own beliefs.

A second example uses the Christmas celebration to view history from the standpoint of symbols. Many artifacts have come to be associated with the yuletide season because of its long history in western civilization. Some of these symbols invite reflection and introspection. In some parts of the world others symbolize midwinter as a social rest-stop in a physically cold time of year, bringing conviviality and release. (Decorated trees, holly and mistletoe fit into this last category.) Any one of the many products of Christmas (even the smell of cut pine) can evoke memories of the entire celebration for those who have had the experience.

History doesn't simply deal with the past processes; history is a continuous process. It is happening right now, and we are all either actively or passively part of it. As future historians look back on our time and rearrange the scattered artifacts we produce, they will probably characterize this period under some general terms in order to see our age as part of the larger process. But we are here and now, and we can begin doing the same for ourselves. All it takes is intentional analysis and a functional appreciation of the process we experience.

WESTERN MANKIND — A BRIEF GENERALIZED SURVEY	WEST ASIATIC PEOPLES MESOPOTAMIA 3000 BC – 331 BC	EGYPTIAN CIVILIZATION 3000BC – 1st CentAD	ANCIENT GREEK CIVILIZATION 3000BC – 146 BC	ANCIENT ROMAN CIVILIZATION 300BC – 365AD
RELIGIOUS CONCEPTS	The sun & nature divinities; gods of plants and animals; strong belief in **life after death**; little separation between **gods** and **kings** in terms of influence (great public efort is exerted to carry kings into state of external life; priests control education; (temporary life—eternal afterlife)	Gods reside "in the sky" and control all human behavior; mysterious, magic, fatalistic; symbolism and superstition. "Man is a **pawn of nature** but must learn to behave as nature."	Highly developed appreciation and **worship of nature**; **gods take human form** as well as animal form. Mother "Hera" (fertility) is supreme deity. Religion is life and growth-oriented; gods are ultimate rulers and growth-oriented; gods are ultimate rulers over crops, families, victories, etc.	Closely patterned after Greeks while evidencing more concern for **social** organizational, governmental problems of greater population. Emperors viewed as near gods; reverence for ancestors and artifacts as opposed to natural processes.
SOCIAL CONCEPTS	**Deified monarchy** (god-kings) rule; build for life after death; dedicate all human activity to prepare for the peace which follows the stress of life; man is subject to kings and gods; most revered tasks are those most closely related to the movement toward the afterlife.	Increasing size of society and its needs promotes **trade** and **social intercourse**; concentration on developing methodology; government; property control; law; organized food production in mutually supportive approach to managing resources.	Simple hierarchy of clearly marked **class levels** (from farmers and servants to "privileged citizens"; slaves serve aristocrats; strong government acts as protector and maker of social decisions.	**Urban movement** and interest in **social orders** promotes need to turn to colonization and acquisition. Urban centers of **trade, government** and **culture**; views rest of the world as a resource (to supply the strong and fit); family oriented.
MAIN ARTIFACTS	Fragile temporary domestic products; **eternal tombs** designed for eternity and to act as gateways to afterlife.	Temporary domestic products; **semi-permanent tombs**; trade and commerce paraphernalia; excellent **records** of use of lands, laws and trade goods **inventories**.	**Temples, civic** building and **cultural/recreational monuments**; literature and law-relating principles of co-existence with nature; fine arts; mosaics, murals, sculpture and carving.	**Temples, civic** buildings and **cultural/recreational monuments**; literature, art.
POPULATION	less than 50 million.	Up to 50 Million	50 Million	100 Million

EARLY CHRISTIAN PERIOD 313AD–800AD BYZANTINE ERA 330AD–1453AD	MEDIEVAL PERIOD 800AD–1100AD *the Dark Ages*	RENAISSANCE PERIOD 1400AD–1800AD *the Age of Enlightenment*	NINETEENTH CENTURY 1840–1880 *the Victorian Period*	EARLY TWENTIETH CENTURY 1901–1915 *Edwardian Period*
Constantine and Pope Gregory determine tenets of **Christianity as official** law. Eventual coronation of Charlemagne and the establishment of the "Holy Roman Empire"; return to living with respect for nature (avoidance of extremes); diversity of particulars.	Education and cultural enlightenment under auspices of Christian priests. **Papal power overrides** most monarchical power; bishops control governments, land use, military, etc.	**Humanism**; breakdown of Papal power; new views of life process (instead of afterlife) as the most viable aspect; Christian ethics (Christ as model) leading to exploration and discovery. Science and earthly "fact" intermingling with traditional mysticism.	Return to strictness and fixed **obedience to rules** of church and state. The 'proper' life leading to a 'satisfying' death and heritage; many variations and translations of similar Christian themes.	New examination of **relationship of man to nature** (and supernature); life-oriented; review of rules and redefinition of man as a life force.
Reaction to domination by invaders leads to **subjugation to religious leadership**. Trade, agriculture and industrial activity must thrive on a collective basis for the ultimate glorification of Christ.	Concentration on life after death; vast expenditure of energy building cathedrals dedicated to achieving a clear path to heaven; to glorify **God**. Commerce and industry are heavily taxed by the church and social purpose begins and ends in Christian mysticism. Individuals and groups are subjugated to the constant threat of marauding armies or feuding neighbors.	**Man** (life process) **oriented**; moral inner-directedness; revival of learning; individualism and general interest in the rights and privileges of **separate citizens; honor derived on the basis of merit instead of birthright; personal protection takes the place of protective custody by church or landlord;** 'universal', 'form-giving', decisive man emerging. Beginning of industrialized society.	Return to abidance by laws imposed outside of self. **Compliance**, conservatism, and hard work. Increased population forces the masses to gather under economic overlords in positions as factory owners or materials distributors); growth of new social movements and labor organizations.	New **social organizations**; Marxism, socialism; the study of human rights; women's suffrage establishes its roots; conventional, traditional, institutional views re-examined for social flaws.
Church and Christian symbols; religious paraphernalia and paintings.	**Cathedrals, churches** and other **religious shrines**; relics (and personal effects) of saints and martyrs; walled cities and towns.	**Houses**, castles, cathedrals, home fortifications; printing and books, the tools of war and mechanical advantages; highly refined arts and crafts, social spaces and public art commissioned as monuments to the wealthy patrons.	**Machines** and tool-crafted products; elaborate machine-made decorations in houses, clothes & furnishings as a result of potentials of new industrial processes; air and water pollution.	**Flamboyant houses, restaurants** and **clubs**; more civic construction (town halls, schools, hospitals, etc.); new industrial products of world war lead to rise in technology.
250 Million	500 Million	800 million.	1.5 billion	2 billion

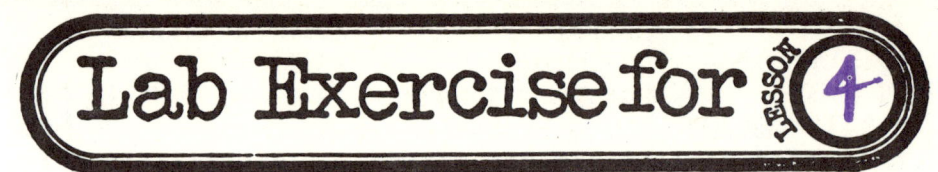

Lab Exercise for Lesson 4

The chart "Western Mankind", a synthesis of many overviews of history, presents a brief survey of the social history of the West from its ancient Egyptian beginnings to the first part of the Twentieth Century. Although it is but an outline the undulations between action and reaction, development and change, and the relationship between product and process can still be seen if a single aspect is followed from period to period.

Religions move back and forth from a concern with the here-and-now to focus on the hereafter. Social concepts change as they respond to population growth and individual and group needs. Because of our distance in time, we can see that 3,000 years of recorded history produced countless bits and pieces of detail (so-called end products). If one person were to try to bring the chart up to date by filling in a final column which characterizes our own time, it might read something like this:

The UNIFIED WORLD
[1914 AD - 2000 AD]

Religious Concepts

A new understanding of the laws of physics, chemistry and biology establishes a new human relationship between the natural and supernatural. Organized religions abound. Traditional religions re-examine their "mysteries" and many provide scientific bases for their tenets. A clean, more physically healthy, socially responsible, natural way of life becomes the typical "religious" way of life.

Social Concepts

Survival of the group is far more important than any individual life; interdependence replaces independence; switch from "do-it-yourself" to dependency on outside services; mass education and mass culture; sharing of world resources on a physical survival fair-share basis rather than on an economics and trade basis; transition from personal freedom (self-regulation and its accompanying responsibility) to control by system (with no individual held responsible for any total decision); change from belief in personal privacy as a human right to the belief that government must have access to the operations of all its members; breakdown of family communications, instructions for living received from TV, radio and magazines; economics and mega-corporations control politics and world decision; international language and measurement standards, rising illiteracy.

Main Artifacts

Superjets; television and communications satellites; computers; the common market; the inter-company memo; paperback books and magazines; world trade centers; diagnostic equipment.

Population

1975 AD - 4 billion
2000 AD - 8 billion (forecasted)

How It Really Was [exploring values]

The preceding summary is perhaps a reasonable description of our current world. But what if we took a different point of view? Then all of the categorized information under it would change also. Consider the following titles and try to re-write the description of our time as it might be seen in these various terms:

1. The Violent Years (1912-2000)
(The Age of War and Energy Control)
Hint: Don't forget Sam Peckinpaw and Andy Warhol movies; the Alice Cooper-Evel Knievel period; wars in the near east and mid-east; the international dash for the control of oil reserves; Kent State and the student revolution of the sixties; the Democratic Convention in Chicago; Watts; people living at the edge of outrage demanding to be shocked more and more.

2. The Years without Value (1930-1985)

(The Time of Imbalance between Resources and Needs)

Hint: Instant, throwaway, all aluminum and plastic-wrapped trivia (where the thing tossed out is far more valuable in terms of the natural resources it represents than the thing kept); Diet Pepsi; air-conditioned patios; ice rinks in the desert and dune buggies in Minneapolis; the "my home town is awful and I've gotta get outta here" feeling; public approval of political dishonesty and the "fantasy viewpoint" which sees everything as an act or game; nostalgia trips.

3. The Space Age (1945-2000)
(Space Science By-Products and Interplanetary Exploration)

Hint: The electronic invasion, new resources bring even greater pleasure and ease to society; the new and the unknown; the power of Man; the fragmentation of processes into specialization; super rationality and seriousness; programmed behavior; "2001-A Space Odyssey" becomes a film classic; "Spaceship Earth" and ecological consciousness is born.

4. The Cultural Revolution (1913-1990)
(Intellect and Information Retrieval Systems Join Forces)

Hint: Renaissance man becomes a mass possibility with the education explosion assisted by TV classes and digested, programmed coursework; self-hypnotism and inner peace; children log more than 30 hours per week of TV fare; domestic use of computers.

5. The New Natural Reality (1960-2050)
(Energy Consciousness)

Hint: Natural energy systems replace traditional use of

fossil fuels; products stop responding to unnecessary savings in time at great environmental costs; slower pace of life causes new respect for time; clean environment establishes renewed appreciation of environmental use and design.

Which point of view (or title description) of past and present and predicted future times do you shy away from the most? Which do you favor the most? Would you like to combine some of them to make a more ideal future for yourself. . .or add new titles?

Record your comments in your notebook. They might represent some values-revealing facts regarding your probable role in your society as it moves along the path of history.

Questions for Today [developing beliefs]

Getting outside your own point of view isn't as difficult as it may seem. All you need is a technique. Here's one: By responding to the following suggestions, you may find yourself in someone else's shoes...looking out of "a fresh pair of eyes" (as Woodrow Wilson once said).

A. Write the outline of a talk you might give to a group of senior citizens on the subject of "Growing up in the 1980's".

B. Try to convince yourself that pleasure is a more desirable goal than hard work. Make a list of pros and cons for each side, and don't give up until there are at least ten arguments for both points of view.

C. Write a series of letters to someone describing yourself mentally and physically after pretending the following:

   you are much younger than you are now

   you are much older than you are now

   you are your same age but of the opposite sex

Guaranteed Forever [value insurance]

Life is full of written guarantees and verbal promises. Some are useful and provide security when honored; others aren't worth the paper they're printed on or the time it takes to listen to them. Nevertheless, we all love the promise of security, no matter how shakily it may be offered. We tend to seek out "eternal" items to fill our safety deposit boxes and treasure chests such as gold and diamonds and furs...we look for "lifetime" and "100-year" contracts and promissory notes...the "sure thing".

Discovering the real worth of a guarantee is another value-revealing exercise. Try it to find out what you believe about guaranteed security.

1. What would you mean by it if you offered someone an "unconditional guarantee"?

2. Write down five things you believe you could guarantee absolutely. Would you include some "conditions"? Which ones?

3. If you borrowed a friend's car and guaranteed you'd bring it back in a week in better condition than before you borrowed it, what would you actually be promising to do? Suppose a tire blew out during the week? What if the battery went dead? What would you do if the car was stolen during the week?

4. When you make a promise to yourself, what "security" do you put behind it? For instance, if you bought a new camera on an installment plan would you also be promising to give up the camera and forfeit payments made thus far if you didn't make a payment as scheduled? Suppose you promised yourself to gain or lose ten pounds of body weight by next month. What would you forfeit if you didn't meet that promise to yourself?

5. Find a guarantee or warranty on something like a TV or refrigerator and read it. Then write a guarantee to yourself, including conditions and penalties for one of the following:

   to take excellent care of a pet

   to produce daily salads from a backyard garden

   to never eat between meals or overeat at meals

   to keep your car in good running condition

   to reduce your natural resources consumption

   to learn to play the flute in three months

HOMEWORK
See page 74 for today's homework assignment.

Section V-1, Values Is . . .

THE BIG VALUES LESSON

The renowned values researcher, Stephen Pepper, begins his 732 page "outline" of THE SOURCES OF VALUES (University of California Press, 1958) by telling us that his book " . . . for all its length, is only a sketch," This is not an expression of false humility. Nearly all experts who write about values draw similar conclusions. Any attempt to "say it all" is defeated before it begins. But even if the study of values is indeed endless, at least we can begin. Up to this point our VALUES TECH lessons and exercises have provided the potential for laying a solid foundation for further constructive value-revealing study.

In most academic institutions values are usually studied in advanced ethics classes, and because of the presumed difficulty of the subject matter, only a few brave souls with persistence to meet the prerequisites have the pleasure of taking the course. At VALUES TECH however we break that pattern by simplifying the terminology and making it available to all for practical application to life.

What we believe and the standards by which we judge the ultimate consequences of our behavior represent our system of values. Collectively they are the by-products of the human search to find cause and reason in experience. Reasoned human values therefore are abstractions, removed from the context of reality for analysis. They are conceptual things and not necessarily universal things. Aside from those made by Man, there are no abstractions in Nature. We observe Nature, abstract meaning from it and proceed to plan a path of intentional relationship to the environment and its components which we have observed. In this process we must evaluate the relative importance of things, people and events as they figure into the life forces which push us from outside our bodies and guide us from within our minds. High values are thereby assigned to those parts of our experience which enhance or support our existence and growth. And we attribute low values to those things which diminish or negate our existence and growth.

Personal drives stemming from human needs generate and determine values. The "worth" of things is influenced by both external natural environment and personal directions and plans. The dynamics of values in general involves an interrelationship of "my values" with "your values" as both further relate to "our values" and to our collective external environments. Thus we see that it is an illusion to think each of us is alone, free to choose and determine the worth of things. We are only part of the total process of interrelationships (as the VALUES TECH lesson in ETHICS pointed out). Although we often fail to recognize such a fact and make decisions as if we were independent agents outside society, the truth is eventually exposed. For without intentional consideration of the forces present in the entire natural system, we would find ourselves victimized by their inevitability. We must either accept their existence or pay the penalty for our refusal or ignorance.

Human values appear to be generated by three primary sources:
Survival: Natural existence and growth

Self-fullfillment: Personal intent, drive, ambition, appetite, foresight, planning

Societal Enrichment: culture, heritage, ethics, group interaction and intent.

Each of these further encapsulate our various awareness levels of time, space and the reality of material things as they relate to our purpose.

Together they comprise our total experience of environment. And whether we live alone or as part of a social group, our ultimate value source is the life we live. Within that context, positive values are assigned to those experiences which help us meet our aspirations . . . either alone or in groups.

Valuation implies self-determination. And consciousness of directions, needs and the worth of things suggests an ability to judge experience with self-conviction. To deny the personal need to assert purposes of our own design is to ignore the evidence of how human beings function as a natural species.

Values awareness is the means by which we measure individual and social freedom. To know where we want to go and what it takes to get there is just another way of indicating that we are capable of taking charge of our own lives. Having no values or criteria for making decisions infers a life without direction. Without value awareness, the worth of experiences is neutral.

Summary

Values stem from forces both inside and outside of us. They represent what we need for existence and growth as individuals and members of social groups. Values are not identical to the things, people and events of experience; instead they represent the personal and social rankings of good-bad, right-wrong, beautiful-ugly, enhancing-diminishing, or desirable-undesirable, which we assign to things, people and events. From our intentions, goals and purposes we derive our criteria for making further value judgments. High values go to experience which enhances our goals; low values go to negative aspects.

In general then, values represent what we believe. And personal ethics grow out of the relationships between what we believe and strive for and the values expressed by the socio-environmental world outside ourselves.

**Section V-2
The Source of Necessity**

Knowing our goals and having the skills it takes to get to our planned destinations is a real leg-up in this increasingly complex world. But no matter how we might state what we hope to achieve, the underlying purpose of all human action is to fulfill basic human needs. That's the fundamental rule of the human life process. Getting to know more about our individual and socially determined needs is, therefore, prerequisite to moving closer to an intelligent, self-controlled and personally valuable life.

Although some behaviorists may express skepticism regarding attempts to develop any complete list of basic needs requirements, we unabashedly present the following facts, comments and conjectures for your consideration. We hope that stimulating your interest in human needs at the personal level will also result in a deeper understanding of the interrelationship of all our needs at the societal level.

Fundamentally, the cost of living can be measured by finding the sum of the energy required to satisfy BASIC HUMAN NEEDS. If we are seeking universals, human needs fill the bill. These are costs we all pay for the privilege of living. And there is no need for these to be "hidden costs," we can put them out front into the light of day through conscious awareness of potentials and intentions. The first consideration is to recognize the word "basic" as a starting point because "basic" needs are those primary urges and instinctual drives which get us moving even before we know (are conscious of the fact) we want to move at all. All of our wants, desires, intentions, emotional expressions and many of our individual differences are built from the raw material of these basic human needs. Even the demands imposed on us by the societies we organize and join are derived from those same fundamental forces which initially drive us as individuals.

Basic needs can also be classified into three generating or source groups: **instinctual** (basic to life), **social** (basic to living in groups), and **cultural** (growing out of and occasionally obscuring the others). Some needs are required for personal survival; some for participation and growth in social situations; and some derive from coping with the demands of the other two.

We can propose that those drives which are basic to life stem from and follow the two governing laws of nature: the Law of Balance (equilibrium) and the Law of Change (process). And we can allow an entire pyramid of human needs to grow naturally from those two assumptions.

The basic theory of needs interrelationships comes from Abraham Maslow, a pioneer and outstanding representative of the many psychologists who have researched human needs. Maslow concluded early in his studies that the urges built inside each of us were interrelated in a dependency-chain-like way: some needs were prerequisites for others. He pointed out that our higher level urges are ignored until the primary ones are satisfied; the most basic needs being the life-sustaining physiological ones and the highest order needs being the "self-actualizing" intellectually fulfilling ones. Just as we recognize that resource conservation and environmental pollution problems mean little to a hungry family, and that usually people don't start looking for a house and garage until they've already acquired a mate and car, we can easily accept Maslow's Theory of first things first.

Here are some facts you'll need for dealing with your needs.

A. When seen from the viewpoint of human needs, behavior is defined as "an expression of needs satisfaction." From that standpoint everything we say or do is an attempt to fulfill instinctual or cultural urges. Through our motions and our emotions we express our personal requirements for living. We act out and describe our experiences in degrees of intensity, pleasure, joy, passion, ecstasy, disinterest, indifference, boredom, ignorance, annoyance, anger, loathing, rage, attraction, interest, manipulation, love, caution, fright, panic, surprise, giddiness, astonishment, shock, vigilance, anticipation, hopelessness, anxiety, sorrow, sadness, empathy, grief, competitiveness, distrust, deviousness, destructiveness, teamwork, trust, support, desire, lust, etc. Familiarization with the kinds of emotional expression can simplify the understanding of what is being expressed through the medium of behavioral observation and training or control. (Exercise: Attempt to define each emotional expressive term and then, taking them one day at a time, observe how often and in what situation you tend to include that emotion in your own behavior. Record the conclusions in your journal.)

B. Just as there are various levels of needs, there are also various degrees to which any one need may be satisfied. Again, the degree of repetition of emotional expression is the key to noting the degrees of unsatisfied need. (There is no current proof relating the degree of physical or mental health to the degree of need frustration or satisfaction, but we can once again assume that "too much" or "not enough" of anything is a clear expression of imbalance and therefore not in compliance with natural law.)

C. Actions, emotional expressions and situations do not determine needs. It's just the other way around. Needs come first. They determine our actions, emotions, and to a large extent the situations into which we place ourselves. They form the basis of strivings, objectives, goals and ultimately of beliefs and values. We are guided by what we believe and need.

D. Our physical and mental health can be measured by the degree to which our physiological and psychological needs are fulfilled. One acceptable view of "mental illness" is to define it as the result of frustrated human need . . . recuperation is the period for unblocking or satisfying a need previously jeopardized. ("Natural" medicine uses a similar argument by saying it is better to attack disease with nutritional supplements than with synthetic preparations.)

E. The intensity of expression fluctuates in proportion to the ratio between the energy required to meet a need and the amount of total energy available. For example: If we desire to fullfill the physiological need for shelter at a high sociological level (by acquiring a very comfortable, high status, single-family house), and we find when we attempt to do so that our bank account does not match the required payments for such a high level of satisfaction, we will probably not wait until our bank account increases to fill the need, but will instead settle for a less spacious, lower status duplex or apartment.

F. Since each of us is concerned with fulfilling personal needs, individual differences can be measured by the particular way in which we assign importance to or rank those needs. We each have our own personalized NEEDS PROFILE, and a society at large is made up of separate subgroups whose members have similar NEEDS PROFILES, which are also uniquely different from each other subgroup.

G. Age, growth rates and environmental factors affect the way individuals and social organizations translate their need levels. Climate, national goals, international relations, technological development and availability, physical resources, population and education are some of the main forces which impinge on needs differences.

H. Until our basic needs are met, we remain unsatisfied. So we usually work very hard to satisfy needs of different kinds. This lifetime chore is compounded by the fact that the more any one need is frustrated, the harder we work to satisfy it. Until they are satisfied, needs serve as driving, motivating forces. Once satisfied, needs no longer serve that function.

I. Occasionally we struggle to satisfy the same need over and over again without realizing that some far more basic need remains unsatisfied beneath it all. For instance, a person might invest a fortune in records and tapes in order to accumulate a "complete collection" without realizing that a more basic need for completeness and flexibility could be better satisfied by utilizing the collection in a good public library.

Here's a proven method for testing the urgency of your needs to see if they are truly instinctual or simply assumed. If you answer NO to any of these questions, it's a good chance that the urge in question is not instinctual but merely the way you are currently translating your true need.

Regarding the "urge", ask:

1. If the urge were not satisfied, would I begin to feel physically or mentally ill?

2. Would the continual fulfillment of this urge reveal a deeper basic need?

3. Does my physical and mental survival or growth really depend on satisfying this urge?

HUMAN NEEDS

A Chart of Human Motivations

NATURAL BASIS

BALANCE
- SURVIVAL
- ADAPTATION

CHANGE
- GROWTH
- ENERGY TRANS-FERENCE

UNDERSTANDING & COMMUNICATION

UNITY	RHYTHM
ORDER	PROPORTION
HARMONY	ILLUSION
CONTRAST	VARIETY
	REPETITION
	DOMINANCE

INSTINCTUAL

SELF-PRESERVATION

Safety Sense
AVOID CAUSES OF PAIN & ILLNESS
RESPECT FOR PAIN AS INDICATOR OF DANGER
FREEDOM OF MOVEMENT TO PROTECT BODY & ACCOUTREMENTS (INCL. PROPERTY)
MOVEMENT IN DIRECTION OF LEAST RESISTANCE
AVOID DANGER
DEVELOP SENSORY SKILLS
   Clarify Perceptual Skills
   Responsiveness
DEFENSIVE ABILITY
   Survive Attack
   Avoid Belittlement

ACCESS TO ALTERNATIVES, ESCAPES
Health Sense
min. daily req; food, water adaptability; tolerance, symbiosis
digestion & synthesis of FOOD INTAKE
MUSCLE & ORGAN EXERCISE
   Avoid Atrophy
PRODUCTION OF ANTI-BODIES
HYGIENE, CLEANLINESS

DISCHARGE:
   Eliminate Wastes, Tensions, Excretion, Respiration, Perspiration,
   Via Excretion, Respiration, Perspiration, Crying, Shivering, Fever, Runny Nose, Diarrhea, Etc.
REST
SHELTER:
   Protection From Extreme Natural or Otherwise Threatening Conditions
Natural Death

GROWTH

Physical	Intellectual	
Expand Species	LEISURE	LOVE & BE LOVED
SEX	Release From Goals	ACCEPTANCE BY GROUP
DEPENDENCE	Playfulness	SYMPATHY, EMPATHY
WORK	Self-Knowledge	SEEK PRAISE
Muscular Development	KNOWLEDGE OF BODY AND NATURE	INTIMACY
Freedom of Movement	SENSE OF PURPOSE (MOTIVATION)	SOCIALITY-COMMUNITY
Create Tension	SENSE OF LIMITATIONS	HONESTY—SEARCH FOR TRUTH
	RESIGNATION TO UNPREDICTABLE ELEMENTS OF NATURE AND AGING PROCESS (CHANCE)	FAIRNESS
		LOYALTY
		GROUP IDEALS, MODELS TO FOLLOW
		EXTEND PERSONAL INFLUENCE TO GROUP
	KNOWLEDGE OF ENVIRONMENT	CONSTRUCTIVITY
	Curiosity	SELF-CONTROL
	Planning	Self-Assertion
	Evaluating	Choice
	PLEASURE/ADVENTURE	Commitment
	Sensory Excitement	Goal-Setting
	FULFILL PERSONAL POTENTIALS	Repudiation, Revenge
	(Self-Actualization)	PRIVACY
	Expand Mentality	Solitude, Concentration
		Meditation, Prayer
		Avoidance of Stimulus

EXAMPLE: Suppose you decided that you just had to have a new car to replace your present "run-down" model.
The three-question "test" might reveal that — 1. the new car would not improve your physical or mental health; 2. Buying a new car every four or five years exposes a need for renewal, social approval, personal acceptance or the products of society (human needs); and 3. Personal growth could be accomplished in many other less-expensive ways.

EXERCISE:
Imagine coming home to your house or apartment to find it in flames. You are very concerned because everything you own is inside about to be destroyed. Someone says you have about five minutes to rush in and save four or five things. Right now . . . before thinking at length about it . . . write down the five to ten things you think you'd grab for first . . take no more than two minutes to do this. When your list is complete, stop to examine each item in terms of why you thought it was more important than those items you left to burn.

CULTURAL-SOCIAL

SELF-PRESERVATION

- SUSTAIN ACCEPTABLE QUALITY OF LIFE
- MAINTAIN BALANCE (by Defining Balance—Achieving Behavior)
- MAINTAIN SAFETY & HEALTH (by Defining Orderly Behavior & Orderly Use of Resources)
- RESPECT INDIVIDUAL NEEDS Of MEMBERS
- CONSERVE SUSTAINING QUALITY Of NATURAL ENVIRONMENT
- DEFINE INDIVIDUAL RIGHTS Of MEMBERS (Boundaries of Governance, Rules of Economy & Standards of Acceptance)

GROWTH

Physical	Intellectual
ELIMINATE EXTREMES EXPAND POTENTIALS SUSTAIN INDIVIDUAL VOICE (With Group Size Increase) SUSTAIN INCREASING PRODUCTION (From Resources) MAINTAIN INCREASINGLY ADAPTIVE SYMBIOTIC RELATION WITH NATURAL ENVIRONMENT SUSTAIN MANAGEABLE SIZE (With Expansion of Individual Potentials)	LAWS AGAINST EXTREME BEHAVIOR (Definition of Healthy Individual and Social Behavior Limits) KNOW PERSONAL POTENTIALS AND EXPANDING REQUIREMENTS (As Related to Realistic Management Record History of Development) SELF-MANAGEMENT (RENEWAL) POPULATION & LAND USE CONTROLS CONTROL INEQUITIES OF RESOURCE DISTRIBUTION DEVELOP LAWS AGAINST ENVIRONMENTAL EXPLOITATION PREDICT ENVIRONMENTAL IMPACT OF ACTIONS PRESERVE NATURAL RESOURCES ON TIME LINE WITH REPLENISHMENT POTENTIALS.

Human Needs In A Nutshell

The Declaration of Independence of the North American Colonialists sums up the subject of HUMAN NEEDS by wrapping it under the blanket phrase "inalienable rights" (life, liberty and the pursuit of happiness).

Section V-3 The Values Pyramid

Values, like Needs, affect our attitudes and our behavior. Some values are "new"; they are at the top of the pyramid and are still being tested. Although not yet accepted and incorporated into overall behavior they are nonetheless obvious because of being "out in front" getting "tried on for size". These are the bits and pieces of other people's ways of life, segments of nature, urges and unaccounted for nagging impulses to try out the untried. Other values are "transitional"; they form the body of the pyramid and provide support for the totally new. Still other "basic" values form the base of the pyramid, providing foundations for the selection of new values and for their progressive development into known forms.

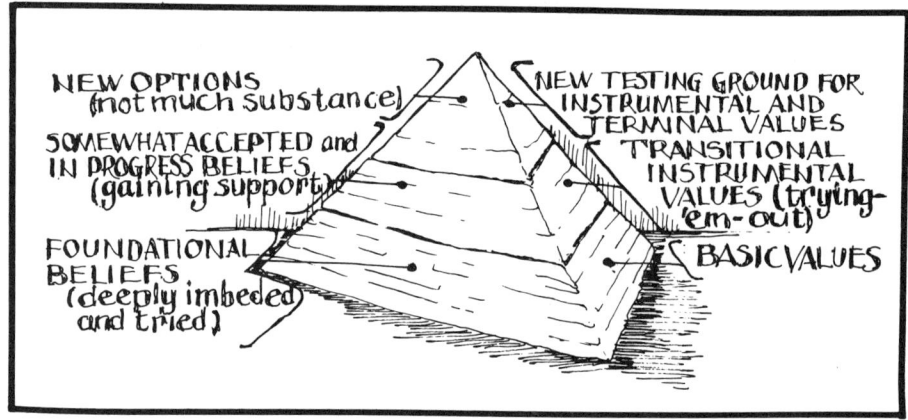

Section V-4 The Values Chain

In the search to better understand our environment we find that all things are related, one thing leads to another. A wink can lead to a smile, a meeting, a date, an arrangement, a legality, a sharing, formation of a family, etc. And values can be sequentially traced backwards through behavior from our statements, attitudes and emotions to the basic values at the other end of the chain. EXAMPLE: If we were to observe a high school student spending $38 for a new carburetor for a customized pick-up truck, we might observe and analyze the chain of values in this way:

"New" values might include:

trying to see what it feels like to behave similar to the crew in the pit stop on last week's TV auto trials; testing what it's like to spend a large amount of money on a mere component of a larger functional system; experimenting with decision-making ability regarding technical performance specification; responding to the urge to try out environmental accountability (trying to tune an automotive system for cleaner fuel consumption), etc

"Transitional" values might include:

having previous support through reinforcements for behaving like "approved" and "responsible" adults; having already spent smaller sums successfully and now ready to progress to a bigger challenge; being able to easily recognize maturity as involving work toward long-range fullfillment as well as instantaneous gratifications (can buy a component requiring work to install which is but a stage in a gratification chain); needing more proof regarding man's responsibility for the quality of environment, etc.

"Basic" values might include:

truly believing that personal worth and accomplishment can best be expressed through large-scale, dynamic, colorful projects; knowing through numerous past experiences that young and old alike pay respect to those who successfully construct or maintain ultra-glamorous products; knowledge that working on personal projects has immediate therapeutic worth due to the obvious personal relevance, etc.

Values Chaining is an organized method for getting past the possible superficiality of what we see and on into the essence of our beliefs and drives. It is a method for attempting to derive deeper meaning from what we sense. It can help us to know more about . . .

how we relate to groups, other individuals and human activity

how we relate to nature and man-affected environment

how we spend resources or allow them to be spent

how we conduct socio-political and intimate relations, the way we spend our money or our weekend or our life, the kind of work we prefer to do, whether we'd rather watch TV or take a walk . . . Any and all of these expressions begin "chains" which can be traced to basic needs, beliefs or terminal values. The links in the chain are explanatory connectors between simple urges on the surface and underlying deeply-felt drives.

At first, the range of values types appears endless. Because it is possible to assign worth to all the things, people and events in life, the thought of classifying values seems somewhat like imagining the task of compiling the ENCYCLOPEDIA BRITANNICA from scratch. But let's try to subdivide this problem into smaller, more manageable parts.

Section V-5 The Encyclopedia of Values

PART A — QUALIFIERS OF VALUE; How values are described. It is important to know how the term "value" is being used. Here are the commonly accepted adjectives associated with the various usages of value terminology.

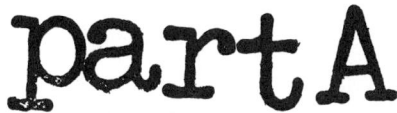

Factual Values — Reality-based, observable, quantitative, measurable, individualized, (primarily) subjective, which includes preferences, appraisals, wants and desires as they are stimulated by survival or human needs.

Normative Values — Cultural-based, expected, qualitative, societal, (relatively) objective, which includes all of the demands social groups impose on their members; socially redeeming, traditional mores.

Survival Values — Directly related to basic needs, growth and existence in the natural, supernatural and man-made environment.

Inchoate Values — Newly formed, unfounded, not yet consciously related to meaning, experimental.

Instrumental Values — Operative, intermediate, undergoing development.

Terminal Values — Basic, foundational, generative, world view.

Positive Values — Enhancing to intentions and purposes, satisfies appetite.

Negative Values — Diminishes purposes, establishes aversions, resistance to basic needs.

Face values — Worth determined by superficial representation without analysis of cause or consequence.

Hidden Values — Basic worth obscured by superficial distractions.

True Values — Basic worth as it is related to all considerations which might be brought to bear on the relevance of cause or consequence.

False Values — Irrelevant considerations applied to determine worth.

Fragile Values — Areas where quantification or measurement is difficult.

Hard Values — Areas where measurement is easy; translatable into dollars, labor, land, property and other resources, etc.

Quantitative Values — Capable of being measured in terms of quantity; how much, how far, how many, how long, etc., primarily numerical.

Qualitative Values — Capable of being measured in terms of quality; what kind, characteristics, degree of excellence or "richness," properties and interrelationships; primarily verbal.

NOTE: Everything we study and anything we can know can be evaluated in terms of one or more of the value qualifiers found in PART A.

part B

A PARTIAL LIST OF THE SUBDIVISIONS OF VALUE STUDY

Self

Psychology	
Introspection	(natural self-id); (intentional self-ego)
Behavior	(actions)
Personality	(sub-selves)
Human needs	(effects of outside of self on self)
Physiology	(body)

Outside of Self

Society	(shared values)
Ethics	(morals)
Symbolism	(meaning)
Communication	(expressed meaning)
Order	(system, logic, law)
Psychology	(social mentality)
Anthropology	(social classification)
Institutions	(social organization)
Aesthetics	(beauty)
Religion	(good-evil)

Survival [Natural-Supernatural Concerns]

Ontology	(existence)
Cosmology	(the universe)
Theology	(God-Supernatural)
Epistemology	(knowledge)
Phenomenology	(thought)
Physical Life Science	(reality)
Mathematics	(philosophy)
Ecology	(natural process)
Medicine	(life maintenance)

AN ANTHOLOGY OF STATEMENTS REGARDING THE VALUE OF VALUES

Value consciousness paves the way for accountable, responsible decision making. Knowledge of our basic and changing beliefs is the surest method for developing the whole self as a total package containing sub-selves, myths, religion, thinking and behavioral patterns. Our new and transitional beliefs may not seem valuable to us at first, and we may put off conscious attempts to know them while waiting for basic values to form, but what we believe at any point in the life process is all we've really got to go on at that time.

"*The greater an organism's powers of discrimination and capacity to have insight into the relation-holding among things, the more extensive and articulated his life space and correspondingly the reality of the situation . . .*"

                Stephen C. Pepper
                The Sources Of Values

Ignorance of value normally results in irregular, unsure and unpredictable behavior; inability to make decisions or to plan ahead and dependence on others or social movements for direction.

According to the TAO, [the doctrine of the 6th Century B.C. philosopher Lao-Tse] Nature is the basis for all values. And instincts cannot be validly considered prior to the proper considerations of the laws of the natural-supernatural forces.

There are relatively few effective image makers in all of society. Because of this, it is the beliefs of just a small percentage of the population which have strong effects on the beliefs of many. Choose your own models wisely.

Values increase in intensity, from the untried to the tested to the proven. We develop them from our experiential relation to self, society and Nature. Basic values are formed, not formulated before the fact.

When behavior is positively reinforced, positive values develop. As experiences and reinforcements are repeated, we are better able to sort out those parts which satisfy our needs and reinforce our intentions. Those positive parts eventually grow to become our primary approval standards called "basic" values.

"Cultures differ in their values; each one shapes, or at least colors, its own values. Christianity is one of the great values of our society and culture; so are the works of Shakespeare, and our democratic institutions and liberty — even the Liberty Bell, as a visible and tangible symbol."

                        A.L.Kroeber,
                        ANTHROPOLOGY (New York:
Harcourt Brace Jovanovich, Inc., 1948).

Because of the many common denominators which link us together as a species [survival and human needs], we find ourselves naturally adhering to a common set of value-forming principles. Who and what we are as individuals and as members of society, where we are headed and how we plan to get there are the universal sources of value.

In an open mind values do not remain static; they are in a constant state of flux between the very simple and the very complex, from the superficial to the profound.

Values are dynamic in their interrelationships. We shouldn't expect to find them once and live by them for the rest of our lives. We can only expect to test, change and develop them. Static values, without potential for change, have caused the downfall of many individuals and institutions throughout history. It is only relationships which are "enduring" or "eternal," not the attitudes men may have regarding those relationships.

The worth of things often changes as new situations and new objectives appear.

Individuality suggests that no two people will have exactly the same values. No matter how similar basic beliefs may be, there will always be differences to be accounted for.

"There is no democracy [in determining a hierarchy-ed.] among human values, however each may cry out for an equal vote. It is the business of the soul to impose her own order upon the clamorous rout; to establish a hierarchy appropriate to the demands of her own nature and by the mere fiat of her absolute choice, if that be based upon self-knowledge."

                Learned Hand, The Spirit of Liberty

Prejudice emanates from conflicting value systems. Since we seek to satisfy our purposes in the most reinforcing way, it is clear that different purposes may well call for different reinforcements, thereby producing conflicts of interest and eventual animosity. Finding valued common denominators is a classic method for repairing broken human relations.

Values judgments are directly relatable to the age and maturity of the evaluator. A baby's values generate from moment to moment, survival needs being the prime generators. Between the ages of 12 and 20, we begin to translate values into goals, and then see them related to the days, weeks and months of time management. The responsibility that comes with age usually finds 35-year-olds making plans for decades ahead.

Values are most clearly expressed when we see them as points existing somewhere between our basic beliefs and disbeliefs. In that way we become more conscious of the full range of value or potential of the situation, person or thing being considered.

Since we are 'and continually become' our own most convenient model, it is normal to value others in the same ways and to the same degrees we value ourselves.

It's not hard to see that keeping an open mind to values can make it easier to cope with the many different value systems we face daily. But being reasonable and open-minded doesn't have to mean being "wishy-washy." We can still be very definite about what we believe without falling into the trap of intolerance or prejudice.

Value-revealing actions fall into two groups: things done consciously and things done sub-consciously. Sub-conscious acts imply underlying values; conscious acts are based on underlying values. Thus everything we do is related, directly or indirectly, to what we believe. And the elements of our environment have little personal meaning except as they are seen to fall inside or outside or our individual value-belief systems.

"The scale of values which determines everyday response to experience is a relative judgment based on accepted knowledge. When this knowledge is seen to be limited and therefore inadequate, the scale of values crumbles."
      Idris Parry, ANIMALS OF SILENCE
      (London: Oxford University Press, 1972).

Without conscious values, the best we can do is to "grope along intuitively," hoping for the best, waiting to recognize and select those things in our environment which move us closer to where it "feels good." It's not a very efficient way to spend a lifetime, but it surely is popular.

The positive concept of Good [and the complementary negative concept of Bad] grows out of values systems. Ultimately it is what we believe that determines the Good and the Bad: those things which enhance existence are good, and those things which negate our existence are bad. And since all value-generating experiences occur within complete contexts [they are never separate events]; there are many forces which act on the good-bad situation.

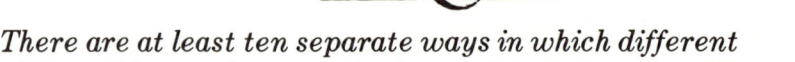

There are at least ten separate ways in which different philosophies tend to explain the good-bad situation. They are:

1. Nature guides us to do what is good. When we behave counter to Nature, we are being bad.
2. God is the source of Good; Bad comes from the Devil.
3. Good is that which gets us closer to a state of joy.
4. The satisfaction of human needs is the basis of good; thwarted needs are the anti-good.
5. Our individual dreams for a meaning-filled life determine what is good and what is not good. If an element of experience gets us closer to where we want to go, it is good.
6. Social goals determine good. Mankind's collective dreams are more important that those of individuals.
7. Good comes from within; people are inherently good, and they instinctively know good from bad.
8. Good and bad are concepts learned from parents, teachers and other models. We derive a knowledge of the rightness and wrongness of things from behavior reinforcement.
9. Good is the result of rational and logical determination. A thing is good when it fulfills its own logical definition.
10. There can be neither good nor bad for a natural creature of the universe. Bad and good are intellectual concepts which imply a

condition of unnaturalness or supernaturalness. They have no place in the natural belief systems of men.

"Whatsoever is the object of any man's appetite or desire, that is it which he for his part calls good; and the object of his hate and aversion, evil; and of his contempt, vile and inconsiderable. For these words of good, evil, and contemptible, are ever used with relation to the person that uses them, there being nothing simply and absolutely so; nor any common rule of good and evil to be taken from the nature of the objects themselves.
                    Thomas Hobbes, (1588-1679)
         (Part I, Chapter 6). LEVIATHAN

Since Good and Bad are the basic expressive terms of value, they form the limits of a scale for making value judgments.

Worse	Bad	Mediocre	Good	Better
Worst	Not Acceptable	Acceptable		Best
	Below Average	Average		
	Poor	Fair		

"Too much of anything is bad" is a value statement derived from the natural need for balance ["too much" being analogous to "imbalanced" and therefore out of order with natural forces]. From this standpoint, "too much good" would also be bad.

The popular Zen theorist, D.T. Suzuki, expresses his supernaturally-based value system as he refers to the TAO: "TAO is nameless. The very moment you say, 'IT is good,' the good loses its goodness. The really good is just so, and no more, no less. The good is just-so-ness. So with the rest of human values."
         HUMAN VALUES IN ZEN,
     "New Knowledge in Human Values," p. 95.

G.E. Moore in PRINCIPIA ETHICA *[1903] sums it all up by writing "Good is good, and that is the end of the matter."*

Some typical GOOD/BAD reactions to consequences:

	Good Reaction	**Bad Reactions**
Basic Sensory Level	*Sensory Pleasure;*	*Sensory Offense; pain, distaste*
Basic Needs Level	*Satisfaction of Needs; fulfillment*	*Unfilled Needs; anxiety*
Personal Level [Self]	*Enhanced Personal Goals; positive reinforcement Personal Goals*	*Negated Personal Goals; rejection*

THE ANNUAL VALUES TECH

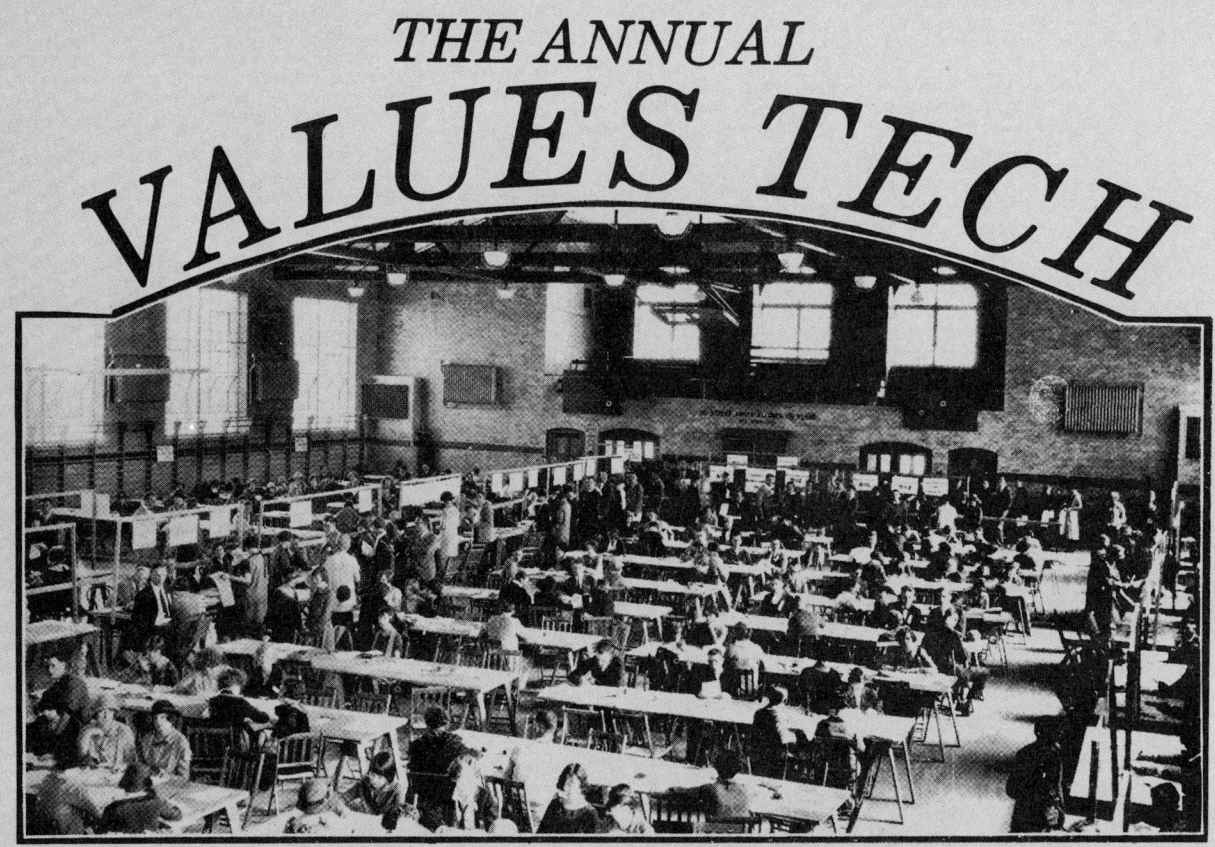

WORKSHOP IN VALUES & VALUATION

A basic values discovery laboratory conducted both as a part of the regular curriculum and as a refresher course for students, alumni and friends of the Polytechnic School of Values.

[**Note to participants:** Although the values workshop is being presented here as a "4-day event," it may take you only forty minutes, or it may require a full four weeks or even as long as four months to complete since you are working on a self-paced schedule.]

Program

Schedule of Events

Opening Prayer
Rev. H.E. Parsons
Chaplain of the P.S.V. Summer Camp
9 a.m. Pendleton Gym

Workshop Kick-off

Elizabeth D. Evans, Associate Dean

1st Day

Conflicts of Values: "Truth out of Friction"
Conducted by Maj. Frank P. Overhill, U.S.A. Ret. Alumnus

2nd Day

Values Via Inference: "The Fine Print"
Conducted by Charles Campbell, Partner,
Wyler, Campbell & Heinz, Inc., Guest

3rd Day

True Worth: "The Dollar Value" Game
Conducted by the Faculty

4th Day

Value Competition: "Intramurals"
Coach Maynard F. Maxwell &
Coach Doris Rose,
Physical Education Dept.

Closing Remarks

Elizabeth D. Evans, Associate Dean

Opening Prayer

H.E. Parsons, Chaplain

"Let us pray.

"We beseech the Almighty to help us study and learn with open-minded tolerance as we participate in this workshop on human values. Help us to maintain an ethical attitude with respect to all our decisions and actions. Realizing that as humans our selfish needs are too often foremost in our minds, we ask for guidance in developing those skills which will also help us apply our new-found knowledge for the good of others in society. We join now with our sisters and brothers in the attempt to make greater sense of our lives through an awareness of our beliefs and an intentional coming-to-terms with our basic human motives and inner drives. As we discover the forces within us, it is our fervent wish that we shall be enabled to meet those forces with objective understanding and clear, unprejudiced thought. We ask thy blessing upon our endeavors, both now and in the future. Amen."

Workshop Kick-off

Elizabeth D. Evans, Associate Dean

"It's good to see so many familiar value-seekers among this class. It is a fine feeling to know that you still think enough of your school to come so often to renew your spirit and to bolster your value-finding skills. I can promise you lots of work, fun and full educational value from the projects you will be undertaking in the coming days. This year we have invited an excellent group of speakers and workshop leaders to introduce the various subjects. They assure me that a full measure of opportunity awaits you. Let's begin."

1st Day
"Truth out of Friction"
[A Session in Value Conflicts]

Major Frank P. Overhill, U.S. Army, Ret.
Alumnus of the First Graduating Class,
June, 1940

"The subject of my life work to date has been warfare; I dealt with conflict. And although I am now retired and no longer on active duty, I still deal with conflict, just as all of you must deal with it, on a day-to-day basis, because that is how we progress. That is how we learn. For, in a sense, anyone who wants to get to know his beliefs and values must become involved in his own war games. Age and experience have taught me one very important fact: Very little is learned where conflict is not present in some form.

"Times of peace can be times without pressures, where societal and environmental forces co-exist in a soft balance with our own inner drives. During such times of peace, no dominant single force strives to subordinate all others. Separate ideologies are not at war. Life is at rest. We relax. (And we may develop wasteful habits.)

"Oh, I know what some of you are thinking: That guy is a war-monger; he should have been named 'Overkill' instead of Overhill. But you must realize that peace is the probable goal of all those who deal with conflict. If I raised the hair on the backs of your necks, I did it purposely. I wanted to attract your attention and start you thinking in new ways. Thus my analogy regarding war as a means to discover personal values.

"Value finding is like military warfare, in the sense that conflicts must be resolved, which in turn requires a strategy. What we are experimenting with in this session is conflict. When values are in conflict, they have the same symptoms and consequences that wars do between nations. For, you see, war is an expression of conflict or difference in values: the values of one group contend with values of another. And rather than arbitrate or compromise, both sides battle it out to the death or at least until the weaker side gives in. Now, we all know that this is the hard way to resolve differences. I have devoted part of my life to minimize aggression and to make human conflict as humane as possible. But today I propose another way. I call it the 'Overhill Underkill Non-Aggressive War Game Approach to Conflict.' War without Bloodshed. Ideological differences without any black eyes.

"This is how the game began. Over the years I discovered that contrast and balance are two of the basic laws of Nature. Along with harmony and order, they comprise the underlying principles of the physical world. I found contrast expressed in complements, differences, opposites. And I saw balance in compensatory, responsive actions. Together they provide the movement which put sparks into our existence. To me they are the basis of 'change,' which is for some the ultimate natural law. I reasoned that our instincts are constantly at war—harmonizing, compensating, becoming alike, seeking to be different—and that life is confused. We are always dealing with conflicts of interest. Because of this everything we do, conscious or not, is an attempt to control the conflict (between our various needs seeking fulfillment) in our lives. In addition, each of us has an ego which is constantly goading us into becoming a unique distinctively different individual. And these distinctions and differences produce further disagreements and lead to the general condition of conflict between life styles and ideologies.

"Painstakingly, we struggle to make sense of all these differences. And just about the time we think we've discovered some absolute which will resolve all future conflict, the truth changes on us. New facts send us off into a sea of new conflicts where we search for a deeper truth until change again prods us on. On and on we go.

"Science and technology have only compounded the problem of changing values and conflicting drives. At one moment we might decide it is wrong to waste fossil fuel on an airline vacation to Greece, and the next day someone may invent a way to use solar energy to speed up production of or a substitute for fossil fuels that would have previously taken millions of years to replace. One moment it is o.k. to be daring, another it is imperative to be cautious.

"But the conflict which generated these values warns us that experience is a two-edged sword. Even while we aspire to one position, we are testing its validity through experiments in the opposite direction. The cost of achieving our ideal is balanced against both opposing considerations. In short, we rarely achieve the ideal we aspire to because its antithesis is always part of the search for its achievement. Choosing beliefs therefore calls for careful and conscious determination. Since our situation is usually somewhere in between the best and the worst, it is good military strategy to plan maneuvers which will insure the most successful resolution of the conflict, even though it may produce imperfect results.

"The 'Overhill Underkill Non-Aggressive War Game Approach to Conflicts in Values' goes like this:

1. Analyze a conflict situation thoroughly to find out what you believe about it. Do this from the point of view which enhances your interests.

2. Next, do a complete about face and take the adversary's role. No doubt you'll be able to build a good case for that side, too.

3. Then go ahead and openly declare war: Set up a mock war between both viewpoints. First sort out the 'Generals'. These are the leaders of the two sides and represent the major differences whose conflicting objectives need to be identified. Next, find the differences which are not so clearly delineated. Call this group the 'Officers'. And finally (if you ever do get down to the 'Enlisted Personnel') you'll see that many elements are common to both sides of the battleground.

4. When the conflict is clearly laid out in front of you you can then declare peace: Write a 'treaty' that does justice to both sides. You may see that the strong belief you once had in the 'good' of one side and the 'evil' of the other can transform into an appreciation for both points of view.

"It has taken me many years to discover the value of bloodless war. The next time you encounter a conflict you might try my simple strategy to possibly discover that value for yourself."

EXERCISES in CONFLICTS of VALUE

"Now we are primed for the first activity in today's workshop session which is to try out my method for yourselves.

Choosing Sides

"1. On the top, left side of a sheet of paper, write down something you strongly believe...strongly enough to want to incorporate it into your behavior...something you presently use as a value standard for judging the goodness of the actions and thoughts of yourself and others.

Example: 'I believe that both sides in a conflict should always 'level' with one another.' (What would you write?)

"2. <u>Next to it, on the top, right side of the paper, write down the antithesis of your belief</u>.

Example: 'All's fair in love and war.'

"3. <u>Then, lay out both of the 'armies' under each heading</u>. Some of you will want to do it one army at a time. Others may want to alternate back and forth.

"4. Finally, follow the 'Overhill' method, and <u>write the treaty</u> which clarifies the new, deeper understanding of both sides in the resolution of the issue you selected to 'fight' over.

"After warming up on that first exercise, I'd like you to spend the rest of the day getting more familiar with the beneficial aspects of conflict by trying out several of the following exercises."

BLOODY MARY OR SOUTHERN COMFORT?

Overheard at a recent cocktail party were two people from very different backgrounds. One was a tradition-bound, society-conscious matron from the Deep South. The other was a liberated divorcee from California.

This exercise requires that you now take the side of one of the two. Which one do you choose? While you tell someone else why you side with the one you do, get that person to make notes about the value and belief statements you reveal during the explanation. Translate the notes into your journal.

THE PRICE IS RIGHT

A typical way to judge a personal improvement goal is to compare it with its antithesis. When we do that we're not so concerned with how "good" we are being but rather with how "bad" we are not being. As Alan Lakein says in his book, HOW TO GET CONTROL OF YOUR TIME AND YOUR LIFE, "Most people spend their lives minimizing losses rather than maximizing gains." But this is natural; we learn from our mistakes and it is easy to learn to concentrate on avoiding dangers after having suffered the consequences of one or more painful mistakes. In contrast, it's not so easy to concentrate on the "good" side of things when there are no obvious "punishments" or costs to pay if we don't really put forth our best efforts.

For most of us, high cost is equated with high value. "You get what you pay for" is a very common belief. It's well known, for instance, that the psychiatrist's high fee is intended to insure a serious intent on the part of the patient. Without it, too many people would miss appointments, hedge on the facts and generally disvalue the entire experience.

1. With the foregoing in mind, can you explain why most people work at getting a "good deal", why they think it's important to buy things at bargain prices and sell them at a profit? Try explaining your answer to someone else. Again ask that person to make mental notes--or write them down--about your statements of belief and to note especially when it appears that ambivalence occurs.

2. HEADLINE: "Plastic Trees Replace Real Palms in L.A."...but Astroturf also replaces grass in many places while recorded bird calls "naturalize" the lobby of the Hyatt Regency Hotel in San Francisco, and other oil-base plastic surrogates replace originals in many parts of our lives. To some giving up real trees, grass and birds for plastic and electronic ones may not seem a very high price to pay for all the instant wonders provided by the industrial cities in which they live. There is, after all, an economic rationale behind the switch to plastic palm trees: they require less maintenance and will probably look fresh all year long while saving on the city water bill (remember that Los Angeles is really sited in a relatively treeless desert area). Plastic grass may also have economical advantages over real grass. It also remains green and clean all year long without sun or water and makes for inexpensively maintained football fields and pool sides. Electronic birds save on feed bills, clean-up costs, legal problems and other expensive factors which accompany real birds. We must conclude that unquantifiable values such as the clean air production of real trees, the beauty of birds in flight, the occasional joy of seeing a nest full of eggs, the seasonal reminders of fallen leaves are not as important as the exacting economic considerations. Or must we?

It may be tough to get started, but do you think you could oppose the above argument with economically valid reasons for why real trees are still superior to plastic ones? (Clue: Try starting out with the counter argument that if money is the issue, it might be better to have no trees at all.)

DICHOTOMY

When the things we believe in get split into mutually exclusive groups, ambivalence or dichotomy occurs in our lives. Richard Brautigan, the modern American writer, is a master at using life's ambivalences to interest his readers. One typical scene finds him playing Chinese Checkers with grandma and catching her cheating. It's left to us to decide which he values more: Grannie's companionship or his sense of fair play. In a similar vein, try to imagine what you would do if...

...you wanted a peaceful walk on the beach but instead arrived to find an old man being beaten by teen-age thugs.

...someone in your family offered you a lot of money to buy something you felt contributed to air pollution.

...you knew it was your extra effort which made your relay team a winner. But at the awards dinner, your teammate receives the trophy and scholarship for it all.

...after working all weekend to help a friend who claims to be broke, you find out the reason for her plight is that she is buying something which you would also like to have but can't afford.

POLYGLOT

Ambivalence is a term which refers to conflicting values. Multivalence refers to manifold conflicts. And yet all attempts to explain our reasons for doing or wanting something merely reveal the many values upon which behavior is based. You will recall the Lesson in Human Needs revealed that mere existence, survival and growth as individuals and as members of society placed enormous demands upon our energies. And we know that any one of those demands can become the initial motive for our beliefs. But without a way to sort out the reasons we have for doing things, conflicting values can lead us to all sorts of unintentional results.

These examples may be familiar:

1. You need to fulfill a long, drawn-out promise you made but you also find that you need rest because you are very tired and run down.
2. You want to think of yourself as a tolerant human being, but you find that there are some definite benefits to remaining separate and aloof.

3. You hate inflation and the unreasonable increases in apartment rents without commensurate benefits, but you get an opportunity to make a killing in real estate and you yield to the temptation.

Now let's see what you can do about those conflicts. Try this exercise:

A. <u>Plan and pretend to give a philosophical talk to a 3rd grade class</u> on the subject: "Peace of mind is more important than material success". What examples would you use? What's your key argument? A tape recorder will tell you (after the fact) how well you argued your point.

B. If as a consumer you truly opposed waste and inflation, what arguments could you make in support of a realtor who planned to convert a fruit orchard into a sales lot for recreational vehicles?

PEACE IN OUR TIME

Consider the following conflict of interests and the way in which it might be resolved: Just like the next person, you too like to relax, have a laugh and enjoy life. At the same time you want others to realize that you are a really credible, serious person. To smooth out any possible frictions caused by being considered either a hedonist or a dullard, you might seek a harmonizing element. For instance, you might begin to take your humor more seriously by upgrading it from puns to thought-provoking anecdotes. Or, you might add more humor to your serious side by loosening up your interests to include lighter matters. Thus, by finding a common denominator, you might bring the two formerly diverse values into a harmonious relationship.

Now, it's your turn. What might you do to resolve these conflicts? (Provide at least two alternatives for each dilemma.)

1. You thrill at the thought of being an "A" student, but you firmly believe that "all work and no play makes Jack a dull boy".

2. You say that you believe "good fences make good neighbors", but at the same time you find yourself writing a letter to the editor imploring your fellow citizens to join together for better communication.

3. As a teacher, you think students should participate in all stages of the problem-solving process, but you also believe they're not old enough to responsibly engage in the stage where they must evaluate themselves.

2nd Day
"THE FINE PRINT"
(A SESSION IN VALUE INFERENCES)

Chas. "Buz" Campbell, partner in the advertising firm, Wyler, Campbell & Heinz, Inc.

"Every morning when I walk into my office at WC&H, Inc., I know my job has grown in importance overnight and I have taken on more responsibility than I had the day before. For advertising, ladies and gentlemen, is involved with getting inside people's minds, and that's a heavy responsibility. I do not take it lightly.

"In my thirty-three years in advertising, I have seen sales campaigns progress from the naive days of appeasing the whims of major stockholders, company presidents and board chairmen to today's scientific approaches, where accurate, statistically-generated, psychological studies of communication, values and motivation are part of every campaign.

"Sophistication has taken over. I'm not going to talk to you about advertising; I could do that for hours, but it's slightly off the subject I was invited to discuss. Instead I want to talk about the tough job we in advertising have made for you, the consuming public: your task of finding meaning and value in the advertising slogans we direct to you in so many parts of your lives.

"What I mean by that is only understandable when you begin to analyze what an advertisement really is. First of all, *an advertisement is a communication*. Someone or some company wants someone else to respond to their message, maybe to buy a product, perhaps to vote for a candidate, maybe even to attend this workshop. To do this effectively, the 'communicating' sender has to know something about the 'consuming' receiver: what motivates individuals in that group, their aspirations, lifestyle, and so on. Because in order to get a message across, it's got to be sent in such a way that it is received as a friendly thought, something that's been there all the time. Wealthy communicators with large budgets and expensive ads can hammer their message into the consumer's head by using repetition and multi-media campaigns. But, for the most part, it's the same for them as for a lower budget one-timer. They've still got to say what they want to say in the language the people understand.

"Secondly, *an advertising message contains a motivational trigger*. It may suggest, in a subtle way, or proclaim in a dramatic or humorous way, that something's got to be done about satisfying an unfulfilled personal or social need. For example: **Ads ask you questions to which you have no alternative but to answer "yes"**

'Serious about staying slim?'
'Got those end-of-the-year financial blues?'
'Don't you want the best for your family?'

Ads make dogmatic statements which are difficult to challenge on short notice

'Everyone loves a lover'
'Innocence is sexier than you think'
'The best way to say 'I love you' is by sending flowers'

Ads command action

'Now's the time to buy a new car!'
'Accept no substitutes'
'Eliminate tooth decay!'

Ads suggest models to follow

'Look for our name. It's the best clue the rest is well made!'
'Men! Give your tired old face a fresh young look!'
'You can turn your bathroom into a health spa.'

Ads imply that life can be richer and easier

'Double your pleasure. Double your fun.'
'You only go around once in life, so you might as well do it with gusto.'
'You can find seclusion and security on a wooded knoll in San Francisco.'

Ads predict a beautiful future, if only . . .

'More than ever you need the publication that helps you cope with the every-day hassles and big problems of life.'
'To get the most from your marriage, you've got to try . . .'

Ads offer something for nothing

'Free frisbees, Kool-Aid and kites for the kids'

"But most of all, *advertisements create images of acceptable, need-fullfilling values in the minds of the consumer.*

Ads bring values to life through symbols

We don't really try to sell a product any more. Instead, we work to trigger a value which is already there inside of every consumer just waiting to be spotlighted and turned into a conscious motive in his or her life.

"Let's also take a look at symbols, for although symbols are quite simple to comprehend, they are often tricky to translate.

"Everything is potentially a symbol. Words are symbols; each word stands for several meanings which relate to processes each of us have experienced. Processes and things are symbolic. Experiences and behaviors, even textures and colors, are also symbols. And because personal experience differs, all symbols have slightly different meanings for all of us.

"If my experience of a cat is that a cat is a soft, warm, friendly and purring animal, the symbols for "cat" will probably be positive for me. But if my experiences with cats taught me to think of them as sharp-nailed, predatory, treacherous or indifferent, the symbols for "cat" will undoubtedly arouse negative feelings in me. That's easy. But that's where the simplicity of communication ends and complication sets in. Because, most of us have had both good and bad experiences with cats, and so we might respond either way to symbols for "cat," depending upon how they were presented.

"That's where the ad business really gets going. We're the experts who choose and present the symbols that will carry out our clients' messages to you. Since symbols are so subject to individual translation, we've got to find the universals and common links between our clients' "messages" and your experiences.

"Well, it's not really as tough as I might have made it sound because there are many commonly understood symbols in every society. For example, the dollar bill is a generally accepted standard symbol in our society. Nearly everyone agrees that the 'buck' represents power, control, security and flexibility. And nearly everyone responds favorably to it. Experts such as sports stars can become generally accepted symbols, too: Joe DiMaggio, Billie Jean King, Rosie Greer, etc. are frequently seen on TV advertisements. People tend to see them as standing for the good and the right. They provide excellent testimonial connections between the consuming public and products. Flags, political paraphernalia, certain mottoes and songs follow suit as being potentially universal in their appeal.

"So our main job is to find the link that will fit the right symbols to each particular message. If we do our job well, we trigger the positive response we're aiming to get. The consumers' job, on the other hand, is to become aware of the value of the messages we are sending by checking in their own minds to see if they fit their own needs. But since we manipulate the symbols and frequently change them to say the same things we are usually better prepared to control the consumers' thoughts than the consumers are in knowing their values. I will leave you with that thought as we try some

EXERCISES in VALUES INFERENCES.

"For the remainder of today, our work will be to deal with symbols and responses via exercises which involve seeking out hidden meanings in the messages we all receive. See what you can do with these:"

THEY, THE PEOPLE

Have you ever stopped to ponder why so many people are influenced by ads which proclaim an unnamed authority?

    "Four out of five doctors tested agree..."
    "Tested in a major hospital"
    "Proven at a leading university"
    "Government tests reveal..."
    "Top authorities tell us..."

Make your own list of authorities worth listening to. Are your parents on the list? Teachers? Special friends? What general relationship do you have with your chosen authorities? Why did you reject the ones you did? Which authorities have you purposely left out?

    BOY-GIRL, BOY-GIRL

"Many ads use a picture of an attractive girl or a handsome boy to get through to your message receiving centers. Since they pull at primary needs, they gain easy entry to the minds of the consumers. In the two ads shown, remark how you might respond to the *male-female symbolism* involved (and why):

Use this checklist as a guide to your responses:

Am I not interested:
Am I barely attracted?
Might I stop to check it out?
Do I relate to the model?
Do I read the text?
Do I study the product seriously?
Do I fantasize myself in the role?
Do I plan to buy the product?

Don't forget to include reasons for each check in your record of this exercise.

    FORTUNE COOKIE

"Free fortunes" have an introspective effect on almost everyone. You can get a non-commercial, predictive message from a fortune cookie or a penny scale. Maybe we believe fate will eventually take control over personal intentions anyway. Or perhaps we just like to muse over the possibilities suggested on the little cards and paper slips.

How would you react to the following fortunes if you opened your fortune cookie or dropped a penny in the slot and read:

1. Be aware of someone who intends to rob you of a precious possession.

2. It's time to put some excitement in your life.

3. Tomorrow will be a highlight in your love life.

What would you think? How would you behave? Would you act differently? Why? Record your comments and any new inferences of your personal values.

 SYMBOL SIMON

Positive human qualities are those behavioral traits which refer to fulfillment of personal, physical or social needs. Negative human qualities tend to imply unacceptable personal, physical or social behavior. When we begin to recognize the relationship between underlying human qualities and the superficiality of symbols, we can better evaluate the commercial messages which are thrown at us from all sides.

Here is a list of some typical POSITIVE HUMAN qualities:

Reliable	Civil	Clean
Trustworthy	Even-tempered	Reverent
Willing to Help	Refined	Loyal
Earnest	Modest	Optimistic
Straightforward	Unemotional	Just
Sincere	Courageous	Honest
Unselfish	Brave	Hopeful
Courteous	Loving	Beautiful
Contented	Grateful	Original
Faithful	Generous	Individual
Truthful	Peaceful	Respectful
Moral	Humorous	Pure

EXERCISE: 1. After each word, describe at least two symbols which might depict that specific quality in a newspaper or TV advertisement. For instance:

    Reliable. Symbols: Yellowstone Park's "Old Faithful" geyser
        and
    A window washer's new safety belt

    2. Next, make another list, this time of NEGATIVE HUMAN qualities, and see if you can find at least one symbol which might be used to represent each of those traits.

TAKE IT OR LEAVE IT

GOLDEN HAIR NEED NEVER DARKEN

Combined dictionary renditions of the various meanings symbolized by the word "dogmatic" add up to this: 'a statement or point of view without sufficient foundation for acceptance; or which expects acceptance without proof solely on the word of the person making such statement.'

The dogmatic statements which comprise many advertisements are therefore kind of "take it or leave it" messages. Advertisers throw out a dogmatic statement and leave it to the consumer to fill in the missing facts which might validate or negate that statement. Since few people will take the time to question or analyze such unsubstantiated messages, they often end up buying products without sufficient investigation or justification.

EXERCISE: After reading the following "dogmatic" statements found in typical advertising copy, spend a few minutes thinking about the underlying facts which lead you to see their truthfulness or fallacy. (Two people can have fun doing this project together.)

1. "You don't have to be big to be good."
2. "Faster is better."
3. "Freedom's just another word for nuthin' left to lose."
4. "Hair doesn't look good when it's a little bit oily."
5. "The more you buy at bargain prices, the more you save."
6. "Don't be penny wise and pound foolish."

What logic or criteria did you use in coming to grips with the various statements? Were you consistent in your analysis?

YUCK, YETCH, BLEAH!

The selective process we normally use to perceive the world is such that after we've sensed what appears to fulfill our needs, we may become blind and otherwise insensitive to all else. Nevertheless, perception and intuition are great aids toward simplifying the decisions in life. They offer short cuts to determined action. We simply scan the available stimulus and pick out all those elements which reinforce our own points of view, thus saving a lot of time by responding to only the personally relevant parts.

Knowing this, advertisers selectively place "probable" reinforcements in "easy-to-find" places in our environment so that we can easily pick them up as personally discovered enhancements of our own belief. It's lots simpler for an advertiser to reinforce our existing values than to try to get us to establish new ones.

One way advertisers do this is by playing on the natural desire to be clean and healthy. Thus ugliness, messiness, abnormality, greasiness, thinness, being broken, warped, aged, dog-eared, etc., are rejected, whereas their opposites: prettiness, newness, orderliness, normality, etc., are accepted as positive reinforcers.

EXERCISE: Which of your values do you think are being appealed to in the following ad copy? Trace those values to their source in the spectrum of your personal needs. (Refer back to the BIG VALUES LESSON.)

1. "Why live a lonely, dull life in your dreary old apartment. What a waste! When for a few dollars more, you could move into exciting, socially-active, ultramodern Tropicala Gardens. Make your decision and call us today at 542-1001!"

2. "Tired of working long, hard hours for no status, low pay and too much responsibility? The United States Foreign Correspondents School can prepare you for a high-paying, important job as a member of the esteemed diplomatic service. Write today for particulars. You owe yourself a better life!"

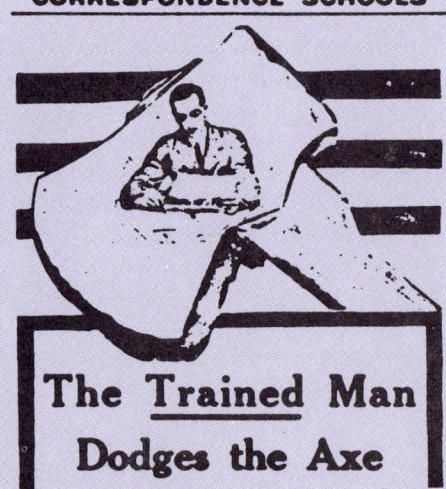

"Before we wind up today's program, I'd like to thank you for inviting me to lead this session in values and advertising. My firm, Wyler, Campbell and Heinz, Inc., is dedicated to honest sales communications, and we believe one way we can make that point clear is by sharing with you the methods and psychologies we utilize to reach through time and space with our clients' messages. I hope you have benefited from my visit as much as I have enjoyed coming to your school."

3rd Day
THE DOLLAR VALUE GAME
(A Session in True Worth)

Conducted by the Faculty. Introductory remarks by Prof. Maurice Whipple

"The task assigned to me in this workshop is to present some principles of values theory. Because of the limited time available, I must warn you that my remarks will be cursory and should be taken as only the briefest introduction to this deep and important subject. I trust, however, that the workshop games which follow will provide ample practical experience by which you may test the theoretical material I now present.

"Although I can't remember who said it, or exactly how it is phrased, my favorite beginning for a lecture of this kind goes something like this:

"The most natural thing a person can do is to always be on the lookout for those parts of life which provide support for personal drives and to always avoid those things which get in the way. You might call it the 'what's-in-it-for-me' approach. It is true that personal, and indeed social, values are related to the positive reinforcement of each person's or group's individualized set of needs.

"Try to think of yourself as a system containing many needs in search of fulfillment and with many outreaching probes into the surrounding environment. Do you have that image in mind? Good. Now add another image to the first: Imagine that the environment is also an active system which contains many forces which prod you back. What are some of those forces? Well, one is the climate and the changing demands it makes upon our attention. Light conditions and other physical realities are also there, such as sounds, and movements and the odors of things. There are also other systems similar to you out there with you, each one probing its part of the environment of which you are also a part. In this way you can see you are a system within a larger system. Each person can therefore be studied as a special model which represents the result of both inner and outer forces. We exist as a set of forces in a sea of forces. And the activity of these inner-outer forces never ends, until we die and then of course, we stop fighting from within and the external forces take over.

"Now we can relate values to this basic model, for they become the screens through which our outward probes and the environmental prods must pass in order to establish a meaningful relationship between the two. They are like a conceptual house we build around ourselves: we create our protection against all potentially deforming external pressures and a home base for our inner drives and needs. Only 'friendly' forces are allowed inside, through the doors of our values-screen house. Forces which do not easily pass through the doors of our values-screen house are ignored until they return presented in an acceptable form.

"My colleagues in mathematics refer to this model as a vector analysis problem. They are always telling me I should establish a basis for measuring the strength and direction of each of the inner and outer environmental forces in my models so that a measurable resultant might be estimated. But I prefer to think of it as a working model which can never have a static resultant and which instead might be better studied on a computer video screen as an always-changing, adapting, dynamic thing.

"How people form their protective values-screen houses shaping the basic judgments necessary to fulfill their needs and to respond to their environments is a subject of much academic discussion. I will only present some of the theories which have developed. Others will surely emerge with time from all the research being proposed. It is my opinion that all theories of value are valid, we just respond to them in different ways. And it is just that individualized response which marks us as unique individuals.

"The most important theories of value are these:
1. Values derive from conflicts. Beliefs are formed by working out the results of opposing views.
2. There is one dominant need inside of everyone, and it is that force which shapes and modifies all others. Since everyone has a different controlling need, unique personalities derive from these differences.
3. External environmental forces are stronger than internal needs; consequently the environment is the prime shaper of human belief.
4. Values derive from ideals; i.e., those things which are hoped for but seldom reached. And it is those ideals which become our standards of reference.
5. Many needs press for equal attention. Some of them, because they are most fulfilled, win the battle for survival and become strong influences over other decisions thus forming a value system.
6. Values are always in process, changing and adapting and developing throughout life.
7. Society and the environment work together to determine the limits of what any individual is allowed to believe. Personal values can only develop after the establishment of group values and natural tendencies.
8. Human needs and environmental factors should be balanced so that neither one receives more energy than we have to spend on it. Because we are apt to devote most of our attention to the need which makes the biggest energy demand at any given time, that is the need which will probably determine our values.

"To summarize: Values come from life and its experiences and demands. They are the abstract by-products of daily activities. And we all have a hand in their choice or determination. Values can be chosen systematically or accepted by default. Free choice is more sought after than acceptance by default or ignorance. Consciousness of values can provide a unified, rational basis for making decisions and they can serve us to guide our general behavior.

"So you see there are many ways to formulate a values-screen house for protection and for dealing with the forces which make up your various and individual worlds. If you become aware of these theories, you can use them to establish more personal control of your values and beliefs.

**"Now, Here Are The Dollar Value Games You've All Been Waiting for:
[The instructions are simple, and the results are revealing.]**

Money is an all-purpose standard of value. It has very little intrinsic value except as metal and paper scrap or as a collectable rarity, or to occasionally fill in as a substitute electrical fuse, screw driver, can opener, poker chip, or heads versus tails decision maker. Instead, money symbolizes energy and resources of all kinds. There is very little in the world that can't be translated into dollars and cents. It's a universal; a common denominator. Everyone speaks the language of money . . . at least a little bit. (To this end, we often hear expressions such as "Money is Power," "Money is God," "Money is the root of all evil," etc.) Its value is therefore extrinsic, deriving from the energy or resource we allow it to symbolize. For instance, one person may use it to symbolize nutrition in the form of a loaf of bread, while another may use it to symbolize recreation via translating it into a bar of surfing wax. Another may use it to invite cognitive growth through the purchase of a book; while still another may simply toss it into a wishing well as a tribute to fate and hope.

"Another characteristic of money can be seen by this example: The U.S. Bureau of Labor Statistics (Office of Management and Budget) reveals that the literal purchasing power of the dollar has fallen steadily from a 100 cent value in 1940 to a 29 cent value in 1975. But during the same time, the actual purchasing power of that drastically devalued money has only dropped 7.5 percent. Put that way, it doesn't seem so bad to be living in inflationary times . . . until you start to wonder who or what is making up for the difference. But how is it possible for the dollar to be literally worth less than its actual purchasing power? Is the quality of what we can buy today inferior to what it was 35 years ago? Is that where the difference is made up? Are more natural resources going into today's products which we aren't really paying for yet? Are we using more low-cost foreign labor to produce the things we buy? Will we ever have to pay to make up for these differences and currently 'free' extras? Who will have to pay? What is the real meaning of 'inflation'?

"Economists see true worth this way: Suppose twenty years ago you could have bought four loaves of bread for $1.00, but that you decided to invest your money at 5% interest instead. Today your dollar would have doubled because of the interest to approximately $2.50. The question is how many loaves of bread can $2.50 now buy? If the answer is more than four, you have gained over the twenty year investment period. If the answer is less than four, your have lost, (even if you actually have more money in the bank, it can buy less that it could before). And if the answer is exactly four, you have neither gained nor lost, unless the quality of bread has decreased in the interim. Thus an economist would state that you've got to maintain a growth rate on your investments which stays ahead of the rate of inflation.

"That feat can be accomplished in several ways: one is to produce more and more and sell it to others (use more natural resources and energy); another is to sell what you buy at progressively greater profits (get ahead of inflation and fan its flames); another is to use resources which are currently undervalued (some kinds of foreign labor, fossil fuels, metals) and increase your prices by amounts which exceed their rising costs or you can work toward improving the quality of your products so that they are more adaptable, long-lasting and satisfying than before; you can be 'true-value' instead of 'dollar-value' oriented.

"The dollar also has these two special characteristics: On the one hand, it is a common denominator—useful for measuring almost anything we wish to examine; on the other hand, it is a barrier against assessing true worth since it is intrinsically worthless itself. Yet is is typically assigned great worth by those who forget it is merely a symbol for the many truly worthy things in life such as comfort, natural resources, freedom, food, shelter, etc.

GAME N° 1

part I "FETCH AND TELL"
(DISCOVERING THE NEED FOR CRITERIA)

VALUES TECH remains a viable institution to a large extent due to the importance of the Universal Life Process (creative problem-solving process) which has become the foundation of our curriculum. Renew your knowledge and skill in using that process to solve problems by applying it to find a solution to the following:

Within a time limit of $2\frac{1}{2}$ hours, go out and spend approximately one dollar (somewhere between 89¢ and $1.15). Your purchase must be tangible (real, capable of monetary appraisal) and something you can show to others without causing embarrassment to anyone present. The criteria you use to make your selection must be itemized for all to see. That's all there is to it. (We urge you to act now. The purchasing power of your dollar may be decreasing daily!)

$2\frac{1}{2}$ Hours Later

"Welcome back to the Values Workshop. I'm sure you know the value of a dollar better now than when you left earlier today. As a matter of fact, you are probably more aware of the worth of things in general.

part II   "SHOW AND TELL!"

Each participant should now show his or her purchase and explain the criteria used to make the decision. During the individual presentations, all other participants are encouraged to make constructive evaluative comments. In this way, the group can establish collective criteria for more responsible buying.

part III   "WISH I SAID THAT"
(COMPARING REASONS)

The following list shows things that some members of one group procured:

1. a roll of film..................................@   98¢
2. two rolls of pennies..........................@ $1.00
3. 27 Xerox copies...............................@ $1.00
4. a potted plant................................@ $1.08
5. one yard of cotton)
   four buttons   ) on sale..................@ $1.18
   one 5-inch zipper)
6. a paperback book..............................@ $1.01
7. an eight-foot tall fluorescent red, military
   surplus practice bomb (rented)................@ $1.01
8. a loaf of seven-grain bread...................@   75¢
9. coffee & doughnuts with a friend who was asked to
   come back for the evaluation session so she could
   be seen as a tangible item....................@   85¢
10. two bars of surfboard wax (for "me") and a bunch
    of straw flowers (for "Mom")..................@   99¢

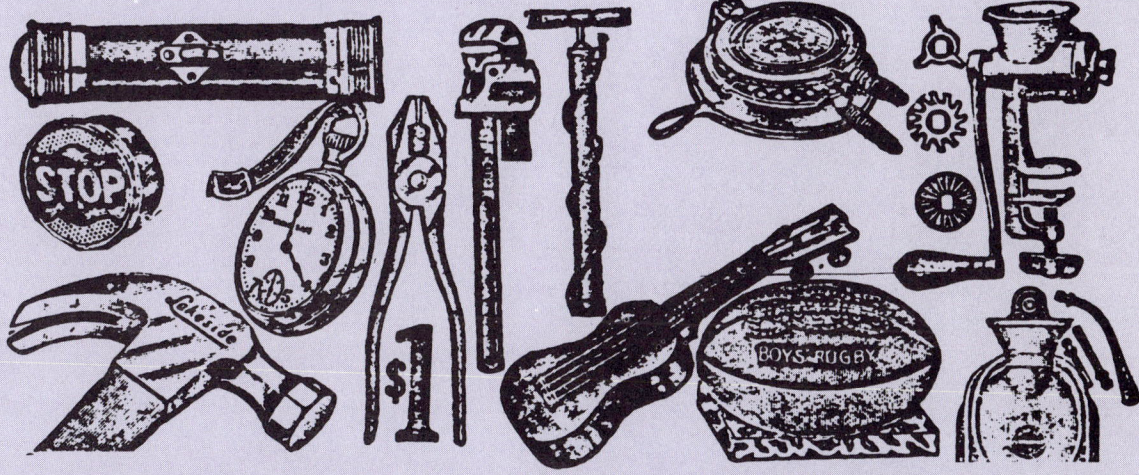

"Which one of the ten purchasers do you feel got the most for the dollar? Why? Can you figure out at least two of the criteria which may have been used for each of these purchases? Would you disqualify the two who went under and over the required limits? How does your own purchase compare with your other favorite on the list? What can you learn from comparing others' criteria with your own?

GAME Nº 2

"PASS THE BUCKS" (ACTUAL WORTH)

A.) Since the penny is 95% copper, it is one of the few things with an intrinsic value that comes close to its stated price. But when we consider all the energy that goes into prospecting, mining, smelting, transporting, minting and distributing; in other words, going through the complete copper-into-pennies process, the true value of a penny goes up and up.

"Realizing that you may know little about such technical processes, we nevertheless ask you to make up a long list of all the possible ways in which energy produced by burning the natural resources of coal, oil or gas might have been spent in the process of locating copper and turning it into the common symbolic item called 'one penny'.

"At the end, share your list and your discoveries with someone else and try to reach some "conclusions" about the true value of the things you incorporated into your study.

B.) Cook a true-value dinner for yourself and a friend. In the process, try to record the amounts of the various kinds of energy used—walking, driving to the store, moving about the kitchen, picking things from the garden, etc.—all the fuel you used, the energy that went into producing each item or ingredient, etc. Spend at least an hour after dinner discussing the difference between the true value and the dollar value of each part of the process. (Your appreciation of the dinner will be heightened!)

GAME Nº 3

"BIG MAC" (HIDDEN VALUE)

From the point of view of energy expended, make an approximation of the true dollar value of all that goes into a McDonald's "Big Mac" hamburger. Don't forget the processes involved in converting raw materials first into basic ingredients and then into McDonald materials (wood into paper into printed napkins, etc.)...all the tools, trucks, gasoline, equipment and work hours involved in processing, manufacture, maintenance and storage before it comes together in front of you at the take-out window. Don't forget the cattle and the many acres of grassland, the human labor (which produced the meat), the wheat fields (which produce raw materials for buns), the tomatoes, onions, etc. (which go into the sauce), etc. A good way to do this might be to start with a large sheet of paper and draw a "Big Mac" in the center. Then draw the separate components around it in ever-increasing circles until you can see the "endless" nature of the exercise. A final task might be to attach an estimated price to the "Big Mac" based upon some standard (such as one worker hour equals $2.00, etc.) to each drawing on the page. (Remember to include the trash process which begins when the throwaways are tossed into the refuse can.)

Note: If you have trouble relating to a McDonald burger, try one of the following subjects:
A can of Coca-Cola
A plastic cup of vending machine coffee
A chocolate-covered ice cream bar
A package of chewing gum

GAME N°4

<u>What does it mean to have a "helpful" place to shop?</u>

1. Go to your nearest or favorite shopping center.
2. List the names of the shops you find there.
3. Establish criteria. What is required for a shop to present an environment of "helpfulness" to you as a consumer? Open displays? Easy-to-read prices? Comparative prices? Friendly, informed staff? List as many considerations as possible.
4. Rank and weigh (factor) your criteria.
   What order of importance?
   Which can be combined?
   Which are repetitions?
   What is the relative importance of each item?
5. List additional comments which may not be directly related to helpfulness but which may make the shop more accessible, pleasant, memorable, etc.
6. Add up the scores

SHOPS	CRITERIA					TOTALS	COMMENTS

"In closing today's workshop I might suggest that if a family were to sit down together and work out the costs and economics of raising a child through 18 to 25 exhausting years, no doubt human life and the value of the family would increase in importance for all involved."

4th day
INTRAMURALS
(A Session in Competitive Values)

**Conducted by the VALUES TECH coaching staff:
Maynard F. ["Maxie"] Maxwell & Doris Rose**

Today, we want to lead you in a series of six games and exercises designed to flex your values muscles still more. You may 'warm up' on the first exercise and you should be going strong when the final bell rings to close the sessions.

EXERCISE N⁰1

PENNYWISE

A popular soft drink* has the following sub-title printed on its all-aluminum can:

"Imitation citrus flavored dietary artificially sweetened carbonated beverage"

The actual ingredients are listed according to quantity: "carbonated water, citric acid, gum arabic, sodium saccharin, sodium citrate, 1/40 of 1% benzoate of soda and stannous chloride as preservatives, natural and artificial flavorings, salt, glycerolester of wood rosin, bromated vegetable oil, artificial coloring. 0.10 mg per fluid ounce (less than 0.04 of 1%) saccharin, a non-nutritive artificial sweetener which should be used only by persons who must restrict their intake of ordinary sweets; no

*Fresca, a product of the Coca-Cola Company

fats or protein, 0.63 of 1% available carbohydrates and ¼ calorie per fluid ounce." (approximate cost, 25 cents)

In this first game, you will investigate just what you get for your money when you respond to a supermarket ad. Some people call it "supermarket consumerism." We call it "plain old physical analysis." For instance, it has been estimated that the amount of "real" meat in a TV dinner costs the buyer nearly $10.00 per pound (S.F. Chronicle 9/6/74). What do you pay for food? And what do you get for your money?

EXERCISE: Go to your supermarket with a note pad, and figure the comparative costs of several things on some single standard, such as "the pound", "the calorie" or "MDR" (Minimum Daily Requirement established by the U.S. Government). Look for the five or six "worst" buys and the five or six "best" buys in the store. Your viewpoint (criteria) will make a difference. For instance, to a child "Kool-Aid" is a bargain. But from the viewpoint of nutrition or economy, "Kool-Aid" will cost you approximately $11.40 a pound, and with $11.40 you could buy approximately 58 pounds of real fruit.

When you have finished your comparison shopping, compile a master list of "bargains" and "luxuries". It should provide a lasting impression of the many different prices charged for similar things.

EXERCISE N° 2

SWEET TOOTH

Here's another supermarket special to tone up your value conscious muscles.

Everyone loves sugar. It tastes so good, and might be considered a nutritious addition (sucrose, carbohydrate) to the diet. But suger "hides" inside many foods. The School of Health at Loma Linda University estimates the following amounts of "hidden" sugar in some favorite American foods:

one scoop of ice cream	contains 4 teaspoons of sugar
one glazed doughnut	contains 6 teaspoons of sugar
one soft drink or chocolate bar	contains 8 teaspoons of sugar
one piece of fruit pie	contains 10 teaspoons of sugar
one banana split	contains 25 teaspoons of sugar

Sure, a banana split is super-delicious. But would you sit down to eat it if you envisioned it as a bowl containing twenty-five teaspoons of sugar?

Sugar is added to almost all processed foods. It's in everything from baby food to canned vegetables, stimulating tooth decay and other suspected and occasionally proven unnecessary consequences. Look for it listed as "sucrose," "sorghum" or as "beet" or "cane" sugar.

EXERCISE: Go back to the supermarket and find as many items as you can which contain hidden sugar. You can estimate the quantity of sugar in cans, jars and boxes by reading the ingredients and noting how close the word "sugar" is to the beginning of the list. (According to law, manufacturers must list ingredients in order of the proportional amount present in the product.) Compile a master list of sugar foods. Even though several good books on the subject have already done this for you, it's a far greater learning experience to do it yourself.

EXERCISE N°3

WASTE NOT — WANT NOT:

The nation's most widely-distributed book is the telephone book. It costs fifty million dollars per year to publish. However it is not as widely read as is should be. According to the phone company, it costs an additional fifty-five million dollars to provide Information Operators for those who don't use the book when they get it.

Another American behavior anomaly is the way we treat the automobile. In our economy, the automobile ranks as the third largest living cost (food and shelter are first and second). The car nicks us for approximately $2400 per year if we drive a standard size, $1950/year if we drive a compact model and $1650/year if we drive a sub-compact. (These are Federal Highway Administration figures based on original cost, maintenance, gas, oil, parking, insurance and taxes for driving an average 15,000 miles per year.) But the fact that is costs nearly $7.00 per day for the privilege of driving a standard car seldom seems to enter the consciousness of the typical driver. Yet that's a lot of money, no matter how fat our budget may be.

Some unnecessary waste derives from an overabundance of things, but much waste stems from the desire for greater convenience. For instance, sunlight prevails over a large part of the earth for a large number of hours per year. By capturing its heat we could get energy for immediate use and also store and transfer that solar energy for later use. From it we could also get vitamin D and the world's top disinfectant action — all free. But instead we burn oil, coal or gas or electricity (which is generated by burning these fossil fuels). We also buy aerosol disinfectants in pressurized canisters and pop synthesized vitamins into our mouths as we dash from house to car, dodging the sun as much as possible . . . all to make up for some things which are really free (but not always very convenient) to use.

EXERCISE: How much are you willing to pay for "convenience"? In 1975 potatoes cost about 17¢/pound in the supermarket. But if you bought them peeled, washed and sliced they cost from 30 to 40¢ per pound (hash brown and French fry potatoes). If you bought them already baked (frozen) with a dab of sour cream, salt, onions and spices, the price rose to 65¢/pound. And the most expensive way to buy potatoes was to pay $4.00 per pound for packaged dehydrated potato soup mix where dry milk, salt, spices and onion are also added. "Convenience" is a very expensive item in a food budget.

As an exercise, choose one of the following typical conveniences and track down the extra cost it entails by finding out what the raw materials would actually cost if you decided to do it yourself. (The objective of this task is to develop keener awareness of the price of services, not necessarily to encourage doing away with them. Don't forget to add on a value charge for your own time and energy.)

1. hiring a packer and mover or moving yourself in a rented truck with supermarket cartons

2. sending your clothes to the laundry or washing them by hand and drying them in the sun

3. drying your hair, shaving and brushing your teeth electrically or doing it the "old way"

4. using instant coffee or brewing your own

5. flying "first class" on a jet or going economy class with less luxury

6. having lunch out or brown-bagging it

EXERCISE NO 4

"WHAT'S IT WORTH T' YA?"

Would you divorce your husband/wife for $50,000? Is your answer, "It all depends"? In this exercise we want to find out what makes up those dependencies we talk about when faced with a tough decision. So, after each question we ask that you provide three candid reasons why you might choose either or both of the alternative choices. By promoting both points of view, you should discover some more "hidden" personal values which you will want to record in your notebook.

A.) Would you sell the family picture album containing the only known photographs of your dead parents to an antique collector for $500?

B.) If you accidentally hit a dog with your car and were sure no one had observed you, would you "hit and run" to avoid the hassle and possible speeding charge?

C.) Would you jump off the roof of a moving freight train for $1000?

D.) Would you take part in a "fool-proof" bank robbery for $50,000?

E.) Would you take the rap of a three-year prison term and public disgrace for someone else's crime in exchange for a guaranteed $100,000 Swiss bank account?

EXERCISE NO 5

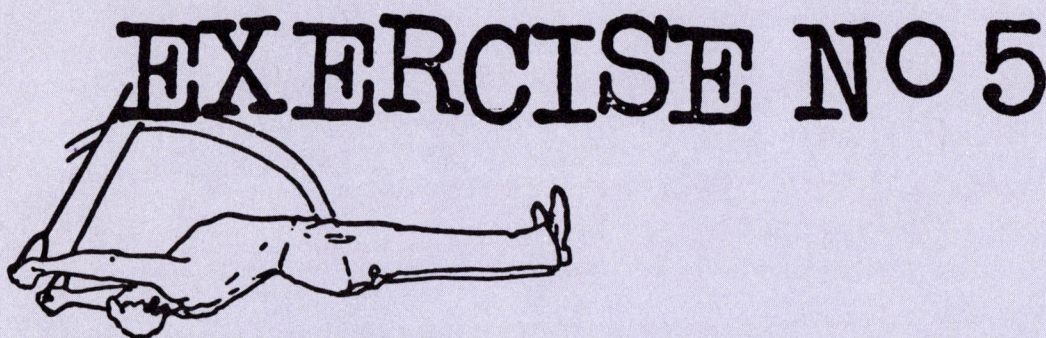

"EROS AND THANATOS"

The next exercise is somewhat similar to the last one in that it involves big issues. But now, the questions involve life and death, and nothing seems to get us closer to our values than that mortal subject. Life and death are natural conditioners of human behavior. "Adventure" may be the drive which combines the two.

A.) In Goethe's famous play, a German named Faust sells his soul to the Devil to achieve certain earthly ambitions. Pretend that you are in that position and decide. What would you ask for right now in exchange for giving up the last ten years of your life? Give reasons for your choice.

B.) If giving up your life could mean saving the lives of two other people, who would your choices be? Why?

C.) What rewards written on slips of paper in the "other five chambers" would you require before you would participate in a real game of Russian roulette?

D.) If your best friend had just sacrificed his/her life for yours, would your life take on a new sense of purpose? Think about it seriously, and then try to answer why.

EXERCISE N°6

NONSENSE?

Our beliefs are important to us. Statements which do not fall in line with our own are rejected as irrelevant, foolish or nonsensical. What do you think is the underlying philosophy of someone who might make the following statements?

A.) "If you plan to enjoy a tree you never watched grow, you must strive to plant a tree you never expect to enjoy."

B.) "Beauty is only skin deep, but $5000 is $5000."

C.) "Being rich couldn't be nearly as fulfilling as having to work for your satisfactions in life."

D.) "Since we are the biggest of our kind, it stands to reason we must be the best."

E.) "Idle hands are the devil's workshop."

F.) "God takes care of fools, drunkards and the good old U.S. of A."

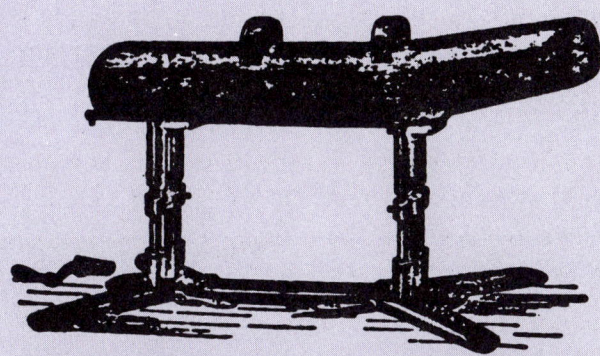

"We see that some of you at the Intermediate level are worn out after all these exercises and that others are just now picking up speed at the end. But most of the alumni have taken this work in stride, keeping their production in pace with changing demands and time requirements. They serve as a fine model and attest to the importance of practice in applying the Universal Life Process to problem-solving situations. All it takes is a little, but persistent, conscious application each day to eventually build the well-balanced and organized mind-body combination. We enjoyed leading this final workshop work-out and we hope to see all of you back again next year in even better shape than we see you now. Remember: It takes daily exercise to remain both physically and mentally fit."

CLOSING REMARKS

Elizabeth D. Evans, Associate Dean

"I know I speak for the President and all who have worked to make this Values Workshop a meaningful event when I congratulate you all for a job well done and some lessons well learned. We staff members have marvelled at your persistence and self-motivation in fulfilling the arduous projects assigned by the workshop leaders. We suspect that many of you must have writer's cramp by this time. So close your notebooks now and take a break. Take time to relax and address your thoughts to some gala happening or desired reward you might plan for yourself either tonight or in the near future. If you have worked hard for these past four days it is only natural to pull back and enjoy a contrasting and balancing experience. The change of viewpoint can also serve as a practical continuation of this workshop which does not truly end today but continues as long as you keep its lessons alive in your evaluative decision.

"Your real reward, of course, are those very lessons you take away with you; some of which you came intentionally to acquire and some of which unexpectedly happened along the way. If you have consciously recorded what you have learned here (in your notebooks) along with some statements of intention regarding how you plan to incorporate that learning into your future behavior, you have already received the biggest pay-off of all.

"Thank you for attending this event and for providing the positive feedback we need to continue in our educational objectives at VALUES TECH."

ADVANCED LEVEL

Turning Values and Abilities into Plans

NOTE! When you have completed the lessons and exercises at the Intermediate Level to your satisfaction, you are ready to proceed to the Advanced final level of work at VALUES TECH.

WORDS to the WISE

"*It may have been a tough climb but we hope it has been a worthwhile one for you from your first pre-introductory lessons to this position of advanced work. We hope that all our students have received educational rewards commensurate with their investment of time and energy. For any of you who may have had trouble and find **your** progress slow or of questionable worth, we ask you to now share your stress with the counseling staff or talk it over with your instructor or other classmates. Sometimes an investment doesn't pay benefits immediately. Perhaps your work has been misdirected or stymied by a lack of concentration or some psychological barriers, and a simple one-to-one sharing session might straighten things out fast. We wish the very best success to all of you as you enter the final phase of our program.*

Before entering school, most students think they are going there with an open mind to replace ignorance with knowledge. However, once they are into the curriculum, faced with real or implied competition and intimidation, many students switch from concentrating on their goal of working toward removing ignorance to the defensive position of spending large portions of time and energy protecting or hiding the very ignorance they came to expose and replace with knowledge. Every student attempting to progress toward a more knowledgeable position will find the journey less tedious and threatening if he or she continually renews their true purpose.

Advancement to higher levels of learning is a special condition of change that calls for special personal attention. As with all change, adaptation is the key. We must either join our force with the other forces of change and bend or be bent. Being aware of this makes it possible to roll with the movement of life instead of against it.

Values change with new information. Although we may spend lots of time and energy trying to put together our beliefs, bad investments should not become chains which bind us forever to those conclusions. It would be better to consider our beliefs as tentative things, things we are always trying on for size, not things which have such a permanent effect that we we no longer need to watch out for how they might cramp our growth. Our beliefs might better be used as guidelines to behavior, not necessarily a fixed set of rules to be held onto rigidly forever.

"Changing our mind" after starting something is not nearly as bad as we may have ourselves believe. It's just a matter of deciding to stop doing one thing and to begin another. [Actually, we have to change our mind about something in order to get started in the first place.]

The crux of making changes involves the extent of our commitments, the promises we've made and the effect our decision to change may have on others. But again, if we had the courage to make the first decision, and if we were able to get others involved in that action, we surely possess the potential for doing it again.

The essence of the problem is fear: fear of appearing weak [yet it takes strength to make a decision]; fear of appearing stupid [yet it takes intelligence to alter values, criteria or priorities]; fear of appearing indecisive [yet it is a decision we wish to make]; and fear of hurting someone who might be counting on us to persist in carrying through with our first decision [which is where the real courage of our convictions gets its biggest test].

THERE, BUT FOR THE GRACE OF GOD, GO I! [A Lesson in Goals, Aims and Intentions]

Everyone has dreams, not just the kind produced by the subconscious during the night out of the many bits of unattended stimuli received each day, but also daydreams—the kind of dreams that are consciously determined—the way we'd like things to be. Motivated by our inner drives and urges, we are all dreamers, trying our best to make life fulfill our intentions.

Standard human behavior is to maximize need satisfactions and to minimize barriers to those satisfactions. The ultimate dream for most of us is the achievement of our goals, whatever they may be.

In the beginning, everyone's goal is happiness, but after that, things really get complicated because we all strive to achieve happiness in special ways. Happiness can be defined by behavior patterns ranging from a frantic search for sheer sensory pleasure to the calm state of prayerful asceticism.

Another confusion arises from the fact that we all begin life in a state of so-called innocence where happiness is a fairly obvious matter: We are either happy (needs are satisfied), or we aren't happy (we are frustrated and cry our hearts out).

But later on, when we're older and not so innocent, it is harder to know when we've achieved happiness. By that time, personal needs and external forces have complicated matters to the point where we aren't sure we will ever be happy and fulfilled. The usual result is anxiety and insecurity. And so the older we get, the more we cling to old securities and habits and resist change.

Becoming conscious of these forces makes it easier to deal with them. They aren't so mysterious or threatening when we know what to expect from them, and the act of reaching out for those things which will satisfy our needs can be accomplished with a minimum of frustration if we are aware of the potential causes of anxiety.

In this first lesson we present a variety of goals and theories. Each item is suitable subject matter for a seminar or discussion group, since the information merely represents what might be the theme of a further elaboration.

Item 1. Goals are directly related to values and beliefs since they are the attempts to express those beliefs.

Item 2. Goals are directly related to behavior because they encompass smaller behavior patterns.

135

Item 3. Before goals can be relevantly defined, values must be clarified. Some values and goals are all-inclusive, and some are just short-range "one-timers." This can cause ambivalent behavior if values and goals are not understood and consciously managed.

Item 4. Since goals are defined by behavior, they can be measured by the quantity and quality of their intensity and duration.

Item 5. Some goals are consciously achieved by systematic adherence to principles and through chosen movements, words and gestures. Other goals are selected intuitively by impulsively allowing feeling and senses to guide behavior.

Item 6. Basic goals are comprised of behavior components. It is probable that no separate act has intrinsic value apart from the contribution it makes to the larger purpose.

Item 7. Goal statements are seldom profound. They become more so as they are clarified and defined. To say that happiness is our goal is just the beginning; then the word must be defined, and behavior must be organized to conform to the definition.

Item 8. We all try to achieve our goals naturally via the route of least resistance. When barriers appear which cannot be overcome by a known response, we say that we have a "problem situation," and a new response must be developed through problem-solving techniques.

Item 9. Needs are not always explicitly set forth in goal statements. Therefore, we often have to go through a great deal of analysis and synthesis to discover the basic cause which is pushing us toward some end. Still, needs are almost always implicit in goal statements. To get to these implications, all we have to do is question **why** we want to achieve some particular goal and keep it up in a chain-like fashion until the real need is exposed. The needs are there. They're doing the driving. All we have to do is pull them out to be seen.

For instance, if you were in training to be a candidate for the Mr. Universe contest, you would probably be concerned with more than health needs alone; publicity, intelligence, attractiveness, press image, etc. Health is an intrinsic value because it is necessary to survival, and all goals having to do with the maintenance or recovery of health can probably be traced to that basic need. A problem arises when goals simultaneously reflect more than one need.

Item 10. Goals are the operant rules that determine behavior. This means that activity grows out of the weakness or strength of personal convictions.

"Goal Mine" [Shopping for goals]

Here are some typical forms in which goal statements occur. Group discussions will help each participant get a better view of their personal response to such statements of intent. Look over the statements. Discuss them. Then choose the points which you deem important and incorporate them into a statement of your own.

The goal of the United States of America is personal freedom and independence. In the introduction to "The Report of the President's Commission on National Goals," we read "The paramount goal of the United States...is to guard the rights of the individual, to ensure his development, and to enlarge his opportunity." It is set forth in the Declaration of Independence drafted by Thomas Jefferson and adopted by the Continental Congress on July 4, 1776.

Americans today want it all. Both/And is quickly replacing Either/Or. They want towns composed of people with diverse interests and backgrounds, so long as they're all the same. They want to live in the sun, near the pool, and stay warm and wet, and yet they want skin forever young and unwrinkled. They hate inflation and hoarding, and yet everyone wants his full share.

"We do solemnly and mutually covenant and combine ourselves together into a civil body politick for our better ordering ...and the general good of the colony." (Mayflower Compact, 1620)

"The National Environmental Goals are the following:

1. fulfill the responsibilities of each generation as trustee of the environment for succeeding generations;

2. assure safe, healthful, productive and esthetically-pleasing surroundings for all Americans;

3. attain the widest range of beneficial uses of the environment without degradation, risk to health or safety, or other undesirable and unintended consequences;

4. preserve important historic, cultural, and natural aspects of our national heritage, and maintain, wherever possible, an environment which supports diversity and variety of individual choice;

5. achieve a balance between population and resource use which will permit high standards of living and a wide sharing of life's amenities; and

6. enhance the quality of renewable resources and approach the maximum attainable recycling of depletable resources." (National Environmental Policy Act of 1969)

In the screenplay "The Pawnbroker", the tortured and broken Nasserman confesses, "I do not believe in God or art or science or newspapers or philosophy or politics. I believe in money."

137

F The philosophic goal of the American Indian has always been "to live in harmony with nature". This leads to clean relationships with the earth, its elements and creatures, and with the gods which govern change.

G The goals of Goddard College (Plainfield, Vermont) read as follows in the 1974 college catalog, p. 8:

> "The specific aims of education must of necessity be personal to and different for each Goddard student. The college has general aims, however. It is expected that students who commit themselves fully to the kind of learning experiences Goddard makes possible will change in certain directions:
>
> They will come to know themselves better as individuals and as members of society.
> They will live as increasingly responsible members of the society of which they are independent and interdependent parts.
> They will become aware of the need for creative thought and action in every aspect of human life, and develop and apply their own creative potentials.
> They will gain wide general information about the world they live in.
> They will gain specialized information and training appropriate to their individual needs and purposes.
> They will grow to recognize and accept the dignity and necessity of labor."

H Yesterday's goals were involved with getting to a place, manufacturing a product, producing power, and making things cheaper and more efficient. Today we search for patterns, principles, concepts and consequences. We're more concerned now with what happens if we do something than we are with simply doing something.

I I believe in trying to do the right thing, accepting the challenge of life and helping others.

J Tai Chi is the essence or ultimate cause, and Tao is the way for those who wish to live in harmony with cosmic principles. Each person must develop a personal sense of virtue. This sense is known as Te.

K The challenge in farming is to stay healthy and make a profit. Health is needed for work and for raising a family, and profit is necessary to beat inflation, to remain solvent and to stay in business.

We must first learn to love ourselves, and then to transcend that self-love into an outward love for our brothers and sisters, and eventually to a love for our natural environment.

Current aspirations concerning the desired quality of life in the United States (1971) are ranked in the table below:

	Relative Importance
1. Love, caring, affection, communication, interpersonal understanding; friendship, companionship; honesty, sincerity, truthfulness; tolerance, acceptance of others; faith, religious awareness.	15.0
2. Self-respect, self-acceptance, self-satisfaction; self-confidence, egoism; security; stability, familiarity, sense of permanence; self-knowledge, self-awareness, growth.	11.5
3. Peace of mind, emotional stability, lack of conflict: fear, anxiety; suffering, pain; humiliation, belittlement; escape, fantasy.	10.0
4. Sex, sexual satisfaction, sexual pleasure.	9.5
5. Challenge, stimulation; competition, competitiveness; ambition; opportunity, social mobility, luck; educational, intellectual stimulating.	
6. Social acceptance, popularity; needed, feeling of being wanted; loneliness, impersonality; flattering, positive feedback, reinforcement.	8.0
7. Achievement, accomplishment, job satisfaction; success; failure, defeat, losing; money, acquisitiveness, material greed; status, reputation, recognition, prestige.	7.0
8. Individuality; conformity; spontaneity, impulsive, uninhibited; freedom.	6.0
9. Involvement, participation; concern, altruism, consideration.	6.0
10. Comfort, economic well-being, relaxation, leisure; good health.	6.0
11. Novelty, change, newness, variety, surprise; boredom; humorous, amusing, witty.	5.0
12. Dominance, superiority; dependence, impotence, helplessness; aggression, violence, hostility; power, control, independence.	3.5
13. Privacy	2.0

(Chart by Dalkey, Norman C. and Rourke, Daniel L. "The Delphi Procedure and Rating Quality of Life Factors" from EXPERIMENTAL ASSESSMENT OF DELPHI PROCEDURES WITH GROUP VALUE JUDGMENTS, Rand, 1971. as quoted in THE QUALITY OF LIFE CONCEPT, A POTENTIAL NEW TOOL FOR DECISION-MAKERS, p.I-51 by The Environmental Protection Agency Office of Research and Monitoring, Environmental Studies Division, March, 1973.)

ADVANCED Exercise No. 2

Lab Exercise for Lesson 1

"Banner Year" [Self-Expression]

Almost everyone loves to march behind a flag. A flag symbolizes what we believe in and lends support to our cause. What kind of a flag or banner could you design that would both express your goals and motivate you to achieve those goals? Start a list of things that could be turned into symbols representative of your values. You will probably want to subdivide the elements included in your list into several columns or groups. As the list grows, make some "idea" sketches along the side of the column which will organize the items into simpler forms. For instance, if peace is one of your values, you may want to symbolize it with a dove or a heart. Eventually, one or more of the elements should emerge as symbolic of the component parts.

Don't try to design your flag at one sitting; mull it over for days or weeks. When you have given it sufficient consideration, consolidate your sketches into one master plan, and either begin to make your own flag by setting up shop or have it made by someone else. (Note! Flags don't have to be rectangular and tied to poles. They can be made of any material or shape. Paper flags are terrific. Have you ever seen a flag made out of bits of wood and seaweed? Sometimes the back of a jacket makes a great "billboard" flag. Or maybe you want your banner to come in the form of stickers, bumper strips or buttons (see your local printer) which can be attached to books, letters or clothes. Your choice should take into consideration how well the colors, shapes, materials and functions reinforce the overall values that are being expressed. When completed, use your banner as a daily reminder of who you are and what you stand for. When your values change, change your banner accordingly.)

ADVANCED Exercise No. 3

Lab Exercise for Lesson 1

"Happy New Year" [Resolutions]

We have found that goals come in many forms, and that their chief characteristic is to express needs through behavior or problem-solving activity. Even though people traditionally make lists of resolutions only at the beginning of a new year, we ask that you take time right now to make the same sort of renewal plans. Don't forget to account for as many needs as possible: the welfare of family, friends, other members of society as well as the survival of the entire species should find their places somewhere on the list because they may eventually play a part in its realization. When you can see your year's work cut out for you, check to see if the work can actually be done in fifty-two weeks or if in fact you are dealing with much longer time requirements.

Lab Exercise for Lesson 1

ADVANCED Exercise No. 4

"That's Not My Job" [Purposes]

If a student's basic role is to learn, and a teacher's basic role is to facilitate learning, what do you think should be the basic role of a school administrator? Write your theory in 25 words or less. But before answering, consider the fact that few students actually see their role as a learner, instead they normally expect "to be taught." And most teachers do not see themselves as "learning facilitators"; instead they think of themselves as "dispensers of facts and figures" and "judges of student worth." The objective of this exercise is to provide a context for discovering how goals actually reflect points of view and personal values. Review what you write and try to extract your beliefs and values from it for recording in your notebook.

Lab Exercise for Lesson 1

ADVANCED Exercise No. 5

"Where Does Love Fit In?" [Priorities]

A general list of goals can be derived from the needs we express as a collective society. Such a list might contain the following items:

- Freedom and independence
- Justice and compassion
- Fairness and equality
- Prosperity
- Relaxation and joy
- Love and friendship
- Security
- Achievement and acknowledgement
- Known relationship with the supernatural
- Health and happiness
- Belongingness and sense of family
- Sufficiency

A.) Using a matrix rank the above list according to your priorities. You may want to supplement the list by annotating each item. For instance, Self-Sufficiency, Autonomy, Privacy, Self-Motivation and Self-Determination may help you explain and judge the first category--Freedom and Independence.

B.) Consciously use your priorities to guide your behavior in the next few days. Stop every so often during that time to see if your actual behavior is in line with what you say your priorities dictate.

"Give Me Strength To See the Light, O Lord"
[Abstracting Intentions]

The following litany was written by the Reverend Cecil Williams of San Francisco's Glide Memorial Church:

"A Time for Coming Together

Leader: We have come together to celebrate Life!

People: Yes! We are celebrating in spite of the conditions we live under--the energy crisis, inflation, war, racism, poverty, greed, sexism, exploitation, repression, guilt and loneliness.

Leader: We have come here to share an experience of Life together.

People: Yes! We have come together and accept our differences--Black, White, Red, Brown, Yellow, women, men, children, poor, rich, middle class, young, old, homosexual, straight, and hip.

Leader: We have come here to decide to live.

People: Yes! Yes! Living is a righteous experience!
Live on, Brother.
Live on, Sister.
Live on, Children."

A.) If you had to explain in a brief phrase (10 words or less) what the litany was all about, what are three different ways it might be encapsulated?

B.) Write your own version of a litany of social behavior.

C. Encapsulate your litany in a title or motto which can serve to remind you of the larger complete text.

Lab Exercise for 1

"Said Another Way" [Restatement: Expressing Intentions II]

We've discovered that one of the best methods for clarifying goals is to make a game of restating them. For instance, find an alternative way to state this goal: "lose 10 pounds." Responses might include, "take the extra load off your feet," "be able to fit into those old blue jeans," "go on a fat-reducing schedule," "trim down to a healthier physical condition," etc. After practicing on the other statements which follow, try to restate one or two goals of your own.

1. earn a promotion to manager

2. write a complaint letter to a company which uses a computerized billing machine

3. become more physically attractive

Lab Exercise for Lesson 1

ADVANCED Exercise No. 8

"A Curriculum in Consumer Intelligence" [Planning]

Almost every school has a curriculum of courses to be taken and a minimal number of grade points to be earned before a certificate, diploma or degree of completion is awarded. Usually the curriculum is determined by one or a combination of tradition, accrediting bodies, changing times, economic pressures, staff capabilities and interests and student needs. In progressive schools a committee composed of both staff and students regularly evaluates the program and keeps it up-to-date in terms of how well the required subject matter and electives reflect the on-going and probable needs of society.

Imagine that you have been elected to sit on a Curriculum Committee charged with planning a new two-year course of study in <u>Consumer Intelligence</u> at the Community College level. (Note! Don't balk at doing this project just because you may not be an "official" educational planner. You are undoubtedly a consumer, so attempting such a task may not be as remote from your abilities as you think.) In approaching the project: you'll find that you need to decide on the kind of courses to offer, and to do that you'll need to analyze the general goals of the school which hold them together as a unified, balanced package.

1 Begin by working out an outline of the entire curriculum. What kinds of courses would you include? (What college goals and objectives would they emphasize?) Which ones are the "key" courses and which ones the "support" courses?

2 Determine the kinds of physical environment you would need and the staff you would hire to make your program a success.

3 Actually name the courses and work out a six quarter program which will probably not exceed 18 units per quarter (six hours per day).

Lab Exercise for Lesson 1

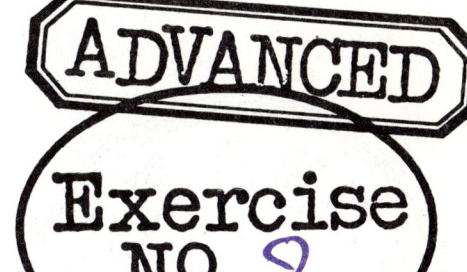

ADVANCED Exercise No. 9

"You Can Only Have One"

Being stuck with the dilemma of what single book to buy at the paperback bookstore which offers a selection of thousands is a typical situation in our highly productive society. Try this simple "conscious" technique the next time you go to buy a paperback.

1. List or try to hold in your memory the criteria (reasons, purposes, needs, requirements, etc.) you wish to fulfill by buying and reading a book. NOTE! We start you off with a few suggestions in

the list below. Add at least 5 more of your own and scratch out any of ours which do not apply to your situation.

2. Following each criterion fill in the name(s) of the book(s) which you think will satisfy that criterion.

3. Thus narrowing down your choice from thousands to but a dozen or more, you will have consciously taken charge of the selection process with the rational application of your own requirements. In the coming weeks, you may even decide to buy all of your choices, one at a time.

Criteria	Titles Which Will Fulfill Criteria
a) helps me to better understand myself	_____
b) helps me to relax and see life with a brighter outlook	_____
c) provides insight into my society	_____
d) increases my knowledge of my special interest	_____
e) helps me to acquire a new skill	_____
f) _____	_____
g) _____	_____
h) _____	_____

See page 74 for today's homework assignment.

ADVANCED

WHAT'S IN A NAME [A Lesson in Criteria and Objectives]

More Facts and Figures Regarding Goals And Objectives

Item 1. A goal statement is more than an intention; it is also a type of conclusion. "I want to get married" is a typical example because it concludes a "solution" to a lot of subproblems leading up to it. Some of the feelings and thoughts influencing such a conclusion might be a strong attraction to a potential life partner, a disdain for loneliness, a desire to break away from parental jurisdiction and to be self-assertive, a need for intimacy, economic cooperation, a desire to be a parent, moral necessity, and so on.

Item 2. Having a goal doesn't mean we know how to achieve it or even that we should try to achieve it. It simply means we've made an initial statement about something we think should happen. A man and a woman might have quite different reasons for wanting to get married, and their differences could lead to conflict and eventual divorce (as statistics reveal).

Item 3. Achieving goals in an accountable and responsible way necessarily brings up the subjects of planning and objectives. is only through consciously planned and measurable objectives that we really put teeth into goal statements. And those same measurable objectives eventually become the basic criteria for measuring our achievement.

A set of carefully planned, interrelated objectives is the key to the achievement of any goal. There's no possible way to get to an "end" except by going through a series of "means." Whether the trip is long and exhausting or just a breeze, there is never a product produced without someone (or something) having undergone a process. But in terms of typical non-systematic behavior this is how the achievement of a goal usually goes:

1. We think we have a goal. We want something and try to describe it. It's vague, and we can't see exactly where it is we want to go or how to get there. But it feels right, and it's the best description we've got.

2. Next, we try to figure out a plan for reaching our goal. But making plans calls for making decisions, and decision-making requires dealing with choice. So instead we think of a couple of things we could do to reach the goal and choose between them . . . selecting the way of least resistance if possible, i.e., we usually work toward what we want in a more natural, intuitive than systematic way. We just use the goal statement as a sort of motto to lead us where it will. We follow our nose; always going, never sure; never knowing how close or far away we are; only feeling better or worse after our experiences when we recognize how something we've said or done has related to that goal, whereas a more determined way would be to work out a serious plan for how to reach the goal, and to follow our plan to its end (or until a better plan convinces us to change course). Afterwards, we may decide that our planned choice was unwise and that a better way to get there exists. But even if that is true, it's a positive result, and we can always learn from our mistakes.

Item 4. If we don't make definite plans for reaching our goals, we are apt to become unfulfilled daydreamers. Like a small boy in a spacecraft museum who sits in all the cockpits, holds the steering mechanisms and imagines all sorts of wonderful trips, we also may never get airborne. Of course, we also will never risk a fatal crash. Yet we know down deep that if we really want to learn to fly, we've got to pay the dues and accept the risks. We've got to take action to make our dreams come true.

Item 5. Objectives leading to goal achievement form a series of sub-destinations; each objective represents some portion of the total task. For instance, suppose your goal is to accumulate $500 in a bank savings account. You could make a deposit of $5 a week for twenty months. Each time you made the deposit, you would be following a plan which had gotten you one week and $5 closer to the destination. A bank book tells you exactly, at any time, just how well you are doing and how far along you have progressed toward meeting the goal.

Item 6. Since goals can't be reached directly, objectives must be clear and include ways to let us know when they are achieved. The bank book is a specific record of weekly $5 deposits. It lets us know exactly where we are. But suppose our behavior was not so regular and consistent. Suppose we deposited $20 the first week, but found that to be too stiff on our budget. Three weeks later when we recovered from the shock of discovering that saving means cutting back elsewhere, we deposited another $10. Thereafter, each deposit required a separate decision as to the amount. Eventually, if we are uncommonly persistent, we might reach our $500 destination. However, the erratic experience would probably have taught us that it is much simpler to plan a regular savings program from the beginning.

Item 7. Because each of us is unique, we have varying degrees of limitations. Some can go farther and fly higher than others. Yet with training and practice, we could all extend our potentials. When planning objectives, it's important not to work out unachieveable chores for ourselves or to be disgusted with ourselves for not completing something on time if it really wasn't possible in the first place. Shooting for marks higher than we know we can reach is only good psychology when we are consciously aware of how we are 'tricking' ourselves.

Item 8. It's important to design attractiveness and interest into the process of reaching goals in order to maintain attraction and interest. This means that variety and balance are key considerations in the planning of objectives. Some objectives might call for "head" work if others are mostly "body" work. Some might be free-wheeling if others require you to be serious. Some might include getting outside in the sun if others are desk jobs, etc. Without variety, we quickly go stale.

Item 9. Objectives come in different forms: Some are long-range activities; some can be accomplished in a flash. Some deal with information which is easy to get, and some call for ferreting out the hard-to-get. This means that an overall time and energy estimate will be a lot easier to achieve if we give consideration to the amount of time and energy required to achieve each separate objective. For instance, in planning to reach the goal of learning to play chess like a master, we can see that it's easy to buy a set of chessmen and a board, find a copy of the rules and read them and to practice setting up the pieces and yet it could be very time consuming to locate practice partners who will give us experience in making opening moves and learning other refinements of play.

Item 10. Objectives are related to goals in a similar way that behavior is related to values. We use objectives to get us where we want to go. They are the actions we plan as a means of realizing our "image-ination." Subconsciously, we often act out a whole series of objectives without ever being aware of the goal behind them. For example we might toy with adventure in a variety of ways, do an outrageous thing or two, get into accident-prone situations, become vulnerable in any way we can think of, because to do so might get us closer to the basic subconscious goal of being noticed in a certain way by someone else.

Item 11. When we make conscious goal statements, we try to decide the relevance of planned action(s) in order to maximize the fulfillment of needs. And when we deal with the products or consequences of goals, we operate as evaluators, determining whether or not the actions or by-products we observe actually do maximize or diminish the generating human needs.

Item 12. Goals begin with subconscious feeling, but should ultimately grow to become conscious and therefore specific, measurable and knowable. As evaluators, we also first respond in a sensory way to the products of a process. Only later are our feelings translated into rational knowledge. The interrelationship between our intentions and needs and the intentions and needs of others is revealed more clearly during the evaluation process than it is during the goal-making process.

Item 13. Whereas consciously planned goals and objectives tend to be expressed at the start of the process, evaluation is an on-going stage of that process which can help us determine the worth of our behavior at any given point. This means that goals and objectives should be kept in plain view from beginning to ultimate achievement. They are our measures of value.

Item 14. Accountability is built into the problem-solving process when we use those intentions we wanted to achieve in the first place to measure what we actually did achieve in the end. This seemingly ideal but nevertheless realistic situation is seldom practiced in our fragmented society. It takes determination to become involved in stating, acting out and evaluating the actions which can get us to our goals, but that is just what the more creative, determined and knowledgeable thinkers in our society do: they not only plan, but they also live out and continually determine the worth of their own course. Sometimes we charge these people with going against the grain and label them rebels, troublemakers, nuisances, show-offs, deviants; but still, for the most part, we respect them for being assertive, self-motivated, creative members of society.

Lab Exercise for Lesson 2

ADVANCED Exercise No. 1

What It Takes [Developing Criteria]

One group of psychological researchers has determined that certain traits typically characterize a leader. Those traits are listed and ranked as follows:

1. Ability -- awake, aware, knowledgeable
2. Accomplishment -- tasks completed and recognized as well done
3. Accountability -- systematic, dependable, persistent
4. Active -- sociable, cooperative, humorous, flexible
5. Socially acceptable -- popular, helpful, harmonious

The list not only describes what it takes to be a leader, but it can serve as a list of objectives for becoming a leader and also as a list of criteria for evaluating leadership behavior. However, this list only represents the conclusions of one research group; your criteria might differ. List the characteristics you think it might take to do the following:

1. win a beauty contest
2. get a glamorous job which pays you to travel
3. be elected to the city council
4. learn to cook like Julia Child
5. make yourself accident proof

Rules And Regulations [Developing Criteria II]

Standard criteria for getting entries accepted into competitions involving manual, verbal and cognitive skills are "neatness, originality and aptness of thought." What additional criteria would you add to each of the following special competitions?

Best soap box derby racer

Best kite design

Best Mardi Gras costume

Best dessert recipe

Best name for a new pet store

Amen [Behavior as an Expression of Criteria]

A contemporary conservationist's oath reads:
"I give my pledge as citizen of this planet to save and faithfully to defend from waste the natural resources of my environment—its soil and minerals, its forest, waters and wildlife."

Outline what you think an entire lifestyle might include if it were based on such a pledge: food, house, clothing, travel, hobbies, property, vacations, buying habits, etc.

Vive Le Difference [Criteria Finding]

It's always easier to see how things differ than to note how they are alike. Perhaps this is because we habitually rely more on contrasts than on harmonies in sensing light, sound, smell, movement, temperature, texture, pattern, etc. These sensed differences are later expressed abstractly, through our words, as we attempt to communicate with others. For instance, we might define the difference between old age and youth by listing two sets of opposing criteria. On the youth side, we'd include terms such as "physically strong, highly consumptive of energy, impulsive," and on the old-age side we'd probably add complementary criteria such as "physical deterioration, low-energy consumption, philosophic", etc.

List at least eight criteria which comprise the essential differences between these pairs of activities:

- A. Catching up on the latest news and taking a walk through the park
- B. Seeing a movie on TV and seeing it downtown in a movie "palace"
- C. Attending a school full-time and taking a correspondence course
- D. Winning at cards and losing at cards

Note! By having one-half of a set of complementary terms, it is easier to get the other half. Developing criteria for one thing can be simplified by developing criteria for its opposite.

If that was too easy for you, think of the listed differences as evaluative criteria and try ranking those criteria in order of importance by attempting to judge from the point-of-view of the "lifestyle" you outlined in the last exercise (2.3).

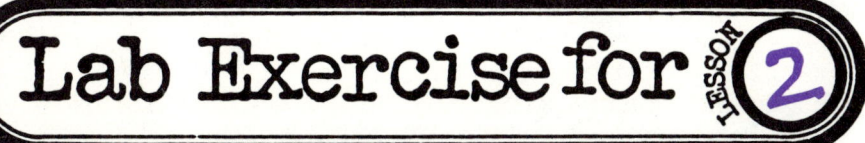

You Can Be The Architect [Responding to Criteria]

When asked what they wanted included in their new campus living quarters being planned, a group of students responded to a survey with the following list of needs:

"Please make them...

    comfortable

    efficient

    humanistic

    practical

    natural

    exciting

    peaceful

    socializing

    easy to personalize

    adaptable to diverse use."

Suppose you were the architect of the new dormitory. What are three things you might consider doing to satisfy each requirement of your student "clients"? (For instance, to satisfy "comfortable," you might consider using soft upholstered chairs and window seats. To satisfy "peaceful" you might try arranging rooms so that noisy hallways are eliminated, etc.) Your list of design decisions becomes your physical response to your personal translations of the stated student needs; they represent three objectives for reaching each of the stated "goals."

Lab Exercise for LESSON 2

Boiling Down [Ranking Criteria]

It takes inductive-comparative thinking to determine the objectives we need to accomplish or reach goals and to determine the criteria for making evaluations. We normally "size things up" by "boiling them down" according to the following common pattern:

1. First, we subdivide the subject into component parts and then separate those pieces into similar groups.

2. Next, we establish a point of view.

3. Finally, we position the pieces according to how they support that point of view, eliminating the pieces which do not support it.

The result is a newly organized and ranked list of elements which support a selected viewpoint. Film-ranking classifications, for example, have been "boiled down" from dozens of possibilities to a brief list of symbols by evaluating films from the point of view of their effect on young minds.

(G)   GENERAL PUBLIC
(PG) PARENTAL GUIDANCE SUGGESTED
(R)   RESTRICTED TO 18 YEAR OLDS AND ABOVE
(X)   ADULTS ONLY (18 YEARS AND OLDER WITH CAUTION)

Another example is the way in which the United States Department of Agriculture (USDA) ranks food products according to color, size, weight, fat content, etc. For instance, all olives eventually fit into one of the USDA categories: large, extra large, jumbo, mammoth, giant, colossal or super colossal. (Is there such a thing as a small or tiny olive?)

For this exercise, first list several points of view which can be used in ranking the given subjects. Then fill in under each viewpoint all the other levels or ranks you think would be there. (If you get into a bind, ask someone who might know more about the subject than you do.)

    an ear of corn

    a new car

    a house of your own

a class gift

a Sunday newspaper

a seat on a 10-hour non-stop flight from Los Angeles to London

Quantity And Quality [Measuring Objectives]

Examining Quantities and Qualities are the two fundamental ways of measuring or evaluating everything from objects, chemical compounds and human experiences to natural events. How old you are, how many inches of rain fell last night, how much something weighs, how often you brush your teeth, and how much homework is assigned are all relatively simple quantitative things to measure. Qualities can also be measured, but they are only measurable if, and only if, they are first translated into quantitative terms. This exercise provides the opportunity to deal with measurements of both kinds.

For example, it's clear that "product cost" can be easily measured in dollars and that it is definitely a quantity (or <u>quantitative</u> criterion). But it's not so clear how we might measure the "sales potential" of a product because that is a qualitative criterion and must be further translated through a series of reductions into quantitative terms; such as

   a.) is visually attractive

   b.) meets consumer needs

   c.) outperforms competition

   d.) is low in cost

   e.) (what would you add?)

and each of these in turn might be further translated to mean:

   a.) visual attraction...has simple, geometric lines, bright colors, bold lettering, etc.

   b.) customer needs...provides satisfaction for adventure, physical exercise and is easily customized, etc.

   c.) competitive...has better fuel performance ratio than other topline models

   d.) low cost...comes within the realm of economic possibility for the average income

   e.) (your turn again...)

It just takes longer to work out measures for the more

abstract qualities of life than it does for things which are easily translated into numbers.

Now examine the list of criteria given below. After each item, first try to determine whether it can be measured directly or indirectly, i.e., whether it is a measure of quantity or quality. In each case, follow your decision by continuing to specify the terms by which one might be measured, making certain to further translate all quantities into qualities as they appear.

cost of raw materials _____

energy required for production _____

sociability _____

longevity _____

multi-use _____

autonomy _____

human need satisfaction _____

universality _____

family-approved _____

independence _____

maintenance _____

usefulness _____

intelligence _____

size _____

efficiency _____

manliness _____

speed _____

neatness _____

originality _____

craftsmanship _____

trade-in value _____

_____

_____

_____

_____

_____

_____

_____

_____

Wheat Bubbles
Puffed Wheat is whole wheat steam-exploded, puffed to 8 times normal size. The taste is like toasted nut-meats. The texture is flimsy and flaky.

POLYVISION [A Lesson in General Studies]

Here at VALUES TECH, we believe in an evaluative point of view, not just for looking back over what we've already done, but also for looking inside, outside, up ahead and all around us in the same analytic and definitive way that we approach the creative solving of any problem situation. Such a "polyvisioned" person is always aware of the here-and-now in a way which relates the present or center of personal existence to as much of the entire time-space continuum as knowledge permits.

Looking backward to see where we've been, how far we've come and how well we've done in terms of where and/or what we set out to achieve is the accepted common-sense definition for the process of evaluation. Undoubtedly, such a retrospective view is valid. With a consciousness of our intentions to guide us, we can move forward into a not-so-dark future, having the benefit of past experience to light our way and point out pitfalls. But evaluation has far more potential for broadening our outlook than can be found by merely looking back. A **pro**spective view, as well as **intro**spective and **extra**spective (outside of our own environments) views are equally valid as life guidance aids. Obviously, we can benefit from a clear view in all directions.

What's so important about knowing where we are, where we've been, where we're headed and what's there to help or hinder the trip? The answer is not always obvious, even though it's usually right there in front of us. To see it, we often have to again be reminded that the source of all our actions lies in fulfilling our human needs. Checking back, we find that "survival" heads the list of a chain of forces awaiting fulfillment in every one of us. And we recall that our urges, drives and motivation stem from those needs which are yet to be satisfied; those which are already fulfilled no longer demand attention.

Everyone has needs to be fulfilled and intentions to be maximized. Discovering how to judge, assess and size up our relationship with the environment is a necessary factor in getting on with that basic work. We want to be sure, as best we can, that we have done all we could to be in the right place at the right time for making our dreams come true.

The argument against polyvision behavior is well known: "Why look back? What's done is done, and nothing can change it"; "Why try to look ahead when we cannot ever hope to exactly determine the future?" And each argument is correct in its own context. Considering both views together in a positive sense we might conclude: We look backward because with the insight gained from retrospection we can better determine the future by changing our behavior from the ways we behaved in the past (exactness being a relative and somewhat theoretical term). Evaluation as part of the Universal Life Process is a way of life as well as a by-product of life. To live evaluatively is to be aware of the present stage of the life process as it occurs, as well as to compare it with the rest of your existence, both past and what you plan for the future. Like anything else, to do this well requires knowledge, skills and attitudes that foster both broad and specific views.

But doing anything well is the result of both inherent potential and developed ability. We don't begin with a high level of skill. That takes practice. Instead, we normally begin clumsily and must work toward doing it well by picking up knowledge and skill through discovery and testing. By trying the same things over and over again and by changing our minds about what is valuable and what is not as new facts present themselves, we progress toward expertise.

Evaluation can be looked at in two ways: the first way is one which views it as a comparative after-the-fact summing-up of experience. The other is the "polyvision" point of view which sees it as a process of progressive improvement through analysis. In the first view, experience is evaluated in terms of where we wanted to go, how far we got and how well we achieved intended aims. But in the second "polyvision" point of view we are more concerned with developing criteria for determining the worth of specific experiences as they occur. "Polyvision" is a "during-the-fact" or "here-and-now" concept designed to develop a dynamic life goals system.

The first view is product-oriented and tends to devalue the importance of life by considering it as something which has passed. From that point of view, evaluation is a chore. If we must wait until the end of a process to evaluate it, we have a tendency to keep looking forward to that day, instead of concentrating on life as it unfolds. Instead of enjoying the preparation and ongoing process, attention is glued on the result. We're so anxious to "go" we forget we're already on the way. The polyvision view, on the other hand, evaluates experience incrementally, making it possible to take the next forward step alert to improvements. Its major requirement is that we must bring our criteria along with us as we go. For no matter how we look at it, evaluation is a process of turning the sensory stuff of experience into new knowledge. It is the way we go about objectifying our experience.

When feelings are put into words, we enjoy the additional experience of knowing and expressing what we feel. For instance, if we go to the theater alone and don't discuss the experience with anyone else its experience lessons may quickly fade away. But if we go with a friend and discuss the various aspects and meanings of the film and consider how its message relates to ourselves and to our personal experience, the whole evening can be more enjoyable and enriching.

The PURPOSE of evaluation is to determine the benefits of experience so that we can better plan our behavior in the future.

The PROCESS of evaluation is one of identifying directions and measuring achievement in terms of quantity and quality.

The PROBLEM of evaluation is the drawing of conclusions without clear criteria or consideration of sufficient alternatives.

The Basic Principles involved with evaluation are these:

1. The determination of worth is a conceptual matter. We can't place a meaningful value on something until we define it and thus form a concept of the thing. Since everyone has slightly different conceptual views of all things, the meanings of values are slightly different for everyone.

2. Concepts are backed up by either our real or imaginary experiences; i.e., we can best conceive of those things which have been experienced. Thus broadening our experiences will result in broadened concepts and clarified evaluations. New concepts can form out of the very bits and pieces of experience which already exist in our brain. We need not have new experiences to form new concepts.

3. Quantity and quality are the basic characteristics of all measurement. Both are determined by comparing achievements with standards provided by planned objectives or desired criteria (which are ultimately the same thing put to slightly different use).

4. Conscious evaluation implies supplanting emotions with facts, of moving from totally subjective response to objective response. The activity of evaluation is to remove as much vagueness and expose as much of the truth as we can.

Evaluation classifications are similar to those we discover when examining thinking processes: they can be classed as . . .

a. Incorrect or ignorant
The result of lack of knowledge and skills or improper, irrelevant attitudes; inability to deal with the situation; concepts untrue; results vague.

b. Impulsive
Inattentive, hasty, superficial, unstudied; speed often produces only a superficial quantitative measure (size, amount, distance, etc.); partial truths; untested conclusions.

c. Preconceived
Close-minded; future limited to continuing the past without additional considerations. Analogy, unstudied as to relevance, used as prejudicial argument.

d. Comprehensive
Sound, open-minded, attentive, objective, comparative, knowledgeable, accurate, complete.

e. Illogical
Inaccurate; concepts not backed up with fact and/or incorrectly related; conclusions misleading.

f. External
Accepts conclusions of another person or group; excessive reliance on opinions or values of others; lack of self-determination.
. . . or combination thereof.

The Different Kinds of Measurements are these:

a. We can measure **Quantity**: how "much"; description of amount
Ex: "He worked hard at the task for **sixteen days, nine hours and six minutes.**"
"The temperature remained in the **high seventies all summer long.**"

b. We can measure **Quality**: how "well"; description of how the basic intentions are reinforced, enriched or maximized.
Ex: "Because of his meditation technique he suffered **little discomfort** while sitting on the pole."
Ex: "The humidity and temperature caused an **insufferable** climatic condition."

c. We can measure **Extrinsic** values: how interrelationships figure into things.
Ex: "The **wind and rain** nearly ended the trial several times."
"Since **we had little to do**, the temperature was of no concern."

d. We can measure **Intrinsic** values: how inner qualities figure into things.
Ex: "The **excitement** which always accompanies graduation makes final exams hard to bear."
"**Friendly** natives help to make rural European travel all the more fun."

e. But in all cases, everything can be measured in a combined systematic and "polyvisual" way: determining worth by comparing achievements with initial intentions and by developing evaluative sensitivity as the process progresses:
Ex: Initial **Quantitative** Objective: to work at the job for thirty full days.

Quantitative Measure after the fact: actually worked for 16 days, 9 hours, six minutes (54% of intended objective). Evaluation: achieved a little more than half of what was intended; perhaps sights were set too ambitiously; perhaps better preparation would allow longer stay; perhaps summer is better than winter to try it again; approximately eight hours per day is as much as anyone could expect to endure.

Ex: Initial Qualitative Objective: to enrich the personality through accepting a demanding job as a challenge

Measures:

A Increased knowledge of personal physical limitations to provide a deeper understanding of tolerances in all human systems;

B Improved concentration skills to allow life to be lived in a lower (but more meaningful) key; etc.

Evaluation:

A Throughout the process I have learned that my personal physical limit for manual labor tasks is six hours at a time. This helps me to understand that all systems have limits and that I must not expect myself or others to exceed them.

B My new ability to focus on a subject and close out all other stimuli for a self-determined period of time helps me to relax while increasing my efficiency at the same time because I no longer waste so much energy.

Lab Exercise for Lesson 3

ADVANCED Exercise No. 1

"Find a Need and Fill It" [Needs and Goals]

Becoming conscious of our needs is prerequisite for taking an active part in achieving their satisfaction. Some needs are insatiable; we must fulfill their demands over and over again. Others can be satisfied once and for all. The important thing, aside from knowing something about those needs as being forces at the base of our motivations, is not to get ahead of ourself; i.e., trying not to satisfy a need which has yet to place demands on our energy. Fulfilling a need before it becomes relevant is a form of meaningless "self-consciousness" (as opposed to meaningful self-awareness).

A. Refer back to the Chart of Human Needs and write down at least two kinds of things you could do to realize some measure of satisfaction for ten needs which you think are currently important to you.

B. Test your response further by trying to establish how you might "measure" the various levels of satisfaction reached by each proposed response. (First decide whether it is to be a quantitative or qualitative satisfaction.)

Note! Your new expanded list represents the start of a working outline for achieving a much more satisfying life.

Lab Exercise for Lesson 3

ADVANCED Exercise No. 2

"Differences" [Measuring Fulfillment]

A difference is something which can be measured by comparing it to two standards or limits, just as knots tied in a rope have a measurable difference in standard metric lengths between them, or as two trees growing side-by-side have a measurable height difference over a standard period of time. The process of measuring achievement differences is simply the process of evaluating fulfillment at various times and then comparing the individual evaluations against some pre-determined standard criteria.

Value statements should also have measurable differences. To find them, we've got to break them down into their constituent parts and determine the comparative worth of each component; as well as the worth of the whole.

In the statement, "Phi Beta Kappa has two objectives: the encouragement of intellectual achievement and the evaluation of academic excellence", two concepts (goals) are expressed. Begin this exercise by underscoring the key words in those concepts, and then proceed to analyze and further define them until both concepts are translated to your satisfaction. Next, lay out a measurable program by which those two specific goals may be achieved.

Lab Exercise for Lesson 3

"Hard Luck" [Contingencies]

The process of life is full of contingencies; i.e., marked differences between what we plan or expect to happen to us and what really happens. At times the task of getting to where we want to go runs on a smooth course. Everything seems to go right. At other times our tasks are more difficult than they should be, as if some force greater than us was blocking our every move. What's the secret key to unlocking a way of life where it is more typical for things to go right than wrong? The degree to which we can control or manage the contingencies. Because although it is true that "accidents" and truly unaccounted for setbacks can occur outside of our plans, it is still possible to minimize their occurance through a strong "accident" prevention program.

Being accident prone is something anyone can control by concentrating on doing things without unnecessary problems. But it does take planning and it does require definite concern over and above a mere intent to succeed. Listed below are some "contingencies" which could pop up to make the achievement of your intentions more difficult. Try to decide two things that might have caused each one to happen and two more things that might have been done to prevent them from happening. Have any of these things ever happened to you? What part of these "accidents" are really outside of your control?

1. You get a bad cold with a fever and a runny nose just before a big test at school.

2. The alarm clock "didn't go off" and you are an hour late for an important appointment.

3. The shirt you wanted to wear most for tonight's date is at the cleaners.

4. After filling out the application and turning it in you find that the closing date for accepting applications was yesterday.

5. You're in constant trouble with your neighbors because your dog is always chewing up their newspapers.

6. The car ran out of gas and you had to miss the concert.

7. You never have enough money to buy what you want when things are "on sale."

8. The teacher always managed to call on you when you were unprepared and never seemed to call on you when you knew your lesson.

You could dip this house in water

9. You would have finished the project on time if it hadn't rained and ruined some parts which then had to be replaced.

10. Even though you worked up to the last minute on the speech, it still didn't go over as well as you thought it might.

"Score Cards" [Evaluation]

A golf scorecard can be used as a model of an evaluation document because most of them contain the rules of a specific local course being played (criteria) along with a chart containing spaces for measuring various points-of-view: yards between holes, number of player strokes compared to the par (or standard) for both women and men players, and handicaps (or advantages for equalizing competition). A game room chalkboard, used to add up scores in games like darts, is another such model and is even simpler with its columns of additive scores for each player all working toward a fixed mutual goal of a predetermined number of points. A restaurant menu with prices listed next to each item so that customers may evaluate and compare their cash resources with their appetites and available selections is another example.

We use evaluative charts and score cards of many varieties to help us observe and make comparative measures of criteria. Some measurements record approximate scores or amounts; some record exact differences in distance, size, price, duration, weight, and other considerations. Measurement scales vary with the changing need to measure very accurately or merely approximately. But most evaluations begin with a set of approximations which may then progress, sometimes over many years, to become very exacting.

Example: To determine the winner from a group of twenty students competing in a graphic competition for the design of a company logo or symbol, the judge used these minimum standards:

1. The foremost criterion selected was "visual attractiveness." Therefore, she eliminated all but those which caught her eye in a first visual survey. This automatically reduced the number of contenders by 70% leaving only seven entries to judge.

2. The second highest criterion was "appropriateness to the organization being characterized" by the symbol. (She comparatively rated this item as being worth ten points.)

3. The next three criteria were all weighted the same (six points each). They were "originality", "communication" and "composition", which she defined in order as "describing a unique viewpoint", "ease in subject understanding" and "ease in visual

recognition." She argued that the last three were only about half as important as the first two because the purpose of a symbol is to both attract attention and to help identify the company more easily.

Entry numbers of the seven contenders who made it past the first visual screening were listed at the top of a Finalists' Rating Chart which also contained the evaluative criteria and their numerical (ranked) equivalents on the side. It looked like this:

Finalists' Rating Chart							
Entry Number	#4	#5	#9	#10	#12	#18	#19
Appropriateness (10)	8	5	9	8	8	2	10
Originality (6)	6	4	6	6	3	5	2
Communication (6)	6	2	5	6	6	4	3
Composition (6)	5	6	3	6	5	5	6
Totals (28 possible)	25	17	23	28	22	16	21

The ranked and weighted criteria made the evaluation much easier because they allowed the judge to work within limits which had a stipulated relative value; i.e., each item under consideration was part of a larger system of considerations where all the components had a relative worth. For instance, as she evaluated entry No. 4, she found that the "appropriateness" factor scored only 8 out of her limit of 10, that it was "highly original and communicative" (therefore receiving 6 points each), and that it had only a slight shortcoming in "visual composition", so she gave it 5 points for that category. After the scores were totalled for all the finalists, No. 10 was the obvious winner; No. 4 came in second and No. 9 took third place.

Now it's your turn!
A. Listed below in alphabetical order are what are popularly known as the Seven Deadly Sins (as gleaned from the work of St. Thomas Aquinas). Your job is to determine their relative importance and to relist them in that order. As you decide on the criteria for ranking one "sin" ahead of the other, explain your own reason for why you have ranked them as you did.

1. anger (hate)
2. covetousness (greed)
3. envy (jealousy)
4. gluttony (imbalance)
5. lust (lechery)
6. pride (contempt)
7. sloth (laziness)
(Is there an eighth deadly sin?)

Sin Rating Chart							
Entry Number	#1	#2	#3	#4	#5	#6	#7
Totals							

B. A complicated variation of this exercise is to critically classify and rank items which are not so obviously different from one another. The list below should provide a challenge to those who zipped through the last part with ease:

1. rock and roll
2. hard rock
3. acid rock
4. soft rock
5. bubble gum rock
6. country rock
7. glitter rock
8. nostalgia rock

How do you rank them? Why?

Rock Rating Chart								
Entry Number	#1	#2	#3	#4	#5	#6	#7	#8
Totals								

C. If you're not interested in rock music you might like to try your skill at TV rating. What specific criteria would you use to rank the following TV shows if you intended to make an "ethical" investment in one of them in the hope of receiving the greatest financial return with the least possibility of encouraging environmental pollution.

1. news
2. variety
3. talk
4. family situation
5. wish fulfillment comedies
6. group comedies
7. action-adventure
8. westerns
9. science fiction
10. old movie reruns as forums for local advertisers
11. educational-documentary

(Hint: Don't forget audience needs, prime time costs, network and sponsor needs, demographic audience factors, women 18-49, young adults while you are concerned with your own needs and preferences.)

TV Rating Chart										
Entry Number	#1	#2	#3	#4	#5	#6	#7	#8	#9	#10
Totals										

"Consensus Made Me Do It" [Self Decision]

Evaluation seems easier when we let others do it for us. But leaving it up to the other person sure puts limits on how much control we can exert over our own beliefs. Still, sometimes it just makes good sense to get another opinion. Deciding on the best restaurant to go to or the best movie to see is often wisely handled by looking around to see where the lines are longest or the most cars are parked. Another way is to let professional critics decide for us by referring to their ratings in newspapers, magazines or guide books. Expert opinion can save us lots of time in our probably over-crowded lives. But just because we decide to allow others to decide for us doesn't remove all responsibility from us.

Because we must often rely on others for information and yet are still tied to our need for independence, we get into trouble, sometimes acting irresponsibly ("what's the use? I couldn't care less!") and sometimes feeling guilty ("I'm sorry; I don't have the answer to every detail you are questioning me about"). Both responses are unsatisfactory because we can't really expect to ever know it all and we can only expect to work with the best information available.

Occasionally, we must give ourselves over to simple faith in others, trusting the rightness of their decisions. The important thing is to be aware of who has the information we need, who it is who is making decisions for us and what their reasons are for deciding that way. At other times, we've got to ask for proof, refusing to believe one more word until satisfied that what we are acting on is acceptable to our own deeper values. In short, we need to set up a self-regulating operation which allows us to rely on others to make some decisions for us while remaining personally accountable by the use of occasional personal check points.

Here's some practice in double-checking some of the typical "decisions" others make for us in everyday advertisements. First, using the advertising copy provided (below), try to read the words all the way through in an "accepting-believing" way. Then record the essence of what you take in by writing a one or two-line synopsis of the message off to the side. Defer judgment as you read. Accept the words as if the person you respect the most has written them for you personally.

Next, read the copy again, this time with all the suspicion of Sherlock Holmes, trying to uncover hidden meanings and untruths or negative values. Once more record a synopsis of your findings.

Finally, compare the two synopses, and explain the differences you have uncovered to a friend or two (not so much to tell them about your discoveries, but rather to reinforce your own evaluative experience by putting it together in spoken sounds as well as in written thoughts).

AD A...ATTENTION, MEN! WHY NOT GIVE YOUR TIRED OLD FACE A FRESH YOUNG LOOK? It's not that you don't look good. It's just that you could look better. Fading sex appeal? worry wrinkles? age lines? a tired, defeated look? Don't despair. Don't give up. Here is help for you. About 3 times a week spread NEW YOU CREAM over your entire face to deep clean your skin, remove impurities, reduce prominent pores and excessive oiliness. It feels so good, as if hundreds of lovely girls are massaging the wrinkles and age-lines out of your face. Improve your looks for only $3.95. Try NEW YOU CREAM today! You'll be glad tomorrow!

AD B...FOR JUST ONE DOLLAR YOU CAN ENTER THE WORLD OF BEAUTY, AND HERE'S WHAT YOU GET:

A fabulous $15 beauty kit brimming with famous-name cosmetics and beauty aids, products you've always wanted to try, from companies you know and trust. $15 worth of luxury cosmetics for just $1.

Plus a magazine chock full of how-to beauty tricks from renowned experts.

Plus a bonus coupon entitling you to extra beauty products at significant savings.

And that's just the beginning! After your introductory beauty kit arrives, you'll go on getting similar kits of prestige beauty products about every two months, automatically, for as long as you want, all on approval at lower than drug store prices. Each kit will be worth far more than the member's money-saving price--many as much as $15, some even more. Yet you pay only $5.98 per kit plus shipping and handling and only for those you choose to keep. No obligation to continue. You may cancel at any time, and the $15 introductory kit is yours to keep for just $1 regardless.

"Consumer Reports" [Criteria Ranking II]

CONSUMER REPORTS, a publication of an independent testing agency, gets a lot of play from people who want to be sure they're going to get a good buy when they purchase an industrially-designed product. It helps people to determine differences between products by helping them to see some of the general criteria for evaluating them and the specific measures of how products compare in relation to that criteria. The published result is a ranked comparison in terms of overall quality, best buys and less-than-best bets.

Given the following groups of alternative items, we ask you to be a one-person CONSUMER REPORT LAB and do the following:

1. Consider at least four (4) criteria by which each item might be judged (these criteria become your standards).

2. Test the items against the criteria by:
   a. determining a means to measure quantity and quality
   b. measuring quantity and quality by your means

3. Rank the groups from best to worst in terms of how well they fulfill your selected criteria.

A. <u>A High-Protein Instant Breakfast containing the equivalent of:</u>

....a hot full-grain cereal with honey and milk
....a glass of orange juice and a cup of coffee
....two glazed donuts and a large glass of skimmed milk
....a stack of pancakes, syrup and cocoa
....two eggs, a piece of toast and a cup of coffee

B. <u>Mother's Day Gifts under $10.00</u>

....a box of drug store candy
....a long distance phone call
....flowers by wire
....a photo portrait of yourself
....two tickets to her favorite play

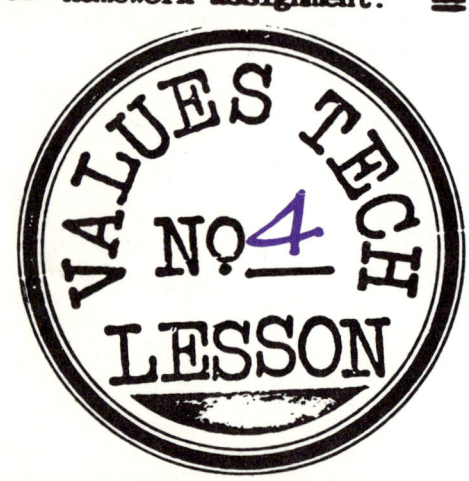

ADVANCED

Good Grades (A Special Lesson in the Evaluation of Student Achievement)

As currently used and misused in many institutions, academic grades are generally considered as a block to getting an education. Instead of being able to concentrate on course materials and the development of knowledge, skills and understanding, students tend to be preoccupied with the variously translated and inferred meanings of a grade. Because so much hinges on whether grades are good or poor, they become the focal point and thus act as deterrents to creativity and open-mindedness. Given the opportunity to change the system, most students and teachers undoubtedly would do away with grades first. (The pass-fail and credit-no credit experiments are usually very popular, a fact which vouches for the no-grade argument.)

But grades shouldn't be the ridiculous problem they seem to have become. After all, we do go to school to learn, and the only way we have of knowing how successful we are is to have an evaluative look at our behavior before, during and after the fact. Theoretically, we should all want even more grades than we get instead of fewer or none at all. So what's the problem?

Well, the problem is obviously not the grades themselves, because like most other things, grades are not inherently evil. But poor grades can cause all sorts of trouble. They can get you kicked out of school or dropped from a favorite club or activity. They can cause ill feelings at home or cut off your funds. They can keep you out of a favored college or graduate school or from doing something you really want to do. Poor grades have even been involved in loss of job promotions and have figured into the draft for military service, divorce cases and suicides. There's no end to the troubles the innocent numerical and alphabetical summations of grades can cause when we lose sight of their basic academic evaluative function and begin to use them out of their context as standards for other decisions.

Instead of seeing them for what they should be—as evaluative expressions of achievement and progress within an on-going ever-changing personal educational process—students suffer from grades being used as irrelevant products leading to bigger products (degrees, diplomas, jobs, etc.) and all devoid of any real explanation of the process they reflect. At grade time the perennial question is "What d'ya get?" not "What d'ya learn?" And when the tests and exams are over and students receive the computer printout of their grades in the mail it's really anybody's guess as to the criteria used for making each separate evaluation. Some teachers are liberal with grades; some are hip; some are tyrants; some are mechanical; and they each grade accordingly. One counts the final exam as 50% of the total grade; another doesn't even bother with a final. One counts attendance as equally important to doing all the homework; Others equate grades with production (three reports earn an "A"; two reports earn a "B"; etc.); Another grades only on the quality of homework turned in. Still another thinks of an A as perfection and therefore unachieveable except in rare cases. It's kind of a game. And as long as teachers continue to use grades as the whip for controlling classroom behavior, attendance and other manipulative functions, the game will continue.

The long and short of it is that grades make everyone nervous. Some teachers devise elaborate self-protection systems using four-point decimal summations to supplant verbal evaluations and to prove their "case" against possible student objections. Students hate grades because they don't learn anything from them. They say grades are meaningless. School administrators don't like them either because they're subject to fluctuation and often upset a smooth-sailing operation.

But the true value of grading still exists beneath it all. Grades are important parts of an intelligent educational system, we need them—or something like them—not as superficial, non-representative symbols leading to certificates and degrees and gold stars, but as tools for maintaining consciousness of the on-going process of learning. To be valid, grading must be an evaluative process which never stops. It must be a way of thinking about learning and improvement. Properly used, grades can really tell us "how we're doing", and they can be helpful in formulating plans for moving forward in constructive ways. But grades cannot be left until the end of a process because process has no end. They must be with the process on the first day and every day of the course (of life) and not just as a judgment-day product, too late to be of more than minimum benefit to anyone.

Handled as a concurrent part of the process, grades can become effective components in achieving what has been called "participative" education, where students and teachers work as a team in making relevant, procedural decisions, where students know at every point in the process where they're headed and where they've been, as well as how they're doin' right now. Treating evaluation in that way as part of an on-going process is also known as "descriptive grading" because it carries a running description of progress and provides a relatively complete view of what has been accomplished and what is still left to accomplish in terms of predetermined objectives. With descriptive grading, no one waits until the end to discover shortcomings. They are clearly seen as they occur—day by day and week by week—and thus can be immediately replaced with positive qualities.

Here is how a descriptive grading process can be established: First, students and teachers must agree that they want to behave in a responsible evaluative and accountable way and that they will all work toward that goal. Initial resistance to this important commitment must be overcome by mutual trust. The next step is to establish goals and measurable objectives. Evaluative Polyvision records of the process should be kept by both teacher and student (perhaps together) noting in an incremental way the quantity and quality of student progress, summing up as they go like accountants making regular daily or weekly balance sheets.

It is mutually beneficial for students and teachers to work together. Because of their experience, teachers can help students to recognize the need for including social and institutional goals into their goal statements. And students can learn responsible behavior by establishing their own standards as well as by observing the standards of other individuals and the school. Thus, grades can help students learn to live in an evaluative way through participation in the on-going grading process; they may even elect to continue this as a self-evaluation process after the course is over.

Books which record the process in an evaluative way become valuable personal documents, much more valuable as products than anyone might have expected or than a traditional grade book could ever be. These evaluative records are valued as the transcripts of existence, as journals of personal experience translated into personal advice. In them personal research and discoveries are accompanied by evaluative remarks: "How an experience got me closer to a goal"; "How an initial objective must be altered to be more relevant"; "How new objectives creep into the picture"; "How experiences relate to the achievement of other goals in life"; and "How they open unforeseen vistas".

The descriptive evaluation process allows everyone to become more responsible by becoming more systematically conscious of their actions and beliefs. Accountability is seen as a way of life, not a thing to avoid. And final grades are easily distilled and understood as meaningful shorthand abstractions rather than as meaningless evils. Instead of merely sensing they are doing "O.K.," "not bad," or "pretty good," students and teachers evaluate progress in explicit terms. As it now stands, most academic grading is a bum substitute for an evaluation process which can be a highly educational experience. If both descriptive and participative, evaluation and grading can be a meaningful reinforcement to all that has gone before.

The incremental evaluation process can be valuable for everyone, not just students and teachers, because progress in personal fulfillment can be slow if it only occurs after the fact and not continuously. It's far better to be involved with evaluation and step by step improvement at the time than to look back only after long intervals, see large mistakes in retrospect and wish we had done something else.

Example

What follows is a typical example of how many students at VALUES TECH conclude their own personal self-evaluative recording processes. Having kept evaluative notes relative to their discoveries and labors throughout the work of each of their courses, the students can quickly review progress in a list of pre-determined areas and tag-on considerations. Although their notes and comments are normally written in a verbal language rather than in numbers they are easily translated into institutional symbols of numerical or letter grades. They evaluate process by reviewing their products: notebooks, tests, comments, projects, reports, assignments, etc.

SELF-EVALUATION
- A. Measurable Content of Course
    1. Class Goals (mutually determined by all relative to subject matter)
    2. Personal Goals (approved by instructor and student; personalization of subject matter)
    3. Classroom participation and contribution
    4. Special activities related to course subject
    5. Tests, exams, hoemwork
    6. Attendance
    7. Extracurricular application of course discoveries

B. Ranked and weighted according to personalized importances as mutually agreed to by student and instructor (using "pyramid" matrix)
1. Personal goals (30%)
2. Class goals (30%)
3. Special activities related to course subject (10%)
4. Extracurricular application of course discoveries (10%)
5. Tests, exams (10%)
6. Classroom participation and contribution (5%)
7. Attendance (5%)

C. Measured progress from evaluative records of student and instructor (by comparison of notes and mutual agreement; subject to arbitration and counsel)

Measure	Evaluation	Value (Numerical)	Letter Grade	Weight Factor	Totals
Nº 1	Exeptional Progress	95	A	30%	28.5
Nº 2	Good Progress	85	B	30%	25.5
Nº 3	Exeptional Progress	90	A-	10%	9.0
Nº 4	Fair Progress	70	C-	10%	7.0
Nº 5	Good Progress	82	B	10%	8.2
Nº 6	Below acceptable	60	D-	5%	3.0
Nº 7	Exceptional	100	A+	5%	5.0
					86.2

D. FINAL GRADE 86.2 (B+)

STATEMENT:
"My progress in this course has been quite satisfactory; even better than that. I can see now that there are innumerable ways to incorporate the subject matter of the course into the practical application of my personal goals. Although my attendance was perfect, my participation in classroom activities has been less than acceptable. I must stop telling myself that it is O.K. to be shy and to always think that its not important to join in with the others at discussions, seminars, and workshops. My plans are to continue evaluating my behavior with regard to this problem of "holding back" and to take every opportunity I can to become more participative in class as well as in my social relations in general."

Lab Exercise for Lesson 4

"Hop Skip & Jump" [Incremental Evaluation]

It can be a mistake to jump from action to an immediate measurement of achievement without going through the verbal or written descriptive stage of explaining what was learned from the experience. In the rush to measure our accomplishment (give it a number or grade), we should not forget to first record the relevance of that accomplishment in words. Remember! The grade is really not significant until we're conscious of the learning it represents. Suppose, for instance, we have just met our objective to photograph the local countryside from the top of a nearby hill. Before we give ourselves a 100% for the finished photos in our hand, we should recall what we have learned: Example: "Hill climbing is twice as hard when you have to carry photo equipment. I need to pare down the weight of my gear." "It's often easier to take the long and easy way to the top than it is to take the short but dangerous way. Shortcuts have more hazards." "A slow, steady climb is more relaxing than to hurry and always be out of breath. I must prepare for assignments like this by doing more outdoor work in the days prior to them." "Sizing up the hill before making the climb can save a lot of unnecessary work."

These descriptions of learning are not just applicable to the special problem posed by that one objective; they also represent principles which can be carried over to many other problems arising in life.

From the three student evaluations which follow, try to determine five (5) things the evaluators may have learned by reaching their objectives to the extent stated in the grades.

1. My objective: "to teach my older brother how to make bread"
   My grade: 60%; he made three loaves, but they were like rocks.
2. My objective: "to finish MY ANTONIA by Willa Cather before Christmas"
   My grade: 100%; Cather is my favorite writer. Her descriptions of experiences are realistic and leave vivid memories.
3. My objective: "to ride my bike to school all winter long"
   My grade: 25%; it rained a lot, and I didn't want to catch cold, so I only took the bike about one day a week.

Lab Exercise for Lesson 4

ADVANCED Exercise No. 2

"Outsight and Insight" [Interpersonal Evaluation]

Have you ever heard the saying, "You can't see your own ears"? It means that it's very hard to see what is not in your direct view no matter how close it may be. And it is used as an argument against the possibility of having meaningful self-evaluation. But evaluation is a process which can act as a "mirror" and allow us to "see" our own ears. Most of us think we can't evaluate ourselves because we're too close to personal situations. On the contrary, we are probably the persons best qualified to do it since, with evaluation as a tool, we can see more of ourselves than anyone else ever could.

But at times it does make sense as we said before to get an outside opinion. In order to gain insight, we might even try getting as far outside of the evaluative situation ourselves. Try this exercise:

A. Draw a full-face sketch of yourself without looking in a mirror. Don't take too long, and don't worry about your drawing skill. Just do your best; you can't do better than that.

B. Next, ask several friends to evaluate your "graphic translation." Write down their comments word for word. Then go back to the drawing board, and with several tracing paper overlays redraw the self-portrait by trying to incorporate their observations in your drawing. Take away what they say "is not there." Change the "features" as they suggest.

Did you get to know your physical image a little better from the experience? If so, outside viewpoints have been valuable additions to your own inside views.

Lab Exercise for Lesson 4

"How to Be a Bookkeeper" [Evaluative Record-Keeping]

If we wait until a task is over before we evaluate it, we've usually lost all interest in doing it at all. And we're out of energy anyway; the process took it all out of us. But incremental evaluation done concurrently can save that hassle. When you evaluate as you go, the evaluation is close to complete when the job is complete. They go hand in hand.

Of course, it's hard to get into the habit of evaluating as you go (just as it's hard to start most habits). Starting a habit means consciously doing something strange and/or new instead of something friendly and old. Think of all the habits you'd have to break to start the new habit of not eating meat or not drinking coffee. Still, when you're doing something you've never done before, no matter how poorly you may be doing it, the simple fact of first-hand experience means you're on the way to doing it better next time.

One way to beat the fears and negative expectations of evaluation is to keep evaluative records, and the key to efficient records is Be a packrat! Pick up, save and evaluate everything that looks relevant to your process. Then, on a regular basis, compare what you've collected with how well it reinforces your goals. (At that time you can get rid of the excess; it's only going to be in the way later on.) Don't make an appointment, read a book, try a skill or do anything without making some recorded evaluative comment about it. Even saying it out loud to some friend is better than no record at all.

Before long everything starts to add up. Because of your enforced evaluative awareness, you know better what you're after, and your "project record" is always there for review, telling it back to you in a way that memory never could. Everything we do has the potential for being evaluated as a learning experience. And even though a sympathetic teacher can certainly help us to be evaluative in school, the bulk of what we learn is achieved through our personal evaluations out of school. The sooner we get good at evaluating the better and the richer our living and learning experiences will be.

This exercise deals with keeping an evaluative record of a project. Follow these steps without skipping a single one (you may find variations of your own later on):

1. Determine some short-range goal, such as: "learn to play bridge," "make a date with the man/woman of your dreams," "walk twenty miles," etc.

2. Outline the objectives for reaching your goal. (For instance, find a bridge player who is compatible and willing to teach you. Take him/her to lunch. Buy a pair of hiking shoes, etc.)

3. Record the goal and objectives in a record book.

4. Set a reasonable time for reaching your goal and begin. Collect all the evaluative comments you can from each experience.

5. Keep a side record about how you're doing in terms of realizing your whole list of objectives. (This is what most schools, teachers and grade computers want to know most.)

6. At each step of the process, stop for a moment to enjoy the cumulative profits of your evaluative learning experience.

Lab Exercise for Lesson 4

ADVANCED Exercise No. 4

"What Can You Show Me?" [Producing By-Products That Sell]

In today's product-oriented world there is little value assigned to the processes of doing things. Much of what we do is considered worthless unless it can be shown to yield a product of tangible worth; something which can be sold in the marketplace. Beginning process-appreciators find this to be a stumbling block since they are always being encouraged by their society to pay attention to production and to further minimize the process for increased efficiency. Even college and university professors, being highly educated specialists in their separate disciplines (having little or no formal education in the facilitation of learning) are just as product-prone as most everyone else in our society. They too want to see the salable results of what their students undergo as process. So that much of what potentially could be learned in school is never openly expressed and reinforced because it has little chance of being translated or incorporated into socially marketable terms.

But we all want to see results. That's the initial purpose of embarking on any goal-journey. It's just that our results are of a variety of kinds and refinement and may not always come in the communicative socially acceptable form of a tangible product. Thus, the many by-products which are produced in the processes of life are usually reduced to but a few end-products, leaving much of potentially valuable stuff by the wayside.

This is a two-part exercise. In it you are asked to sift all of the by-products that you can find from a mental review of a selected process and to then figure out how those by-products could be "saved" by turning them into marketable (socially or institutionally acceptable) end-products.

part A

Select one or more of the following processes as a context for imagining and recording as many by-products as you might produce along the way of going through such processes from beginning to end. After listing the obvious tangible benefits don't forget the intangible benefits to be had by learning new skills of a variety of kinds, learning from your mistakes, discovering more about yourself and your potentials, developing more appreciation of things, acquiring new knowledge and attitudes regarding the values and behavioral patterns of others as they relate to you and to one another, etc. Try not be be concerned at this time about whether or not there is value in the by-products you list. Just list all that you can uncover in a freewheeling manner.

1. Buying a new pair of shoes
2. Selecting a book to read on vacation
3. Painting your room
4. Touring a local museum or gallery
5. Making homemade ice cream
6. Writing a poem
7. Shopping at the supermarket

part B

After realizing and listing such intangible things as "discovering how a supermarket is departmentalized" along with the tangible things such as "bringing home a bag of groceries," sort out all of the by-products into groups, separating tangibles from intangibles. For the items in the tangibles list, try to assign a market value (approximate) to each one. For example, a bag of groceries might be listed as being worth $10. For the items in the list of intangibles, write a one or two sentence statement explaining the potential value of those items. For example, "discovering how a supermarket is departmentalized" is of potential value in that it can save time in future shopping trips (calculatable in terms of minimum wages). At the end, total the value of both tangible and intangible by-products to see (and show) how salable end-products can be derived by a balanced valuation of both product and process.

WORDS to the WISE

HOW NOT TO BREAK A HABIT!

Habit-breaking is a universally unpleasant frustration. Why is it so hard to break a pattern?

Bit by bit we become 'programmed', just like a computer, through our own repetitive behavior. We simplify our lives through repeating the same things over and over again . . . eliminating the need for decision. Since much of the work is solved through pre-decision, life runs smoothly. Then a change of intention or new goal interrupts the pattern and requires that we begin another way of doing things. Intellectually we want to stop and physically the urge is to continue on course "as usual." The conflict causes anxiety; the fun is over.

To stop goes against the active mode of life. There is no process in NOT DOING something; there is only process in DOING something. CONCLUSION: Don't waste time by attempting to stop an unwanted habit . . . invest your energy in the process of beginning a new, more desirable pattern or in reinforcing an existing constructive pattern. For example: if you want to stop smoking, don't waste time worrying over learning to live without a smoke. Invest your concentration on other behaviors. Focus your attention elsewhere, such as on using your hands to play a musical instrument, writing notes, sewing or whatever else you might decide to use as a reinforcement for your positive intentions. When you start doing something else you'll find that there is no room in your life for doing the old, unwanted thing. The habit still exists; there is simply no way for it to fit into your behavior.

Silver Bullet [A Lesson in Contingency Management]

It's almost impossible to have an evaluation without some contingency getting into the act which gives us the excuse we need for having done poorly in some way as a goal achiever. "I just couldn't do any better; this (contingency) kept working against me!" No one "gets the blame," it's all the work of some contingency which we had nothing to do with.

Although there are positive contingencies (things which work to

help us achieve our intentions), negative contingencies are far more common. It's all tied up with the classic struggle between the strong and the weak personality characteristic called "will power." And will power is just another way of saying "self-control."

At VALUES TECH we'd like to see you strengthen your self-control by writing and working out a set of procedures for reaching those goals, Both of these require will power. When you define and set out to achieve a personal intention, you are taking charge of your own behavior. You become self-motivated, self-determined, self-manipulated and self-controlled, for at least a greater portion of your future existence.

To get that far is quite an achievement in itself. When we set out to conquer the unknown, many stumbling blocks are encountered along the way and each must be dealt with according to our strength and commitment.

Once we have decided to take charge of ourselves, there is still a long way to go in terms of overcoming or circumventing obstacles. There are going to be many "dragons" en route to the glorious "quest," and we must find the best way to conquer them. Strength, intelligence and purity of heart simply increase the chance for winning the prize.

It is really not so tough to beat most contingencies when plans are worked out ahead of time. But if we're unprepared, the unexpecteds seem to win everytime. Example: Suppose you have a goal which is to "learn how to draw." The measurable objectives might include the following: buy a pad and pencils, get a good book about drawing, register for a drawing class, set aside time to draw for an hour a day, etc. Now, let's imagine some of the contingencies that could block those objectives and thwart the goal.

Contingency No.1—I forgot I had scheduled a previous meeting the first night of my drawing class.
Contingency No.2—The enrollment fee for drawing class is $75.00. I can't afford it.
Contingency No.3—The art store is out of the special book I wanted, so I can't start now.
Contingency No.4—I don't know what to draw. I think I'll take a walk to look for subjects.
Contingency No.5—I'm too tired after work to draw for a whole hour. I'll put it off and draw for two hours on Saturday.
Contingency No.6—I think I'm catching the flu. I'd better rest.
Contingency No.7—My favorite film is on TV during class time. I'll go next week.
Contingency No.8—I don't think the drawing teacher likes me very well. I think I'll drop out.

With all the potential contingencies we face in life it's a small miracle that we ever achieve anything! But actually there are only a few contingencies that are beyond our control or are so big that they could stop us from achieving our goals: death, injury, broken contracts, storms, earthquakes and other natural disasters; everything else is within the range of personal choice. And we win or lose depending on how we deal with our choices.

Here Are Some Tricks for Taking Control of the Contingencies In Life!

Don't be overly ambitious. Wanting more than you need is the mark of a beginner. Thinking you need more than you can use is natural but an unreasonable reaction to an unfilled need. Keep your new objectives in line with your older commitments. Don't allow a low-priority goal to take over your life. It'll give you too little return for the heavy dues it will cost, and you may become disenchanted and give up the whole thing.

Don't be too easy on yourself. Change implies a reaction to a force. You can't have your cake and eat it too. If you really want something, you've got to start working toward it. And that usually means you must stop doing something else. However, if along the way you discover the old way is really superior to the new way, then give up the new goal as a bum idea, and relax in having tested the new and found the old to be still a winner.

Set up the things you want to do in a systematic measurable way so that when you've gotten off the track you'll know it.

When you settle for less than you thought you wanted, be sure your decision is really the result of reason and care and not just temporary fatigue or a case of 'copping out."

Regularity and consistency strengthen goals and weaken distraction and whims. Driving headlong, too fast and furiously into your work may cause a quick burn-out. Pace yourself. Getting acquainted with something new takes time. We don't usually make friends with strangers instantaneously.

Don't expect more of yourself than you are capable of giving. Start where you are, not where you want to be. (Where you want to be is your goal, not your current behavior.)

Like a tourist, try to be conscious of how new things look and feel. Be sensitive to things that "natives" take for granted.

Be a "generous task master." Reward yourself everytime you see measured progress. But crack the whip, and penalize yourself for backsliding. Some people need others to censure them in some way if they get off the planned schedule and find that making a bet regarding their success or failure helps them to succeed.

Remember too that contingencies do come from outside and must be dealt with in an evaluative decision-making way. These include

so-called "acts of God," institutional rules, a social consensus that rules against us, etc. These insurmountable contingencies can help us to redefine our goals and to take a new direction, or they can force us to delay our plans by rearranging our schedule to solve them as additional problems.

But most contingencies are only imagined blocks to achievement and not real barriers at all. "Mathematics is too hard to handle" is an attitude that keeps many of us from using numerical models as efficient tools. "I don't feel like it today" is also probably more of an imaginary than a physical barrier to getting on with it. In short, most progress is stymied by a negative point of view, founded and supported by some earlier negative experience, and far more imaginary than real.

Regardless of the pain and anguish they may cause, contingencies act as valuable checks on our goals. They tend to keep us honest by reminding us of external forces and consequences not considered in a typical first goal statement. If we don't know that most contingencies can be controlled, they can stop us almost immediately from taking part in our life-planning process. But for those who can spot a contingency and deal with it, progress toward self-control is increasingly smoother and easier. Contingency management can be just the Silver Bullet needed to keep the vampires, werewolves and other demons from your life process.

Lab Exercise for Lesson 5

"Go Ahead, Hit Me" [Negative Reinforcement]

Finding ways to stay in line with our personal goals and with those of society seems easier if we put the responsibility for our good or bad behavior on someone else. "If I take one drink too many, I want you to grab me by the arm and yank me right out of there." Or "I hope you will never trust me again if I am unfaithful this time," etc.

In this exercise you have to think up ways to keep yourself on the path to your goals. Write down at least five different ways you could rely on someone else to help you stick to your guns in achieving each of the three goals listed below. Look for ways that might be fun for the other person as well as effective for you and won't cost too much of your friend's energy (because these will be the ideas that are most likely to last).

Goal No. 1--to learn to play the piano in the next year.

Goal No. 2--to send myself a photo postcard every day while away on a three-month vacation so that I will have a photo record of my trip.

Goal No. 3--to keep a daily list of ranked priorities for at least two weeks.

Lab Exercise for Lesson 5

"Booga-Booga" [Blocks to Achievement]

The four primary objectives of many young men might be stated briefly as:

> to get a prestigious, highly-paid, exciting job
> to be loved by a compatible woman
> to own an attractive home and have money in the bank
> to own a sports car
> (but not necessarily in that order!)

A. Pretend that you are on a fun and education-seeking bicycle tour of Europe with a close friend. Make two lists: one a list of those things which may be helpful to success; things which will increase your chances of completing your entire journey as planned. The other list should attempt to predict things which might occur to block the achievement of your goal. Don't stop until both lists have at least twenty entries.

B. Repeat the process in terms of your personal needs for the following objectives which represent the basic dreams of many modern members of society:

1. to be involved in creative work and recognized as a constructive member of society
2. to have a reasonably unique lifestyle
3. to have a reasonably complete love and sex life
4. to control personal decisions

"Ad Valorem" [A Lesson in Consumerism]

Paying dues is part of our existence. As actress Lillian Gish says, "What you get is a living; what you give is a life." Sooner or later, someone has to give up something for everything we take. Everything has a fee; even marriage, where privacy is exchanged for intimacy. And there's a different price to pay for working or living alone. We pay with time for all of our pleasures, even for those which are normally thought of as being free such as stopping to watch a sunset, and we give up part of our freedom when we stop to pick up a hitch-hiker on the highway. Each benefit has a cost; give and take go together.

The main problem caused by the fact of give and take is that costs are not always so clear. And it is well to consider all the costs of any life experience. Sometimes we end up paying too much. Sometimes we get too little. Sometimes we get a bargain. Some things cost emotional commitment as well as physical energy; other things require money. Still others tax our nervous system. For some things we pay only once and are done with it, while still others require that we set up regular payments for life. Confusion reigns unless we try to establish a decent price and an acceptable value for what we want out of life.

Life can truly be a bargain for those who know how to arrange it so that the benefits outrank the costs. We all know people who "have it made": a good job, able to buy anything they want, a fine house, cars and other material possessions, but they never seem to be satisfied. Although they have it all, things do not seem to get them closer to the happiness which comes with fulfilling their basic human needs. We might say what a shame it is that those folks can't see the error of their ways by analyzing the problem, eliminating wasteful ways and getting down to cases with real priorities. "If only they'd stop satisfying their wants long enough to start consciously fulfilling their needs, life could be beautiful for them."

We know that it doesn't take lots of money to achieve fulfillment (although we'd be the first to admit that lots of any kind of energy resource, money included, helps to smooth out the life process at times). Down deep, most of us do believe in old adages: "Money can't buy happiness," and "The best things in life are free." (we just don't always behave that way on the surface.)

It's not difficult to see why TV and film tales about people who find strength to ditch the rat race and do something outrageously personal are so popular. Anyone with the strength to attend seriously to his own happiness is a hero. But why? And how do we become so committed to that rat race that we forget our own goals and dreams?

The Ad Valorem lesson is designed to help us deal with the theory and practice of getting the most out of life through the conscious budgeting of our resources. In it we shall take the point of view of a consumer-accountant, always watchful to see that the value received is in fact as beneficial as advertised and that the price charged is within our ability to comfortably pay. This is a lesson in bargain-making instead of bargain-hunting. And it includes several techniques for increasing the value of our own experiences without having to wait for someone else to come along to lower the cost we must pay for things or to increase the quantity we receive. In business, costs relative to benefits is another way of describing customer satisfaction or meeting customer expectations. For example: If we walked into a store and found a "sale" going on, we'd expect one of two things:

either a **discounted price** - 50% off; drastic reductions, marked down; items priced somewhere between what the store paid the producer for the item and the price they normally sell it for. Sometimes the price might even be less than what the store initially paid in order to clear out old merchandise.

an **increased quantity** - more of the item than usual ("two for the price of one," "one cent sale," or "an extra serving free," etc.)

We are easily attracted to such sales because they promise the opportunity of getting more than we expected—even something for nothing.

But suppose that instead of such a sale you walked into your place of work and your employer announced that this year the company was offering a new deal on vacations, and that instead of three weeks with pay, all vacations taken from April to September would be longer . . . five weeks with pay! Or imagine how thrilling it would be to reach the fifteenth payment on your twenty-five payment automobile mortgage and receive a mysterious notice from the bank saying that the next ten payments are cancelled due to a prepayment deposit made in your name.

(Wow! Daydreams can really be fun.) But now let's look closer at these terrific deals in order to consider them in terms of realistic costs. Suppose the "five for three" vacation deal had a price tag which called for contracting to stay with the company for an additional year upon your return. Or suppose the mysterious depositer wants a favor from you and has greased the way with a favor to you.

Interesting daydreams?? Sure they are. Crazy examples? Not necessarily. Either example could happen. The basic difference between these examples and what happens normally in a local store sale is the frequency, scale and context. Many people can have five weeks vacation instead of three right now. All they have to do is decide whether the value of the deal is acceptable to them and work it out with their employer. And parents "help out" their dependents with payments and other subsidies all the time. But what they usually ask or expect in return is love and respect, obedience and appreciation.

When we think we're in line to get something free, everything looks rosy, but the subject of dues must also be remembered. When costs are high, interest wanes. It's all in our point of view and is based on our needs and expectations. If we see a proposition as beneficial, then life is beautiful and bountiful. If we see it as too costly, then life can be a pain in the neck. Turning life into a series of bargains can be an exciting adventure. It is still for the most part left up to each of us, since getting the highest value out of our experiences is determined by our own conscious expectations. But the "same old thing" will remain the "same old thing" until we begin to see it in our minds as a new, challenging and viable experience.

Lab Exercise for LESSON 6

"How To Be A Satisfied Customer"
   [Developing Positive Expectations]

People tend to satisfy their needs in accordance with their expectations. If we want something badly (and realistically) enough, the vibrations get so strong and we become so attuned to that thing that we can hardly fail to achieve it. Wishing is not only a first step toward making dreams come true. It goes with believing in ourselves is also a goal-fulfillment catalyst.

The reason positive expectation helps us is simple. We exist in the midst of a constant bombardment of stimuli from the environment. Everything that exists out there not only makes itself available for us to receive, but much of it even cries out to be noticed. When we make it easy to receive what we want to receive and shut out the rest as best we can much of the rest goes unnoticed while certain things become intensified in our minds. That's where our attention is focused. There is, of course, more to making something happen than just willing it to happen, but when we focus attention on what we want, several important things occur: First, we get a vicarious preview of what we want through our imagination, so we visualize the ideal event before it really starts to happen; second, since we are concentrating on the happening, we are the first to notice changes and we can facilitate them; and third, we smooth the way of the happening by removing obstacles which might cause a delay.

We have to focus on the good aspects to get the best out of anything. Jobs don't go flat all by themselves. Marriages don't sour without cause. School doesn't become boring unless we allow it to. What normally underlies those common disasters is a failure to recognize and accentuate the <u>benefits</u> instead of focusing too much on the <u>costs</u>. If being satisfied means that we have received all we expected from an experience, then it's clearly an important part of good planning to direct the necessary attention to benefits from the beginning.

Being a satisfied customer depends a lot on what we expect. We've got to want to be satisfied and we've got to help that process along. It's difficult to be happy if we keep placing orders for what we don't really want out of life. Things run smoother when we develop an attitude which lets us, as the old song suggests, "accentuate the positive" and "eliminate the negative."

Try to find only the good characteristics in the following; i.e., those things which reinforce your own expectations for happiness:

    your mother

    your car

    your present age

    an old building

    taking a driver's test

    learning another language

    having a "blind date"

    writing a letter to the editor

    our VALUES TECH curriculum

(Aim for at least half a dozen good points, but don't stop there if you're on a hot streak. Also if you'd like to continue this exercise for even greater benefits, find two or three things you could do to increase your awareness of those good characteristics in your environment. For instance, if one good point about Mom is that she's always there when you need her, you might decide to reciprocate more often by being there when she needs you. For instance, you could give her a call today, and ask if she needs you for anything.)

Lab Exercise for Lesson 6

ADVANCED Exercise No. 2

"Off With The Old, On With The New" [Renewal]

You say your Levi seatcovers have lost their appeal, the thrill has gone out of your subscription to "Playboy" or "Viva" and even your SXT-8-track tape deck doesn't get you high anymore (with six payments still to go)? Don't break down and cry. It's all just a matter of how you look at those things. Newness and oldness are not so unlike. In analysis they will probably contain expressions of the same things merely seen from different points-of-view.

Change always brings something new and something old along for the ride. If we deal with change from the standpoint of time, we see things passing by us as a series or sequence of events. Growth and deterioration are easily seen that way. Some things are used up or worn out and fall apart; people get wrinkled and buildings get weathered with age.

But there is another way to view the aspect of change, and that is from the standpoint of altered relationships. Since change constantly alters things, interrelationships are always in flux. No matter when we examine something in our environment it is new and different from the last time we examined it. From this point of view, the world is always fresh and renewed.

So depending on whether our point of view is time-oriented (things develop, age and die) or altered-relationships-oriented (everything is always new) we determine our own expectations and behavior toward life experiences. Time-oriented people tend to see their time as running out and feel they must crowd more into life. They may work at retarding the aging process by acquiring new youth-oriented things. Those who find direction from the interrelationships of things tend to see life as a continuity of newness and they may hold onto things until they are beyond functional usefulness. The natural tendency is to adapt to change by dealing with it in one of those two ways, preferably with a healthy balance between them.

Find a partner who will give you a run for your money to assist you in this exercise. Begin by choosing sides: one of you will be "time-oriented" and the other will be "altered-relationships" oriented. Get it clear in your minds what your delicate point of view differences are through a discussion before you begin the next step.

Then split up and concentrate on seeing everything from only the side you have chosen. Work alternately so that

every time one of you offers a viewpoint, the other can counter. For example, suppose the subject you choose to debate is "the school cafeteria." One of the many things the time-oriented side might say is "I wish we could have a different dessert once in a while. I'm tired of the same old strawberry Jello." And the altered-relationships oriented side might reply, "Have you ever noticed how beautiful the kitchen lights appear as they reflect in the tops of the Jello cubes?", etc. Allow the same amount of time for each side to respond until you've had at least twenty-five pairs of views. Then change sides for a second round in order to better see the other point of view.

"Have a Nice Life" [Quality Lifting]

Trying to make things better than they can be is a losing battle. But intentionally trying to look for the inherent goodness in something is a different matter. With that in mind, degrees of goodness could be imagined that have no basis in apparent fact. Here are a few examples: Imagine that two people have brought their lunch to work in brown bags. One of them looks on the contents of the bag as "just a plain old lunch, nothing special," and eats it unenthusiastically. The other acts as if a banquet were about to begin. Everything gets special attention; each morsel is allowed to treat all the senses. But when we examine the contents, we are amazed to see both bags contain the same stuff: a meat loaf sandwich. One of the two saw the sandwich as "leftovers." The other viewed it as something exotic, "meatloaf burlingame." To one, lunch is a chore. To the other lunch hour is another exciting part of the day.

Or imagine two families preparing to go to church. For one, it is a hectic affair: hurrying to get dressed, finding what to wear, never being sure of having money for the collection plate, rushing to the car, arriving a little late, having trouble finding seats and afterward returning home exhausted, glad it's all over for another week. For the other family, church-going is an important ritual and exciting part of life. For them it is incorporated into the whole week; it is not just a Sabbath event. Certain clothes are set aside and kept ready and clean. Everyone interrelates with peace and orderliness. In the church they carefully choose seats which will enhance the service perhaps because of some special lighting and acoustical benefits. Afterwards they discuss the experience and attempt to find ways to incorporate its meaning into their attitudes and behavior for the coming week.

In still a third example, imagine that you have just received two gifts for your birthday. One gets set aside as unimportant. The other gets special attention:

you use it everyday; you make sure it's never lost or broken; you show it to all your friends; you keep it "out front." The cost or size of the two gifts doesn't enter into it. One is valuable; the other is not. Why? Perhaps because one came from a "special" person, someone you love and wish to be reminded of all the time.

To one person, an object may be just a "thing." To another, that same object may be sacred, to be wrapped in silk, stored in a protected place, touched only with clean hands and used only on special occasions.

To see something special in anything takes a special viewpoint. Having a nice day or having a nice life is in large part a result of how we focus our attention.

TRY THIS:

How many ways can you think of to enhance the value of the items listed below? (Remember, your point of view will determine whether something is "good" or "bad" and hence its value to you.)

    tomorrow's breakfast
    a bath and clean clothes
    spending Sunday all alone
    celebrating an old-fashioned Fourth of July
    the next dental appointment
    a flat tire
    having the car washed and waxed
    a hard day's work
    the VALUES TECH curriculum

Lab Exercise for Lesson 6

"Bargain Day?" [Evaluative Thinking]

When prices go up and quality goes down, it becomes increasingly important to learn how to utilize our resources to their best advantage. And since the nature of advertising is to point out the qualities of things, our everyday advertisement-filled environments provide the best classroom possible for developing that important skill. The things we commonly see and read in ads, on billboards and in store windows suggest the values of things, such as:

BARGAINS: "Buy two boxes and get the third free."
                   "Earn extra money in your spare time."
                   "Valuable free gifts in every package."

INVESTMENT: "Buy the gift that keeps on giving."
                   "If you had bought a Fox Hollow home two years ago, it would be worth 35% more today. There are still some lots available. What will your money be worth tomorrow?"

SAVINGS: "When it's 11 a.m. in New York, it's only 8 a.m. in California. Call New York between 5 and 8 a.m. and save big money on your business phone bill."

183

"Why pay more? No aspirin works better than the cheapest you can buy."
"First class mail is usually just as fast as airmail."

All your life you've been bombarded by helpful hints for boosting the value of your economic resources. And now it's your turn to reciprocate through a conscious attempt at making life a bigger bargain than it already is by writing your own helpful hints, figuring out your own bargains and, in general, increasing your own expectations of what you want to receive at a price you are willing to pay.

First, an example: Suppose you decided to go to a concert. What would you expect in the deal? Here are some obvious answers:

EXPECT TO RECEIVE
a seat with a clear view; some new compositional material along with some old favorites; approximately two hours entertainment, etc.

EXPECT TO PAY
somewhere between $2.50 and $7.50 (depending on the importance of the performer) 3 hours of time or more (depending on the difficulty in finding a parking place, waiting in lines, getting a program, etc.)

After listing the obvious and the not so obvious, we could go on to imagine all sorts of things that might make the concert a real bargain, things which would increase the benefits without increasing the cost too much such as:

- to go backstage to meet the star and get a photograph
- to go with someone and share the experience
- to use the program and notes as the basis for a letter or term paper we must write
- to take photographs and have them blown up into personal posters
- to have our records or tapes autographed by the star performers
- to pay for a cheap seat but at intermission move to an unclaimed expensive one
- to go in costume and get our picture in the newspaper
- to make a tape recording on a portable recorder

Can you think of some more ways? Sure you can. Go ahead and find at least five (5) more. (Once you get going, it's hard to stop.)

Bargains are always available. All we have to do to reap their benefits is incorporate them into our act. But remember that everything we add does have some cost. And although plans to increase our pleasure and the value of the concert experience are terrific, let's examine the extra costs just a bit. Sitting in a seat other than the one we paid for might get us thrown out altogether; we might feel nervous the entire time we sit there; we might be publicly embarassed; and we might lose our cheaper seat in the deal. Also, it'll be tough to carry that camera or tape recorder to the concert and then, of course, we might have to drive to the drugstore to get film or a fresh tape which would raise the costs. Going in costume might mean paying for an expensive taxi. So to make a truer estimate of a real bargain, we've got to balance the far out ideas for getting the most out of an experience along with the extra costs involved.

Make a balance sheet of your own for one or more of the experiences listed below. First put down what you'd normally expect to receive and then list what you normally expect to pay. Next, list all the ways you can think of to boost the value and get a better bargain. Later, list the extra costs you figure you'll have to pay for trying to get a "better deal." This will take some time, so you may as well relax and enjoy it once you elect to get involved.

Experience A. taking the train to visit friends in a small town for a weekend
Experience B. going to a political rally for a party other than your own
Experience C. walking or biking to work or school
Experience D. attending a meeting of Alcoholics Anonymous
Experience E. presenting your case against a proposition at City Hall

Lab Exercise for Lesson 6

ADVANCED Exercise No. 5

"Free Kittens" [Hidden Costs]

A "sucker" is a person who is an easy mark for sharpies, a dupe who has to pay over and over again for having been talked into believing there is such a thing as "free lunch" As long as there's someone waiting to be taken for a free ride, someone else will do the taking--for an appropriate fee. Accepting anything "free" entails some measure of gambling. Not being able to see the hidden costs of the "offer," we learn to proceed with caution. Unless we trust the dealer, we must be suspicious of all the "good deals" that pop up daily in our lives.

For instance, the mail-order business was built on the fact that most people have faith in the printed word. Many innocent customers have even been gullible enough to send thousands of dollars to no more than post office box numbers which advertise a terrific deal in a magazine or newspaper. And yet there are some people who having been taken in once are so suspicious of free offers that you can't get them to accept anything free no matter how the offer is worded. Also point-of-view often determines the difference between a good deal and a bad deal. Again, it depends on our particular expectations of benefits versus costs. But the common thing about most advertised offers, whether good or bad, is the fact that benefits are always out in front, clearly visible, while costs are typically on the back or at the bottom, in small illegible print, unintelligible or hidden altogether. One obvious example is at the used car lot where the most lavish "Mach-10" TV Specials are on the front line with their low, low purchase prices painted in big numbers across their windshields; apparently excellent deals. The gas guzzling and high maintenance costs of these big beauties don't emerge until days after the contract is signed.

To avoid being taken for suckers, we've got to learn to read between the lines and determine the true or actual cost...which is not always clear from the asking price or advertised benefits. For example, many kids would give their brothers or sisters away to own a horse. But owning a horse is a very expensive proposition. Hay and oats are costly. Stable rents are expensive and rarely near home. Hardware is also expensive. Daily maintenance is very demanding. Cleaning the stable is no fun at all. Veterinary services are as high as most other professional medical services. Boat owners and racing-car owners suffer through similar problems until they philosophically learn to enjoy the process of maintenance as being a vital part of the process of sailing or driving as they must if the deal is ever to "pay off."

But the all-time "hidden cost" item is that "absolutely free" stray dog or cat that was dropped on your doorstep or which "just followed me home" where humanitarian concerns and social responsibility soon require registration tags, shots, food, daily maintenance, exercise, tolerance, love, boarding fees when you leave town and other considerations. That cute little "free" puppy or kitten is not nearly as cheap as it seems. But it still may be a good deal. Calculating actual costs can be a meaningful and profitable game if you don't allow yourself to become too cynical in the process.

When is a bargain not a bargain? When it doesn't fit your personal or social needs. The Sunday newspaper is a rich resource for use in the game of searching for hidden costs. By using ads in the "magazine" section, the Travel section, the Real Estate sections, etc., as your playground, find the true cost of some of the things offered there. Example: "Come to Sunny California; enjoy the beaches, warm deserts, only $99 from New York." Analysis reveals that $99 pays only for a one-way trip. And what about the icy water at those "sunny" beaches and the need for a car or additional transportation to get around easily because deserts and beaches are miles apart.

Try at least ten ads. Keep going until you feel confident in finding the "truth" underneath the advertised benefits. And remember that a bargain is not really a bargain until it fits into your needs, desires and dreams. Then you are willing to pay top prices and highest fees for satisfaction.

VALUES TECH LESSON No. 7

OUT BEYOND GOALS [A Lesson in Planning for Interdependence]

Planning for the future isn't something we can do once and be done with. It's an on-going task, a regular necessity for an independently controlled life within a mass society. Making planning an habitual part of our behavior allows us to test the specific things we do against the relevance of our overall attitudes and aims, thereby keeping ourselves up-to-date with our own beliefs, the beliefs of others and society at large. They may sound unimportant until we realize that there is often a wide gap between what we do and what we say we want to do.

There are four major approaches for considering one's life on a long-range basis.

Each presents a workable format for self-fulfillment. All confer benefits, and each levies its particular form of "dues." We can observe their differences in the behavior of those around us as well as in our own activities because although we may take preference for one of these views no one of us tends to be all "one way or the other."

1. The EXCELSIOR approach: Imagining and planning for life to continue in much the same way it has in the past but with a steady increase in activity and production. Under this approach, life plans include an accounting for ever greater consumption of resources because of the mistaken belief that resources production will continue to increase faster than they can be used . . . motto: "growth as usual . . . bigger and better."

2. The WOE IS ME approach: Imagining and planning for life to continue in much the same way it has in the past but with a steady decline in activity and production. With this attitude, the satisfaction of needs is commonly sought through mysticism or medicine in an attempt to salve the pains of this life and to prepare for the better afterlife to come . . . motto: "life on earth is the cross we must bear."

3. the LUCKY ME approach: Imagining and hoping that some new insight or sweepstakes prize will eliminate life's problems overnight, turning it into the bright and shiny but undefined paradise of our subconscious dreams. Since gambling generally replaces planning with this approach, such life plans may be described in terms of the ups and downs which go along with wins and losses.

4. The EVERY DAY IN EVERY WAY approach: Imagining and planning to enhance and develop the positives in life; i.e., intending to work for satisfaction of the needs of survival, self, society while eliminating the negatives (blocks, contingencies, deterrants). Setting up a program for achievement in a regular, controlled and systematic way characterizes this approach. Progress and prospects are readily compared, and life is managed in an incremental, evaluative way.

Lab Exercise for Lesson 7

"Hot Links" Finding Interpersonal [Connections]

In the attempt to make sense (find meaning) of the bits and pieces of our lives we all search for key interrelationships and essential connections between things. Not unlike the thinking and reasoning discussion held previously (see Prerequisites) key interrelationships are found by abstracting large groups of elements into more similarly related smaller groups or patterns of organization and reducing those small groups into essences by determining the relative importances of their functions within the whole body being considered. We boil things down until only the remaining components are those which are most effective and crucial remain. Whatever our viewpoint tends to be, it is our conscious involvement with essence-finding that brings us closer to the truth or heart of things. Once distilled, that common denominator we reveal becomes the key to understanding the whole system under consideration.

Along with looking carefully for the essentials or "hot links" within a system it is also necessary to consider the relationships that overall system has with other systems. The reason for doing this is due to the fact that essentials tend to vary with changing contexts. What may be seen as vital to the survival and growth of a system operating under one set of forces could easily change in relation to another set of forces. It is not uncommon to imagine having found the "ultimately essential" interrelationship between the parts of a whole only to discover still another and yet other relationships equally essential as the system we consider changes its position relative to us and other systems.

Human relations provides many examples. The one most familiar to many of us is probably the one of people changing from one role in life to another. Just when we feel that we may have discovered what it takes to relate to a person in one of their roles they switch to another...and the "hot link" we had going for us must be replaced by another, more essential relationship. Using the classroom situation as an example, suppose we determine through experience that the best way to relate to the other members of the group is through the subject matter medium, i.e., if we want to maintain a recognizable unity for the group, we see that it is the subject being studied which is the foremost bond for the entire system or group. Our conclusion: the subject of the class is what holds the class together. But now suppose that the class as a group changes its relationship to the teacher or to the school at large. Then the essential link for holding the group together as a system would probably switch from "the subject matter of the course being studied" to perhaps something like "their mutual case against the teacher" or "their active interest in another school project."

part A

Listed below are three familiar "systems." After analyzing them, what do you conclude to be the essential "hot link" ingredients of each system?

    a) a Cub Scout pack
    b) a brown bag lunch
    c) 2 weeks with pay

Result: the statements you make represents what you believe to be essential about each system examined; i.e., what you think is the most important part or ingredient of each. And your values are being revealed to some extent in this way.

After examining the internal organization of the three "systems" and drawing conclusions as to their essential compositional ingredient try to look at those same systems in terms of their external relationships with other systems. (Note: It may simplify the process by using graphic diagrams similar to radial lines stemming from a centrally located subject or the "organizational" charts which show how other officers and employees relate to a leader or president.)

part B

Through the experience of helping things become more natural and harmonious, we discover that the really hot links in life are those connections which pull various and sometimes contradictory goals into mutually beneficial relationships. As a final part of this exercise, you might like to try your hand at connecting a few apparently unrelated things into a more harmonious union.

Here's an example: In attempting to harmonize the following three apparently unrelated elements one student decided that it would be mutually satisfying for all three if "the friends were invited over for pie to discuss the problem before going out together for an evening of fun." The three elements were:

1. plans for going out on the town
2. an unexpected call from some friends to help them solve a problem
3. hot apple pie in the oven

Now it's your turn! What connections can you find to harmoniously link the following groups of apparently unrelated items:

1. you wanting to go to the beach
2. your wife wanting to go to some antique store
3. the kids wanting to go to the movies
4. only one car available

1. cheese blintzes with sour cream
2. a meeting with an enemy
3. anti-semitism
4. Kurt Vonnegut's BREAKFAST OF CHAMPIONS
(or another novel you may have just completed)

ADVANCED Exercise No. 2

Lab Exercise for Lesson 7

"Mythology" [Enhancing Connections]

Because children are less socially bound and more receptive to change than adults, they tend to interact more with their environments. Always testing things and people around them and trying everything on for size, they are relentless mimics. Out of this play-acting, some children manage to find their way into adulthood with a conscious realization of their own self-enhancing expressions. They learn to extract from their environments those things which actually do enhance their beliefs and values and to capitalize on those elements.

But some children never seem to grow up and stop the game of playing other people's roles. They waste their entire lives trying on one style after another, never getting much closer to finding their own personalities. As adults, when they feel the need to be authoritative, they "become their parent" or some other authoritative figure. Because they are always acting out their needs, it's hard to tell who they really are underneath it all. Theirs is an irresponsible world of myth and fantasy.

Because today's world is packed full of pre-selected, idealized models to mimic it's much easier to be a perennial child, a role-player, than it is to be a self-finder and enhancer of one's inner self. Resisting the temptation to follow other models is a tough job unless our inner purposes are fairly clear. Newspapers, TV, magazines, movies and billboards tempt us to stop being who we are and to start being someone else: why not be the beautiful young wife and mother, the competent father, the adventurous boyfriend, the great lover, the passive Granny. Their motive is to get us to buy their product: insurance, the automobile America loves best, the chewing gum favorite of the year, a vacation trip, cosmetics, the latest gadget and countless other things.

Being able to act independently in the face of social pressures takes more than mere knowledge and skill. It requires having the courage of one's convictions. To openly reject what a friend accepts can be a real test of friendship, and most of us are quite unwilling to jeapordize our friendships for what we believe or value only subconsciously. Fortunately, true friendships can usually withstand the strain of such "tests." And we tend to admire those who do stand up for what they believe and risk public censure or the loss of friends. Their courage and self-assurance is attractive and tantalizing.

Whether we behave according to the model behavior of others or by building our own personal styles, our viewpoints eventually become the expression of that behavior. And whether the dues are higher for going at it one way or the other can only be settled through continual or eventual self-evaluation.

This is another two-part exercise. Part A deals with
following models and fulfilling the images set by
society. Part B deals with the problem of building our
own images and models out of the realtionships we discover
for ourselves in our own experiences.

part A

BEING OURSELVES IN EXTERNAL TERMS: A PARADOX?

When we are primarily concerned with how others see us,
our point of view is shaped by factors outside and
depends mainly on model behavior and social approval.
Answer the following questions as completely as you can:

1. What are the two most "in" restaurants in your
   circle of friends? Would you like to go there
   more often? What's so "in" about 'em?
2. What's everybody wearing these days? How many
   of those clothes do you have? Would you like to
   have more?
3. What's the prestige car to own? Do you want one
   too? Why or why not?
4. What are the latest verbal cliches in your group?
   How often do they appear in your speech patterns?
5. Can you name two best-selling contemporary novels?
   Have you read them? Why or why not?
6. What's your current favorite song? Do you know
   a few of the lines? Is it in the top ten?
7. Who's your favorite movie star? Is she/he fairly
   new on the scene and also on TV talk shows, too?
8. Where would you like to vacation this year?
   Have your friends already been there?
9. What do you do on a sightseeing excursion?
   Is that what most folks do?
10. How independent do you think others think you
    are? Are you a style-setter, a style-follower
    or are you fairly unconcerned about style?

Stop! Don't think for a minute that just because you also
want to test the things, places and beliefs in life that
others are testing, you will lose your own identity.
Checking out for yourself just why it is that some things
are so popular with others is an important way to build
a value system of your own. We all tend to learn from our
environment and from the many "teachers" within that
overall context. To mimic them for awhile is how we
discover for ourselves if what they do is equally valid
for us. The problem arises only when we forfeit our own
identities in the bargain; losing that precious expressive
potential which might be our own in the attempt to take on
the already comprehensive appearing expressions of others.

part B

BEING OURSELVES ACCORDING TO RULES FROM WITHIN US

When we become the evaluators of other things, people and
events instead of thinking of all things outside ourselves
as our judge, life brightens up considerably. Different
points of view and open-minded comparison help us to
become more and more of what we can potentially become...
our own expressions of the selves within us.

Now try answering these questions:

1. As you examine your group of friends and acquaintances, which of them is your candidate for:
   - Best Dresser?
   - Best Manner of Speaking?
   - Best Smile?
   - Best Figure?
   - Best Intellectual Powers?
   - Having the Best House?
   - Having the Best Car?
   - Being the Best Teacher?
   - Being the Best Friend?

   How could you allow each of them to influence your own behavior without letting them remake you completely?

2. What are the titles of your all-time favorite novels? (Name at least two.) How have the "philosophies" of your favorite characters in those novels affected your own behavior? Did you tend to read other works by the same author(s) in order to learn more about those "philosophies"?

3. Do you think that some character on TV tends in some ways to think the same as you do? (Which came first: your thinking style or the TV character's thinking style?) Describe what you consider the similarity to be.

ADVANCED Exercise No. 3

Lab Exercise for Lesson 7

"Your Own Dice" [Increasing Your Chances]

Planning ahead has saved many a day. Positive plans can protect us from being victimized by many negative contingencies. As successful people have been heard to say:

"I prefer to test my skills on a familiar course; it helps me to concentrate on my performance when I am not distracted by the unexpected."

"I always use my own dice. That's my insurance of a fair game."

"A familiar environment and familiar tools are all-important. I could never do as well using strange tools in a strange place."

Through planning we simply increase our chances for success by eliminating as much of the strangeness as possible

For each of the following situations, figure out at least three ways to increase your success by making the strangeness more familiar.

part A

(Example: Buying a car...
   Try a dealer you've used before.
   Buy a brand you already know something about.
   Test drive it to be sure it will meet your particular needs.)

1. Taking a course in the martial arts of Judo or Karate
2. Buying a special gift for your wife or husband
3. Asking your employer for a raise
4. Being elected Mayor

After listing several of your personal qualities or skills, determine how you might better use them to succeed at the following:

1. Becoming the physical fitness leader in your club or group
2. Learning to water ski
3. Overcoming an illness
4. Standing in for the guest lecturer in life management who couldn't make it to your club meeting

part B

HOME-WORK
See page 74 for today's homework assignment.

the end of **ADVANCED** level ...
HOW·YA·DOIN ?

Pendleton Gymnasium: 8:30 a.m. — 4:00 p.m.

Session One

Throughout our work at VALUES TECH, we have become increasingly familiar with the concept of self-control. The determination of personal meanings and the establishment of personal goals are old friends to most of us by this time. We see that our primary choice deals with the selection of the decision-makers; we must decide who will decide for us; ourselves or others. We conclude philosophically that no sound decision of importance is possible which excludes some contribution from both. Of course we want to decide for ourselves, but not without considering the needs and inputs of others. Each individual must consider not only his own needs but those of society and the environment as well.

What will be your self-determining lifestyle? What beliefs have you chosen to serve as the foundation for your behavior? These are personal but essential questions which you now know must be answered again and again. They are not settled once and for all. They must be tested and retested through the introduction of new information not previously known or considered. Evaluation is basic to an intelligent way of life. Evaluation is your framework for growth, your protection against ignorance and irresponsibility and your window to the broad world which exists outside your own limitations. We hope this day will be as valuable to you as previous classes have reported it to be to them.

Accepting the viewpoint just developed, we proceed to the task of fulfilling our needs and starting the search for techniques to pave the way. For no matter how fundamental it may sound at this late date in our curriculum, each of us must still find answers to certain basic questions.

"What do I need?"
"How will I decide?"
"What are my values?"
"What work will I do?"
"How will I spend my time?"
"How will I relate to my environment?"
"How will I relate to others?"
"How will I relate to society?"
"Where will I live?"
"What will I acquire?"
"What are my resources?"
"What are my aims?"
"What is my plan?"

The sum of our experience can then be examined from two points of view: from the inside (we will look ahead with self-generating concepts to the fulfillment of our conscious needs) and from the outside (we will look to others for help in determining our behavior, how we dress, what we do, how we speak, where we go, what we buy, how we achieve our purposes).

The general name we give to the summation of our behavior patterns is **System of Values**, within which is included our beliefs and overall decision-making criteria. We use our System to help us classify our needs into manageable groups so that we can begin to give form and expression to our beliefs through our behavior.

In choosing our values, we choose our mode of life; and by virtue of our decision, we reveal—inadvertently or intentionally—the interrelated parts of our individually dynamic beliefs. Through our style of living, we act out our personalized plans for fulfilling needs. If our Life Plan is vague, it is difficult to act out intentionally, thus making life difficult to understand. But consciousness of direction helps provide an outline for the whole story chapter by chapter and insures the possibility of a clear and predictable script.

Let's begin this exercise with an example:

Suppose you are chosen as a contestant on a TV game show. You have just earned the privilege of being able to take home all you can accumulate in a shopping cart in three minutes by rushing around inside a supermarket. Where would you dash to first? The expensive foods? The staples? Long-lasting foods? To those that require refrigeration? To cans or bottles or boxes or bags? Meats only? Liquors? To foods with water and excess fillers removed? Cigarettes? So many choices!

Obviously, you could choose only the first things that come along until your cart overflows and then return for more and more as time allows. Or you could evaluate your choices ahead of time and establish a set of personally and socially respectable needs-based criteria. One approach is haphazard; it carries no dues before the fact. If you follow the first approach you may have to regret consequences afterward and so you hope for good luck. The second approach is self-directed and calls for intelligent planning. It doesn't guarantee a thing, but it does allow you to expect more beneficial consequences as a result of paying out some planning "dues" before the fact.

The Tragedy or Comedy of Being Myself

Although today's exercises use the analogy of drama instead of the supermarket, they represent essentially the same tasks. We not only must know the choices available (characters, heroes and heroines, villains, sets, acts, scenes, theatre, audience, costumes, etc.), we must also write the script which gives meaning to each of our choices.

Reaching beyond foreseeable goals into long-range planning takes us to the problem of determining plans for the rest of our lives. As we tackle this awe-inspiring project, it becomes increasingly apparent that the more we try to delineate an outline for the total journey, the more we realize it can probably be defined in detail only a piece at a time. Each move forward brings with it new amounts of insight and experience which in turn alter the master plan. Sometimes getting closer to a life goal is like getting closer to a mirage; the more progress we make, the more elusive it becomes, until eventually, as we enter its closest boundaries, it disappears altogether. Or moving onward to what seemed to be our final goal merely opened up new horizons which we could not see before. Consequently, we must spend much of our lives planning for and going step by step toward intended places of great and little importance. And we are wise if we learn early in life that much of the fun is in going as well as in the arriving.

Whether the drama of our lives will prove to be tragic, comic or a balance of the two is for the most part left up to us, since we write most of the script and act out its roles. Outside influences will, of course, figure into some of the staging, but the responsibility for establishing how the scenes are written and played continues to remain in our hands. Each of us creates our own personal drama within environmental and hereditary limits.

Exercise

Although this first session includes only one project with simple limitations, it will probably cost each participant the full amount of time. We ask that you now proceed to scan the following series of lists with three rules or guidelines in mind:

1. Imagine that you are preparing to write the script for a play about who and what you are now as related to who and what you may want to become later on.

2. Try each item in the lists on for size; try to become familiar with how it feels if it were part of you. Try on the various roles; put on the different costumes; and try to imagine others who have played these parts before you. Try out the "age groups" to see what they may feel like; have fun experimenting with many of the languages, dialects and accents you know to be there; pick up the props and use them in some way so you might get a feel for what they can do for you. Get onto the stage and sense the impact of a complete setting. <u>Take your time</u>. <u>This is just a familiarization session</u>.

3. After imagining what it feels like to incorporate each separate item into your behavior, go one imaginative step further by attempting to see yourself and others you know and love as actually playing out those singular and combined parts as real-life roles.

Note! While reading through these lists which represent a mere sampling of the various combinations and variations of choices open to us in life, it may be helpful to make notes regarding items which seem to stand out as more or less appealing than others. Please make sure to add other items you feel to be missing (and do it when you think of it so as not to forget them later on).

The Roles [functional behavior]

Obviously, there are more options open to us in life than the stereotyped family roles we might initially imagine: "nine-to-five husband-father-breadwinner" and "twenty-four-hour wife-mother-homemaker." The possibilities seem unlimited as we attempt to classify all of the many functions which need attending to in a large interdependent society, but an outline might look like this:

The Providers
Farmers
Fishers
Ranchers
Agribusiness Persons
Nursery Persons
Miners
Refiners
Foresters, Lumber People, Mill People

A-1

197

Shopkeepers

Power and Utility Suppliers

Water Protectors and Purifiers

2 The Trades and Crafts People

Practical artisans—potters, stained-glass workers, tailors and seamstresses, sign painters, etc.

Designers—interiors, store windows and displays, advertising, etc.

Maintenance Personnel—repairmen and women—TV, mechanical equipment, etc.

Industrial Workers—machinists, mechanics, welders, boilermakers, sheetmetal workers, etc.

Construction Workers—carpenters, plumbers, electricians, concrete workers, painters, plasterers, tile setters, glaziers, telephone crew personnel, etc.

Computer Data Personnel

Assembly Line Workers

3 The Traditional Professionals

Doctors—M.D.s, surgeons, psychiatrists, dentists, oculists, veterinarians, etc.

Lawyers

Architects

Engineers

Teachers

Religious Leaders—Ministers, Rabbis, Priests and Priestesses, etc.

4 The Service Personnel

Public

    Police officers; guards
    Secret or special intelligence agents and investigators
    Military Service Personnel
    Firemen and Women
    Water, Sewer, Streets, Power, Garbage and Refuse Personnel

Commercial and Domestic

    Secretaries and stenographers
    Contractors
    Butchers, Bakers, Cooks
    Janitors
    Window washers
    Butlers, maids, laundry workers, companions
    Gardeners
    Delivery Persons—milk, water, coal, oil, gasoline, bread, laundry, mail, newspapers, etc.
    clerks and salespersons

Restaurant operators

Computer and switchboard operators

Elevator operators, doormen and women

Hosts and hostesses

Bell boys and runners
Ushers
Waiters and waitresses
Dishwashers and kitchen workers
Drivers, conductors, pilots, railway engineers
Stewards, stewardesses
Morticians
Credit, real estate and insurance investigators
Prostitutes—men and women
Bodyguards

The Recordkeepers
Librarians and archivists, file clerks
Historians and curators
Private collectors, hobby collectors
Dealers in antiques, junk, estates, auctions
Members in historical clubs and groups
Statisticians, accountants, bookkeepers

The Decision Makers
Politicians, officials, assessors, commissioners, judges, city planners
Landowners, landlords
Bankers and lending organizations
Executives, board members, chancellors, regents
Environmental and natural resource managers
Land developers
Image makers, advertisers
Unethical manipulators, racketeers, exploiters

Artists, Philosophers, Wizards & Wierdos
Painters, sculptors, ceramists, weavers, musicians, dancers
Poets, writers, song writers, filmmakers
Mystics, cultists and occultists
Inventors
Town "characters," self-appointed street lecturers, cranks, provocateurs

Scientists
Biologists
Physicists & Chemists
Data manipulators
Program designers
Mathematicians
Medical, biological & physical researchers
System analysts
Environmental Scientists

9
Natural resources Scientists
Poly-ologists
Social Scientists

The Entertainers
Actors
Night club, TV, radio and film showpeople
Performing musicians, barroom pianists, singers, etc.
Street painters, caricature artists, fortune tellers
Columnists and newscasters
Satirists and cartoonists

10
The Sportspeople
Athletic team members and coaches
Professional and amateur sportspersons, golfers, hunters, sailors, skiers, etc.
Sports writers, announcers and newscasters

11
The Middle Persons
Realtors
Manufacturers' representatives
Insurance agents
Travel agents
Promoters, entrepreneurs, event organizers
Door-to-door salespersons

12
Apprentices and Surrogates
Students
Understudies
Part-timers, moonlighters
Aides, stand-ins, "yes" men (and women)

B
Characters [Personalities]

Because of the many different selves within each of us, no one descriptive word can say it all about a person. But we can use descriptive terms to express behavioral tendencies and predominant characteristics. From the following list, you might to consider the "predominant" traits of the characters you will choose to express the content of your life drama.

Some major personality varieties may be described as follows:

The **thinking** person (who expresses the process of thought instead of action)

The **judging** person (who expresses the use of evaluative criteria over emotions)

The **feeling** person (who expresses emotional response to sensory stimulus)

The **sensing** person (who expresses physical response to sensory stimulus)

The **nurturing** person (who expresses support of other people and other systems)

The **assertive person** (who expresses personal goals being pursued)
The **aggressive** person (who forces personal goals on others)
The **dependent** person (who expresses a lack of personal goals)
The **introverted** person (who expresses self-orientation)
The **extroverted** person (who expresses social orientation)
The **impulsive** person (who acts on the first clue to every stimulus)
The **reactionary** person (who acts counter to every stimulus)

Sets [Physical Environments]

The elements which we can manipulate to meet our environmental staging needs and to give physical context to our plans are the following:

Inside Orientation: Rooms and Spaces which we can describe as being either

open	or	closed
small	or	large
organized	or	cluttered
single-functioning	or	multi-functional
changeable	or	fixed
light, airy	or	dimly lit, den-like
sun-filled	or	electrically illuminated
shadowless	or	contrasts in lighting
avant garde	or	traditional
colorful	or	low-key
soft-edged	or	hard-edged
simple	or	complex
private	or	public
intimate	or	public
exciting	or	relaxing
formal	or	casual
dirt revealing	or	dirt concealing
individualistic	or	trendy
low ceiling	or	high ceiling
related to outside	or	inner-related
quiet	or	noisy
scented	or	odorless
ascetic	or	feast for the senses

Outside orientation: Spaces which we can describe as being somewhere between totally untouched by man and highly civilized

Wilderness
    a. Mountains
    b. Forests
    c. Deserts—sand plains, grass plains
    d. Verdant valleys
    e. Jungles
    f. Swamps
    g. Ice fields

Remote camp and cabin sites

Farmsteads

Farm villages

Country towns

Small cities

Highway-related beaches, campsites, mountain trails, streams, rivers and lakes

Cities
    a. Medium-sized
    b. Large
    c. Metropolis

Downtowns: commercial areas, streets and spaces between buildings

Urban areas: neighborhoods, streets, front and back yards, empty lots, parks

Suburbs
    Streets
    Yards
    Decks
    Patios

3. Geographical location

    Northern hemisphere
    Southern hemisphere
    Continent
    Nation
    Region
    State

D. Costumes and Make-Up

The first clues to recognizing the players in a drama include their build, sex, race, coloring, age and what they are wearing. Here are the main possibilities:

1. Male
   Female

2. Oriental
   Negro
   Indio
   Latin
   Caucasian
   Semitic
   Nordic

3. Popular garb
   Individualized garb
   Heavily clad
   Lightly clad

4. Slim
   Medium build
   Husky
   Overweight

5. Senior citizen
   Middle aged
   Young adult
   Teen and youngster
   Baby

Props
Pets and other animals
Tools and equipment
Automobiles and other vehicles
Libraries
House furnishings and street furniture
Landscape elements, mountains, lakes, rivers, streams, trees, etc.

Dialog and Action
Native language
Foreign language
Multi-lingual speech
Proper, formal diction
Slang or jargon of role being played
Accents and personalized lingo
Profanity
Non-physical, predominance of non-movement
Easy-paced, moderate physical movement
Frantic, helter-skelter movement
Balanced activity, fast and slow, organized and casual
Physical exertion predominance

Motivations

Since members of the cast will be driven by their own unique combination of unfulfilled needs, they will all translate their need to achieve satisfaction into customized belief statements and/or behaviors. Some of the more commonly observed motivations take the following form:

(Note: Although it appears that many of these beliefs are typically assigned to either male or female, it must be realized that either sex can play most parts with equal success.)

The Little Woman — "Give me a good man, and I'll take care of him. I'll wash his socks, bear his children and keep his house."

The Breadwinner — "I'll work hard for my family. I'll give them a good house and all they'll ever need in exchange for their devotion."

The Loner — "I can get what I need without asking for help from a demanding partner of the opposite sex."

The Playmate — "Hooray for the opposite sex! Here I am for the asking. The whole world is my bedroom."

The Archie Bunker — "I am the center of the universe."

The Brute — "The only way to get what I want out of life is to take it by force."

The Thief — "The only way to get what I want is to steal it."

The Victim — "There's absolutely nothing I can do about the shape of things. I'm a victim of my environment."

The Non-Person — "No individual is as important as the group; the needs of society come before anything I might want for myself."

The Philosopher — "There is good and bad in all things. My role is to maximize the good and minimize the bad in terms of enhancing the potentials of myself and society in order to help insure our mutual survival."

The Thinker — "Through reasoning and systematic problem-solving, I can work out a well-balanced continuance of the human-natural state."

The Guilty One — "My standards are set so high that everything I say and do falls far below perfection. Consequently, I am always ashamed and apologetic for my behavior."

The Innocent One — "I am not responsible for what happens to others and bear little responsibility for my own fate. I'm just doing my job in the best way I know how."

The Patriarchal Stereotype — "I am a hard, goal-oriented, controlling, manipulating, righteous, strong, tense, traditional, rule-maker."

The Matriarchal Stereotype — "I am a soft, process-oriented, nurturing, facilitating, tolerant, stable, relaxed, merciful and forgiving person."

The Bandwagoner — "If we all want to do it, it's got to be all right and natural to do it. I find no need to question the power of consensus."

The Child of God — "The forces which govern my existence are beyond my comprehension. My role on earth is to keep myself receptive to love and to the supernatural."

The Taoist — "I believe in the necessity of achieving a symbiotic relationship with nature by seeking harmony, balance, contrast and order in all things so that I can fulfill my needs in the most direct way."

The Revolutionist — "Change is the primary law of life. I must get behind change and push and never resist its presence."

The Counter-Activist — "The dire consequences of what others propose must be constantly monitored. I can keep the world honest and on a natural course by resisting all unplanned change and by taking corrective measures to balance those changes already in operation."

The Subverter — "Traditions and institutions are in need of constant renewal. My task is to get them to behave more naturally, systematically and accountably."

The Institutionalist — "Traditions cannot always be explained, but they must be good to have endured. Therefore, I will follow them unquestioningly and do my part to keep them alive."

The Teacher-Humanist — "My purpose is to help others select ways to achieve their own purposes and potentials. From that work I, too, will learn."

The Teacher-Scientist — "My purpose is to illuminate the dark corners of life."

The Teacher-Egoist — "My purpose is to communicate my knowledge to others so they may see the world as I see it."

The Hedonist — "Life is short and should be enjoyed to the fullest. The ultimate joy of sensory satisfaction must be extracted from all experience."

The Hero Worshipper — "I choose to believe exactly the same things as "X" and to pattern my life after X's behavior."

The Loser — "Every situation contains the potential for crisis, and every crisis is a potential danger. I therefore feel I must sacrifice myself to my purposes, knowing that since I cannot win, I may at least be able to hold back the tide for a while."

The Winner — "I insure the success of my purposes by conscious involvement in their achievement."

The Chicken — "What I do is bound to turn out wrong and be chastized by society. Therefore, I'd better do as little as possible and hide what little I do from the critical eyes of others."

The Dramatist — "There are no small concerns in life. Everything is an important event and should be noted as the epic it is (especially those things which I personally chance to experience)."

The Child of Nature — "The greatest evil in life is to abuse Nature. The best way of life is to have an ongoing love affair with Nature, to enjoy a long and satisfying courtship, and to eventually lie down together in harmony."

The Moralist — "Prudence, justice, temperance, courage, faith, hope and charity are the guiding rules by which I live."

The Superman — "Nature presents a challenge to me. My ultimate purpose is to conquer and subdue its forces. Man is destined to supervise the universe; I work toward that day."

The Apollonian — "Reason and intellect supercede emotion and sensory response. I assertively work to grow, to mature, and finally when it is time I will be ready to die."

The Dionysian — "Impulse and feeling supercede fact and logic. I sensually respond to the romance, poetry and play of the life process."

The Manipulator — "People are so gullible; some of them actually get pleasure out of helping others. Most of them are too weak to complain when being used by others. The best thing I can do for these weaklings is to direct them according to my own good and strong purposes."

The Goal-Oriented — "Let's get on with it. I can't wait until we're finished . . . or until we get there . . . or until I'm graduated . . . or until I'm older . . . or until I'm married . . . or until . . ."

The Alive and Well — "Today is the first day of the rest of my life, and it is to be enjoyed as if it were my last. I take things as they come and savor them all as important components of a total existence."

The Critic — "Most of what we experience is in need of improvement. It's my task to point this out to society."

The Inventor — "I wonder what would happen if I took this thing apart and tried to put it back together another way. I wonder what would happen if I joined this thing to that other thing. I wonder . . ."

Question: Do you find yourself playing more than one of these roles right now? If so, it is normal to have those different 'selves' active at the same time. Yet when it comes down to a final judgment, you could probably characterize yourself as some one or combination of the roles presented. If you do not find yourself here, we hope you will take time to try to write that part as you now envision it to exist. Give it a title and a basic statement of belief. (Yes, this is still another opportunity to encapsulate your values and beliefs.)

Remember that titles, concepts and role translations are very personal things, and that two people may see an otherwise identical behavior pattern in entirely different ways. After trying out the previous listings to see how they fit your own abilities and/or interests, take a break and let the experience sink in for a while. Muse back over some of the fantasies you may have had while trying out something totally alien to your experience. Incubate.

 SESSION TWO

Writing scripts for the dramas of our real dreams is an important task; it should be approached with a sound balance of humor and seriousness and with both freedom and caution. In short one-way, closed-minded thinking is probably the greatest enemy to the planning of a full, natural life.

But designing the script of our lives need not be a search for "the greatest story ever told," nor must it require superior foresight or writing ability.

For the most part, life dramas are composed of interconnected vignettes instead of grand pre-ordained epics. In these fast-changing times, not everyone can plan for five or six years ahead. It's far more common and natural to think in terms of weeks or months. To do otherwise is to ignore the potential impact of facts which come with daily change. (That's where institutions often get into trouble with their long-range "unchangeable" plans.) Beyond those few probabilities which we can clearly assign to the near future lie only the possibilities for very general planning images: the farther into the future we plan, the more vague the image must be.

Still there is great value in having an eye to the distant future as well as having specific plans for the weeks and months ahead. Only in that way can we judge the collective meaning of the parts as they unfold and are acted out. Also, survival quite often depends on a long-range view. Financial security and physical health in old age are usually strongly dependent on plans enacted in the prime of life. Formal education normally requires a commitment for years in advance.

Following our earlier session which merely dealt with browsing through some of the many options available to life script writers, we will now attempt to summarize that experience and use it to give form to those personal concepts revealed all along the journey through VALUES TECH. On with the show! What will be the actual story and play of your life as you might write it for yourself? What approach will you take to plan far ahead into a somewhat vague and non-specific future? What criteria will you establish to work out your plans for the immediate and incremental steps which will lead you into and through that future?

How do you envision your role . . . as the star of the piece, as a supporting member of the cast or merely as one of the extras who will fill your stage? Which settings will you choose? How will you choose to be dressed? What will you select to be doing? Who will you choose to be working alongside you?

Now is your chance to consolidate all you have learned in the many workshops, laboratory exercises and lectures at VALUES TECH, for in writing your life script, you will once again be involved in the process of giving form to your intentions and dreams. As you enter this decision-making process, we again remind you to relax in the security and knowledge that no problem is so complex that it cannot be subdivided into manageable parts by following the UNIVERSAL LIFE PROCESS.

Exercise

The procedure for this session is as follows:

1. Review your notes and thoughts from the previous session.
2. Set up a master criteria list of factors which must be satisfied when you make your decisions in the course of designing your play script.
3. Organize your notes and favorite criteria into patterns or interrelated groups. You might want to pull together several motivations, roles, settings, etc., into a relationship of greater harmony, contrast and order.
4. Write an outline of the "play." Use your master criteria list to determine which costumes, which sets, which languages, etc. will probably tend to reinforce your motivations and which will probably work against them.
5. Write at least three alternative outlines of a short or long-range life script within the next hour. Force yourself to produce results within the alloted time.
6. Select a favorite or combine them to produce a script you could be happy playing.
7. Write the outline for the entire play, and describe or draw the costumes and sets. (Later on you might try using scrap cardboard and paper to actually build the sets in order to get a better picture of what they will look like in three-dimensional terms.)

Here are two sample outlines from last year's Life Style Review. The first was written by a California student who now lives in Alaska and works for the Forest Service while she also works in her sparetime to build her own farm and cabin.

Title:

Mother Nature and the Midwife

Characters:

Me, the midwife (age 23), wearing both handmade and "city made" clothes

A forest ranger and his wife (ages 30, 28) in government uniform and city clothes as neighbors and friends

The friendly trading post operator (age 50), wearing work clothes

An Indian tribe (all ages), wearing handmade clothes and skins

Many animals and birds

Setting:
Edge of the wilderness; various deciduous and evergreen trees; snow in winter, cool lakes in summer, green and rich all year; in the Sierras or Canadian woods; perhaps Colorado, Wyoming, South Dakota or Washington. My own cabin in a small clearing next to a creek. The nearest neighbors are at least a mile away. Clean, slear skies, quiet, slow moving, healthy, brilliant sunrises and rainbow sunsets, the smell of pine, wild flowers and bread baking in my own oven. The simple life.

Props: A large dog (German shepherd) and all the paraphernalia for natural, near-independent living. Stone fireplace, dulcimer, cast-iron stove, old pickup truck.

Plot:
I'm a midwife and work occasionally with a regional Indian tribe or local pioneers. I spend most of my time on personal survival: planting, cultivating, working at sewing and weaving, cooking. My life is lonely, but sweet. I have my dog and some meaningful work to do. The big problems are fairly easy to comprehend and cope with. There's little deception in this simple life because so few people are involved. I'm a kind of child of nature, and my neighbor, the ranger, checks on me to see if I'm safe every other day. I love my life. It contains everything I need.

The second example was by a student interested in the world of business and community He was just promoted to assistant manager of the 3M Special Products Division.

Title:

The Happy Tinkerer

Characters:
A crowd scene (thousands of indifferent people moving in all directions, dressed as "people of the city." The rarely speak and then mostly to themselves.)

The Tinkerer (me): part of the crowd but special in that I almost never change directions as they do. We all dress pretty much alike.

My Wife: pleasant, intelligent, average, but special in that she cares little for the crowd's opinion.

Mr. & Mrs. Friend: our neighbors; involved with their own interests and a lot like us.

The Scene: My laboratory workshop; containing my tools and projects; good light, pleasant working conditions (pretty much on my own), lots of available experts to help out in a jam; experimental stuff all around me but the place is not too crowded; there is plenty of room and resources to try things I've always wanted to try.

Our home: soft, warm, private, quiet, a garden, a pool, good music, a dog, probably no children to compete for our attention.

Our neighborhood: aloof, quiet private.

Our town: small, suburban, impersonal, unassuming; some local characters; not very progressive.

Plot: I do what pleases me most, and I am tolerant and respectful of others. My friends smile and chat with me occasionally, but we rarely get serious about what one another does. I stay put (unlike the crowd around me), spending most of my time either in my shop at work or in my home, working mostly on my projects. My wife spends most of her time at home. Occasionally, we walk around town or drive to the city together for a private night amid the crowd. Life is not a big thing; it is just a quiet, private working existence without hassles."

If you get stuck in making up your own script the following list of HELPFUL HINTS may prove useful:

1. Select two of the favored "motivations" from the previous lists and connect them into one combined statement of philosophy. Use that statement as your "concept" of definition of life, and make all the rest of your decisions according to its premises.

2. Select one or two desirable "roles" in life, and write a plot, etc., to fit those characters.

3. Choose a favorite "environmental setting" and tailor everything else to that place.

4. Chose two roles, one setting and three beliefs, and write a harmonizing plot around the combination of limitations.

5. Envision your self in a favorite "costume," and enjoy a fantasy about all the rest which "goes along" with it.

Here's an additional Lifestyle Review classic game for those who finish the major exercise early or who need a break from heavy thinking and writing. It's called: "WHAT'S MY LIFE?"
1. Take a sheet of 8½" x 11" paper, and cut it lengthwise into three strips.
2. Fold each strip upward from the bottom in alternating fan-like back and front folds until it has been divided into 5 sections with only the top showing.
3. Keep one of the folded strips and give the other two to friends.
4. Have each friend draw a "speech balloon" in the top section (facing up), and have them write one of your favorite "values statements" in it...something they think you believe very strongly. Write one yourself also.
5. Pass the strips around so that everyone gets a strip containing someone else's version of your beliefs.
6. Each person then draws a head and shoulders in the next folded section of the strip. Have everyone try to match their drawing to the words above it.
7. Pass the strips around 3 more times until everyone has tried to match (a) a drawing of chests, arms, and hands to the heads; (b) torsos and hips to the chests, arms, hands, and tools; and (c) legs and shoes to the torsos and hips.

In the end, the three of you will have produced three different composite cartoons conforming to three different views of three different values statements pertaining to you. Retrieve your personal statements and see how your friends envision a person who would say, think or believe such things. The true value, of course, comes with a discussion about why each of you thought your particular drawings enhanced and elaborated on what came before them on the strip.

the Final Week REVIEW

REMODELLING: A FRESH START

As you approach commencement, you may still not have any long range and specific ultimate end in view; however, you should be prepared to go on and on within the life process of growth and development. If you have participated in these lessons and exercises you have traveled through dark unknowns which are hopefully now somewhat brighter. And you have revealed many of the previously hidden selves within you. You may now observe that your feet are slightly "higher off the ground" (as the Zen philosopher, D.T. Suzuki, is reported to have said).

Again and again you have attempted to clarify your values and concepts, always striving to get closer to the truth or essence of yourselves. You may have sought the ultimate but have only discovered the parts; mere clues to the spiritual whole, and never the whole itself. And to confound matters even more, you may have watched those clues change before your eyes as they continually respond to new information. You have undoubtedly found yourself to be not one but many selves, composites of many sub-personalities; and you should have learned to see that you are, in fact, your own common denominators; the hero or heroine of your own life. Words and friends have been your medium of travel, and the many value-revealing and self-finding techniques have been your guides on the journey.

Now you begin a final week of formal study, while knowing that the study of life continues on an informal basis thereafter. During this week, you should focus all you have learned thus far regarding your plans for moving forward into your own ever-expanding individual and collective futures.

How To Avoid Getting In Your Own Way

The principal subject of education is change, that irresistible constant we have all come to respect. But notice that we tend to include the concept of change in our plans indirectly. For the most part we tend to resist change; expecting the worst. We seem to be caught in the middle, not knowing whether to give in and fatalistically enjoy the inevitability or to stand firm and yet still be pushed against our wills. Planning implies change—throwing out much that we have paid dearly to learn over the years. It is a process which requires maturity and decision-making skills.

Coming to school, reading a book, practicing theory in an

experimental lab are all evidence of the willingness to change. (Undoubtedly our foremost reason for coming to school was to learn or to alter behavior from what it once was to what it might yet become.) If measurable learning has occurred since entering VALUES TECH, it can be noted by observing those things that we now do differently from before.

Changes are rarely revolutionary. It is much more common for changes to occur in little, evolutionary, almost unnoticeable ways. Then one day we wake up to a world where everything seems totally different from before, not because everything changed overnight, but instead because bit by bit it developed and grew. Perhaps we dress differently or eat different foods. We behave in different ways. We may be more or less satisfied than before, depending upon whether or not our needs have been resolved.

Yes, self-fulfillment requires a plan, but not a plan to change from what we are into someone totally different. Rather it requires a tactic of becoming steadily more like ourselves, better able to deal with our own special limits, potentials and unique characteristics.

Some examples might better explain just how simple the task of self-enhancement can be. Suppose, for instance, that during self-examination we revealed a "wanderlust" tendency as a distinct personality trait. Our immediate question might be: "How can we further enhance and satisfy that wanderlust characteristic?" Many potential answers could follow: "We can develop a circle of friends all around the country (or world) in order to make it more friendly and comfortable to jump around." "We can find a job which helps us to move around: work for the airlines or a travel bureau, be an international salesperson, join the military service." "We can steer clear of long-range commitments which might tie us down." Any one of those answers would enrich our enjoyment of being more like ourselves by satisfying our special needs.

Another example is to note that a physical characteristic such as red hair or blue eyes can be enhanced very easily through proper understanding and selection of color. For instance harmonizing tints and shades of analogous or complementary colors in clothing, cosmetics, wall paint, room upholstery, automobile interiors, lighting, etc., can make blue eyes seem much bluer and red hair much redder. But the simplest enhancement is also the most natural: Keeping our hair, eyes, skin, clothing and behavior fresh and clear or clean; keeping them open to view and easy to see; "allowing" them to be appreciated is the simplest enhancement of all.

Earlier, during your first days at VALUES TECH while coping with the Entrance Exams, you began a "Vade Mecum." In it you recorded all you could find about the many selves within you. By deriving connections and patterns from the disconnected information gathered, many of you even constructed models of your separate selves. Hopefully, through the course of your studies, those journals and models have now become the priceless companions we intended them to be at the outset. And participants who invested time and energy along the way now have a better knowledge of the interdependent changing selves within them and are more aware of their personal needs, limitations, behavior and potentials.

Before we begin our final set of exercises in self-enhancement, let's reexamine the "model" of yourselves as it currently exists by following this procedure:

first, organize all the "self" information gathered throughout the entire curriculum into sets or groups of similar or closely-related items;

second, determine patterns and predominances by noting repetitions, linkages or relationships;

third, identify your resources, energies, powers, assets;

fourth, identify constraints from within yourselves and your environment (forces, limitations);

fifth, identify directions, goals, intentions, aims;

sixth, identify conflicts and paradoxes.

This may take some time and persistence but when you have finished, you should have an up-to-date record of all you currently know about yourselves:

>your personalities
>your heritage, background, ancestry, upbringing, education
>your knowledge
>your attitudes
>the tangible and intangible things you control
>your behavior
>a "guess-timate" of your remaining lifespan
>your hierarchy of needs
>your dreams or goals

And you should also have a better understanding of the conflicts between your goals and your limitations. Once that "model" of your existing selves is organized, you should be well on your way to a state of enhanced reality.

This final task, therefore, is to establish and implement a plan: a practical scheme for achieving a renewed, enhanced, self-directed you. A seventh step will be added to the six which comprised your self-assessment up to now, a final planning step which provides directions for making the most out of what you've got and plan to get.

To assist you in planning ways to become more like yourself and to make the most of what you've got, we offer the following twenty-three techniques (which may be varied, combined or tailored to meet your individual needs). Try them all on for size. Have fun. You have everything to gain.

TWENTY-THREE SELF ENHANCEMENT METHODS EXERCISES

PINNOCHIO (All strung up?)

Once you stop thinking of yourself as a victim manipulated by others or by fate and start thinking of all the terrific possibilities of self-control and self-direction, you will stop being a "puppet" and can start being the "puppeteer" or guiding spirit behind your many selves. As puppeteer, you might visualize yourself as the kindly Gepetto, the evil Svengali or the jovial

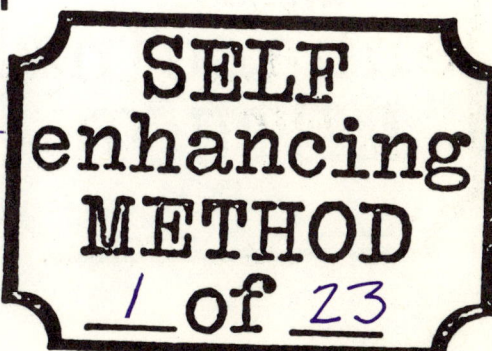

Buffalo Bob. You will then have determined how you have chosen to express yourself; as the clumsy but adventurous Pinnochio, the sweet but anxiety-ridden Trilby or the carefree comic Howdy-Doody, etc. As you pull the strings, so your part will be played.

AN EVENING AT HOME (Glad you could drop in!)

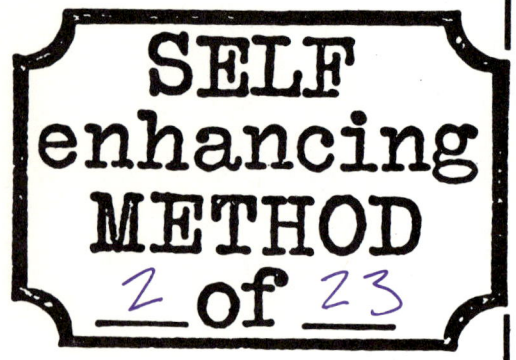

By imagining that the many selves within you are a family which lives in the house called "you," it might be pleasant to spend an evening "at home" with those intimate companions, getting to know them better, listening to their complaints and satisfactions, trying to decide ways to help one another in the days to follow. You might begin the evening by making it "comfortable" for your physical family (a warm bath, clean hair, perhaps some cream, oils or perfume, a pleasant drink, etc., etc.) and "at ease" for your psychological family (removing as many fears and anxieties as possible, giving in to the situation, closing out distractions, etc.).

TALK TO THE ANIMALS (Feeling extra-sensitive?)

Idealizing ourselves means taking a positive stance. When negatives are ignored, they wither away. For instance, if you found that one of your predominant selves was a highly sensitive person who got its feelings hurt at the drop of a hat, a positive response would seek ways to put that sensitivity to work. You could do things like learning to "talk" to the animals. You could become more conscious or aware of relationships or points of view not typically noticed as in biology or astrology or cooking, etc. Make it easy for your senses to function. Search out the exotic textures, tastes, odors, light-color-form combinations. Help others to sense what you sense. Turn your sensitivity into increased energy for yourself.

HARMONY, CONTRAST, BALANCE, UNITY AND ORDER
 (Try it. You'll like it!)

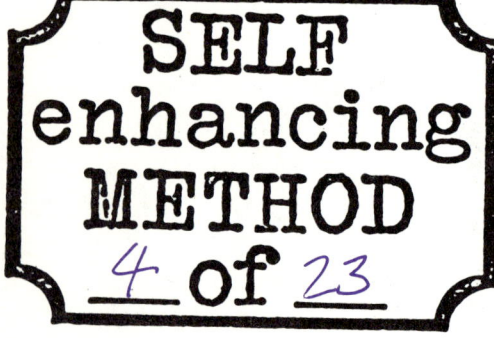

The natural laws which govern your existence can become conscious guides to expressing your natural selves in the simplest ways possible. It is natural self-management to keep your self components in tune by enhancing the similarities between them in order to provide "family" resemblance, by enhancing their differences to generate life, by encouraging their equilibrium to keep you from the unpleasantness or high dues associated with extremes or conflicts and to reinforce their overall togetherness to provide direction and purpose within a recognizable <u>organizational</u> framework. Ignorance allows a state of natural bliss. But once we stop to learn about our behavior as it relates to nature, it takes planning to be "naturally" yourself.

ADAPTING TO CHANGE (Feeling a bit older today?)

Another nature-based technique is to harmonize (get in tune; vibrate) with change. If you consciously realize that your body is undergoing change and organic aging every minute, you will be better able to see that everything else is also undergoing growth and transition. And if you can become sympathetic and empathetic to this basic flow, you can cheerfully accept life as a fact containing both gains and losses, both ups and downs, and perhaps come closer to being the satisfied ruler of your own kingdom. Swing with age; don't try to remain forever young or act too much older than you are. Stretch your fabric to its limit, but don't let it rip.

SELF enhancing METHOD 5 of 23

SENSORY TOOL KIT (Turn on your receivers!)

The five senses give you information from within your own self system as well as from their translations of the outside environment. Getting to know your senses better can help you to improve what you have or step-up your conscious sensory intake and thereby enhance your sensitivity. If you begin to think of your senses as tools, you can call on them at will to scan areas you intend to study.

SELF enhancing METHOD 6 of 23

Your sense of Sight - gives overall clues to what is there in terms of form, color, shape, mass, texture, movement and other symbolic aspects of reality, including meanings of words and other images in print and other media.

Your sense of Hearing - provides additional clues to position, distance, material qualities, operations, etc.

Your sense of Smell - provides both animal and intellectual clues to reality.

Your sense of Touch - provides additional clues to the physical reality.

Your sense of Taste - provides more overall clues to reality; i.e., chemistry, physics, biological components.

SELF enhancing METHOD 7 of 23

DATA BANK (Don't forget what'sis name!)

Every conscious, subconscious, and (as some believe) unconscious experience you ever had is stored in the memory portion of your brain. It's all there, if only you know how to retrieve it. You can learn how to store information so that it is easily retrievable by using the following conscious techniques:

A. Become more intentionally observant. Keep your five senses turned on by consciously using them to scan your environment.

B. Become concerned with more attributes and aspects of people and things.

C. Find interrelationships between the elements you sense, so that as they are stored in your memory they are also filed as parts of bigger systems and thus have less chance of getting lost in the shuffle.

Basic Rule: Never file anything without connecting it to something else in a relationship so you can retrieve it when it is needed. The more consistently you use a "code" to make connections between the new things you encounter and the things already on file the easier it is to recall experiences.

MOTTO TIME (What's your line?)

SELF enhancing METHOD 8 of 23

Once you have identified your dominant personalities, propensities and abilities, it is easier to direct and order them. But some people reject a unification of their aims within some overall direction statement because they fear that to do so would close the door to other experiences. They want to experience all of their potentials equally without any one part of themselves being thought of as more or less important than another.

This is a valid approach, but it also tends to produce mediocre "generalities" instead of higher-level "specialties." Whatever your choice, the act of clarifying direction is tantamount to self-improvement--getting closer to what you believe and can become. An entire value system can be summarized in just a few words as in a motto. Often while reading a book, a statement which seems to sum up our own beliefs will stick in our minds. Or we may experience this when listening to a lecture, a sermon or while watching TV or a film. By finding a few mottoes to live by of your very own, even though they may have originated with someone else, you can set yourself up for improvement. Just make sure that the mottoes you choose are not over your head and can be enacted with reasonable effort. Some typical examples are: "By helping others I help myself." "By helping myself, I learn to help others." "It's everyone for himself in this dog-eat-dog world."

BITS AND PIECES (Where do I begin?)

Just as there are many separate but interrelated pieces that go together to make you what you are, so you can enhance your entire self by improving those pieces one at a time. It makes little difference where you begin (unless certain limits, dependencies or priorities exist to help decide the point of beginning).

You can start in little ways and work toward larger improvements. For instance, by improving your handwriting you can get closer to having that skill symbolize your chosen values. By altering the way you arrange your hair or by choosing your clothes differently, you may be able to enhance your physical appearance. A changed diet could yield all sorts of beneficial effects on stamina, health, comfort and behavior if it were designed with your particular physical and psychological needs in mind. Improved physical fitness through Aerobic exercise of heart and muscles is a basic way to begin a self-improvement plan. Just start somewhere, and keep going.

MORE BETTER (Making a good thing better)

Certain things reinforce us, and other things diminish us. Identifying reinforcements is the positive task of life. The other things are of little importance unless they get in our way by diverting our time and energy to other tasks. It would seem that distinguishing between reinforcers and diminishers would be a simple matter, but it's not, because reinforcers often hide behind apparent unpleasantness, such as work, and diminishers are often disguised as pleasurable experiences which nevertheless contain disastrous consequences, such as overeating and obesity.

Here is a "positive" technique whereby you can accentuate the positives and eliminate the negatives. As usual, the first thing you do is make a list of all the things you like or dislike about a particular trait. Then, after each like and dislike, list all the ways you can think of either to encourage it or get rid of it. The resulting ways become guides for enhancing your best qualities. Once you know what they are, you can consciously work them into your existing time schedule.

ST. IGNATIUS (Out, damned spot!)

Anyone who has ever been on a Catholic religious retreat should be able to tell you about the book entitled, THE SPIRITUAL EXERCISES OF ST. IGNATIUS, for in it they discovered that centuries ago this Christian leader worked out a basic plan for clarifying and eliminating negative behavior (sin) so that there would be more opportunity to concentrate on an individual's "redeeming" qualities. One of the classic exercises of St. Ignatius goes something like this:

A. In the morning when you wake up, select a personal defect you would like to eliminate during the day. Become aware of that defect by keeping it in your consciousness all day.

B. After lunch, mark down the number of times you fell into this particular defect and ask God for help in reducing the number (examine the naturalness of what you are doing).

C. Repeat this process after dinner.

D. Continue the exercise for as many days as it takes to reduce the defect to insignificance, unworthy of your attention.

HONEST ABE (Are you a self-actualized person?)

In his famous book, MOTIVATION AND PERSONALITY, Abraham Maslow outlined what have become the standard guidelines for becoming self-actualized. (He later referred to the process as one of "following your own star.") These Maslow self-improvement suggestions may help you as they have helped others:

Find humor in the human condition...not just in gags or jokes.

Love others for their "being," not for what they can do for you.

Develop "clear eyes." Ask the obvious questions, ones which get to the point and don't beat about the bush.

Realize that the miracles of life are repetitive. Enjoy nature. Different sunsets happen every evening. Seek out new views of the real, not new realities.

Try to consciously realize and enjoy your experiences.

Be comfortable in your own "home" (body).

Be spontaneous; unguarded. Drop your audience awareness.

Try to love things so much that you are willing to allow them to be themselves without your manipulation.

Refer to your own "inner Supreme Court" for judgments.

Trust yourself to be casually great instead of having to show off and prove your greatness.

CANCER CLUB (What's the secret clawshake?)

People who are interested in astrology find great quantities of information about their behavior and about how to relate to the behavior of others. Don't be put off by the non-scientific basis of astrological readings. The results are often as clear and trustworthy as many of the more accepted psychological personality inventories. Following this technique will lead you to get together with others interested in astrology and to make friendships with one or more persons of your own astrological sign. Perhaps you could form a club and give the club a name. A Cancer Club, for instance, might be named THE SILVER MOONS or THE CRABS. The purposes of the club would be to find out more about yourselves and also to find ways in which to further enjoy being what you are.

SWAP MEET (What'll you trade me for three bad habits?)

If you've ever been to a Flea Market or Swap Meet, you've undoubtedly had some thoughts about the relative values of things. Perhaps someone offered to sell you a scarf for 25¢, and you remembered the same scarf cost $5 when you bought one for your mother just five years ago. You wonder what the seller plans to buy with the 25¢. Will it be better than that fine scarf? The trade-off doesn't seem reasonable until you realize the seller no longer wants or feels the need for a scarf and instead wants to cast it off. (The bigger question is whether or not you need to take it on, despite its current low cost or former value.)

Using this line of thought, try taking your un-wanted values to an imaginary Swap Meet to see what you might get for them. In your imagina-tion, someone may be able to give you something in exchange which will be far more useful to you than your no-longer-used beliefs.

Begin by going through the drawers, closets and

hidden corners of the attic (of your mind) and throughout your house (body) to collect all those things you wish to unload: things like clothes that no longer enhance your body; books and records that no longer increase your perception; furnishings which no longer fill your needs; junk food which produces excess weight which holds you back; robot-like TV watching which steals your time and your planning potential; etc. Then see what replacements you can find to meet the needs of your new consciousness. (Another way of looking at this is to consider the effort as a Moving Sale; you're moving on to richer, greener pastures and must leave some old, unwanted things behind.)

MUTATIONS (Has anyone seen Igor?)

SciFi stories and movies are replete with "mad scientists" and their unsuccesful or monstrous mutational experiments. Trying to build a superior creature, they fall short of their goal and are left with a misshapen horror. Without stretching too hard, it should be easy to see a parallel between such stories and our own self-improvement project, because we are also put together from bits and pieces, and we also strive like Dr. Frankenstein to make something better of what we have. The moral of the story is classic: When you tamper with nature and go too far to manipulate people, all hell breaks loose. Work only to improve yourself, not others. And don't hope for a magic machine or a fiendish injection or potion to change you into a totally different superior being overnight. You can only become a superior version of what you already are...and that will take time.

Here is another mind-stretching and dream-planning technique. Spend ten minutes to an hour or so in private. Imagine yourself in your "laboratory" working on this project. There you are, bits and pieces all over the place, awaiting the loving, careful, revitalizing synthesis of your benevolent scientific efforts. How will you reconstruct and remodel your components? How will you improve what already exists?

FAT FARM (Europe on $5 a day)

A new breed of dude ranches dedicated to renewed health and self-improvement is increasing in popularity throughout the world. Some of them are for the renewal of tired executives; some are for relaxation and psychological renewal after some traumatic life experience; some are for "fatties" to lose weight. Users affectionately refer to them as "fat farms". Their programs typically include relaxation, yoga, dieting, self-centering, better nutrition, imagination games, physical therapy, good food and rest--all the ingredients for a healthier, more relaxed "you".

You might consider spending your next weekend or vacation at one of these self-improvement establishments. Magazines carry ads for dozens of them. Some are even long distances away if you really want a change from the old familiar environments and experiment with what you might become. An alternative and less expensive way to do this would be to turn your own home or apartment into an imaginary health spa for the weekend by utilizing your bathtub, sun deck, kitchen, bed, etc., as substitutes for the special hot tubs, whirlpool baths, herbal baths, sun rooms, diet-conscious menus, massage rooms, at the real ranches.

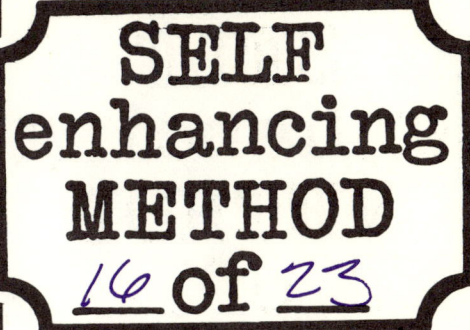

RITES OF PASSAGE (Recipe for a new you!)

In RITES OF PASSAGE, author Arnold Van Gennep stresses three distinct levels of growing up: SEPARATION - TRANSITION - INCORPORATION: Breaking away from old patterns...entering into a confused, yet absorbent intermediate phase...and working out a set of new patterns. By adding a few stages more from the VALUES TECH Universal Life Process, your continued-growth program might look like this:

A. Declaration of intent to change
   (decide you really want to improve and set up your intended goal and rewards)

B. Preparation for change
   (get everything you will need to start the journey)

C. Definition of the desired change
   (discover what specific problems or goals are involved and in what order of importance)

D. Ideas for making desired change
   (familiarize yourself with alternate ways to implement the changes)

E. Selecting ideas for change
   (compare your alternates with your concepts and criteria of definition)

F. Implementing change
   (Use your selected alternative to help you:
   1. "SEPARATE" from the old
   2. "TRANSITION" between old and new
   3. "INCORPORATE" selves into new patterns

G. Evaluate the change by comparing results with intentions

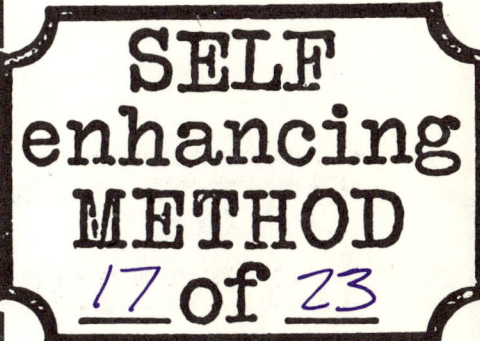

SELF enhancing METHOD 18 of 23

NEW HEROES (Follow Me!)

We seek models to guide us for each new step in our development. Whether those models are merely the people next door or famous and popular statesmen, athletes, musicians, theatrical personalities, teachers or gurus makes no difference. In these models, we see the qualities we want to attain, so we watch them and their behavior. We listen to their words to discover what and how they think; we observe their clothing; etc. Then we try out similar things for ourselves. The theory is that if we take on the images of what we aspire to become, there will be at least a "tendency" to facilitate those changes in our personality.

Go ahead; try it. Focus your attention on a new hero. Allow the old one (if any) to take a back seat for awhile. (You don't have to throw off the old ones completely. After all, they helped you get where you now are. But you will need to pay closer attention to the new ones for awhile.) Who will the new models be? How do they represent what you want to idealize in yourself? How do they go about doing what you'd like to do yourself? How can you overlook their shortcomings in order to learn from them?

Another way of using this method is to view it as a process of disidentification with what exists and identification with what is proposed. In any event, it is simply a process of becoming the new you by no longer behaving as the old you.

SELF enhancing METHOD 19 of 23

HOW, NOT WHAT (Just a matter of orientation)

Anxiety is a typical companion to those who concentrate on what they have done or plan to do instead of how they plan to do it. "What" refers to things or events as products outside the context of doing. But "how" is a process word which precedes activity and behavior. For instance, if you want to improve your physical stamina by jogging, don't waste energy concentrating on "what" type things such as, "I ran 10 laps today". "I hurt my foot when I ran across the railroad track." "I saw four other joggers on the road today." Those things do nothing to improve your stamina. Instead, focus on the process of "how" you controlled your breathing and pace to reach your new 10-lap record; how you were inattentive to ground conditions when you injured your foot; how your running techniques compared with those of the other joggers; etc. Find out about the "hows", and you're on your way to improvement.

SELF enhancing METHOD 20 of 23

SUPERMAN & WONDER WOMAN (An unreal path to reality)

In working toward self-idealization, you may have formulated unrealistically god-like plans for your own perfectibility as a self-controlled, self-sufficient, totally wise, superior person (chuntzu, as the Japanese say). Still, the fantasy of thinking that we might leap tall buildings in a single bound and run faster than a speeding locomotive is harmless if it helps us reach the top of the mountain by shooting for the moon. Things which initially seem far-fetched are often quite possible

to achieve. As the saying goes, "Don't adjust your mind. The fault is in reality." The following format may help those who need to try overshooting their mark in order to hit it squarely in the center.
(It's just another way of looking at the VALUES TECH Universal Life Process.)

RELAXATION	(acceptance)	give in, take it easy
CONCENTRATION	(analysis)	focus on parts and interrelationships
IMAGINATION	(definition)	develop imagery of that which is to be achieved
SPECULATION	(ideation)	choose alternatives
DIFFERENTIATION	(idea-selection)	choose the best way to follow
IDENTIFICATION	(implement)	try to become the superior person
REALIZATION	(evaluate)	awaken yourself to reality

CIRCUS PERMIT (If you've got it, flaunt it!)

A simple, positive approach to self-improvement is to put what you've got out front, on-the-line. Let everyone see it. Flex your muscles; let your hair blow in the wind; fly your flags; put it all to work. Go ahead. Write your own ticket. (Just don't be overly assertive; that's a bore.)

Issue yourself a permit to begin working on the "glamorous" "attractive", "intriguing", "colorful", New, Improved You. Having such a permit helps you to realize that it's perfectly alright to have a circus parade of your very own. So follow through and design a poster which tells of the wonderful event. Include drawings or photos of the "star" of the show (that's you) with all the side-show attractions depicting "strange and wonderful" improvements to your physical and psychological selves (they are also you). Design the floats or circus wagons to depict the stages of change yet to come. If you're good at building models, you might even want to try your hand at some three-dimensional expressions of your intentions and concepts—an actual model of the parade or circus show.

WILL POWER (I can become what I dream of becoming!)

There is no better technique for reaching out to a more idealized state than the classic, low-dues use of the power of our mind. Will Power, often referred to as "the power of positive thinking" or Psycho-Cybernetics, is really nothing but a concerted effort to realize the self-improvement intentions inside of all of us...a personally instigated, self-improvement program based on a direct or indirect satisfaction of one or more human needs...the amateur self-hypnotist at work.

"Every day in every way I am becoming a more sensitive, socially responsive person."

"My body is in better condition with each hour that passes."

"My ability to see other points of view improves each time I meet someone new."

"Those people who return my smile are able to see the beauty inside my mind."

The secret of will power is relaxed self-credibility coupled with a focus on the positive as opposed to negative aspect. Persistence is also important to the achievement of most efforts involving a change in hard-earned "programming." But concentration on what you <u>will</u> do, instead of what you want to do, is the all-important point.

SUCCESS FORMULA? (Is there really such a thing as a failure?)

By collecting the several theories expressed thus far into one overall formulation of philosophy, we derive the following equation:

$$\frac{\text{Goals/Objectives} + \text{Self (Selves)}}{\text{Resources Outside Self}} = \text{Potential for Success}$$

which translates into prose in this way: The things we wish to achieve in life and the means by which we intend to achieve them (G/O) plus our own Self (Selves) with our particular skills and knowledge are either further enhanced or diminished by the supports and constraints of external resources to yield our total potential for success in reaching goals. To increase our potentials, we must either increase the enhancements of our selves and the resources outside ourselves or decrease the diminishers. Which will it be for you?

WORDS to the WISE

A. Values, beliefs and intentions are very personal things and should be respected as such. Don't try to make value judgments for someone else, and make sure your plans don't rely too heavily on others. The more you depend on someone else, the more you become like that person. Since your dependencies greatly influence your future, your intentions and dependencies should be in harmony to avoid conflict.

B. Our little traits and quirks are neither good nor bad in themselves; they are simply what we do. Some of them are not even our own, but merely borrowed to test and to try on for a while.

C. The self-improvement process often puts you out of phase with others and their concepts of self, and it disturbs the images they project onto you. The success of your own efforts depends to a large degree on how well you can integrate your personal improvements with the needs of others. As William Butler Yeats wrote "In dreams begins responsibility."

D. Negative thinking blocks self-enhancement. It produces fears (mostly imaginary) of not being able to persist or of not having the necessary resources, energies or support, or worst of all that the outcome may not be worth all the effort. Positive thinking, on the other hand, produces abundant opportunities for development and experiment. It is assertive and dynamic; it can both facilitate the task and be flexible in its expectations. A vivid imagination can also figure into positive viewpoints, but such an imagination will concentrate on successes and realized intentions, not on losses and blocked efforts.

E. Some people fall into the trap of thinking that the satisfaction of continually defeating others in competition brings self-enhancement along with it. In truth the act of climbing over others to realize your own whims can be a destructive and inhuman one with very high personal and social dues levied at the end.

F. Staying within your physical limits is not only an ultimate necessity, but also practical planning advice. You can only enhance what you've got, not transform yourself. A trout can become "fillet of Colorado mountain trout, gently sauteed in breadcrumbs to a delicate golden orange crispness" on a restaurant menu only if it was indeed a trout in the first place.

G. Analysis does not imply improvement. Just because you take yourself apart to see what makes you tick does not mean that you are any improved for it. But improvements can occur by efforts to enhance the facts about yourself as you have discovered them.

H. Being yourself means taking on and generating more of the attributes, thoughts and behaviors which fulfill your personal needs within the limits of your potential. In a sense, it is a process of enhancing and stretching your limits.

I. The ideal or perfect you is a false dream, a fantasy, an unrealizable dream. The words are theoretical; not practical or possible. But what is possible is improvement and refinement. It is possible to work toward the realizable dream of an "idealized" you; the you with renewed and enhanced positive qualities; the you that you and others like the best. No one is as beautiful, handsome, intelligent, skillful, etc., as he or she wants to be. We can only do our best and make the most of what we have. We can stretch and we can expand and we can enjoy the challenge of existence. That is the most anyone can realistically dream of doing.

· the end ·
LIFE STYLE REVIEW

THE 25th ANNUAL COMMENCEMENT EXERCISES OF THE POLYTECHNIC SCHOOL OF VALUES

Pendleton Gymnasium; Caps and Gowns, semi-formal

Convocation Address:
 "Deciding for Yourself"
 State Representative, E. Leroy Thorne [D. 12th District]

Farewell:
 President T. B. Brandywine

Diplomas:
 President Brandywine and school administrators [guests are requested to refrain from applause until all diplomas have been issued]

Convocation:
"Deciding for Yourself (While Standing in a Crowd of Decision Makers)"
Rep. E. Leroy Thorne, Class of '58

"Mr. President, school officers, faculty, guests, graduates, I am honored to have this opportunity to share my dreams with such a well-prepared group of graduates; you who stand on the threshold of achieving many dreams of your own. However, I wonder if our positions should not be reversed for, as a politician, it is my function to listen to your needs and your dreams and help make them come true. Because in that capacity I have come to realize that just as it is a right for each of us to have beliefs of our own, it is also our privilege in this Democratic Republic to make those beliefs publicly known in the hope that eventually they will be approved and implemented by society at large.

"You who are now graduating from the Polytechnic School of Values have been trained to think for yourselves. Open-mindedness is your stock in trade. Your ability to make decisions related to purposes of your own choosing makes you unique in the world today. However, this uniqueness may prove a social stumbling block to the realization of dreams which require mass approval. And undoubtedly because of your new creative abilities you will also face opposition because of the atypical things you will propose to do.

"Now that you have new knowledge, skills and beliefs, you are anxious to begin. I can sense it in this auditorium today. But even though our world truly needs solutions to many situations in need of improvement, I beseech you to proceed cautiously and with care. For you must be responsibly accountable not only to yourselves and to your society but to the environment which affects all societies.

"I wish you well in your endeavors, but I also bring you a lesson of experience which may provide you with some peace when the earned privilege of being yourself seems far away and almost impossible to assert. It has served me well in the world of politics. My advice is this:

"Communication is our first line of survival in mass society, so don't

despair when your personal interests conflict with the personal interests of others. Realize that your right to have dreams is only sanctioned by vesting the same rights in others. There are many decisions to be made daily by everyone in our ever-crowding world, and your own decisions will have a better chance of realization if they are adaptable and compatible with the needs of others. When you see your humane and socially-redeeming plans opposed by exploitative financial interests, don't give up. Instead, retreat just long enough to translate your purposes into the language of money so that 'the other side' can at least 'hear' your position.

"If you strive to be totally different, you will soon become an outcast. And if you strive to be exactly like others, you may lose your own identity. The consciously natural way is (and I find this true in my political endeavors) to seek a balance between the two: Be yourself while also being compatible with others in your social milieu.

"With your education, your potential value to society is high, for you have the ability to establish criteria and priorities in the face of confusion. You can identify and interrelate the component parts of both simple and complex problematic situations and detect and expose the true values which lie beneath the surface of things. And you can direct those who would wander irresponsibly from the course of survival.

"When the going gets really tough, I'd like you to consider this set of rules which has eased moments of great discomfort in my own career. I call them my DECISION-MAKER'S SIMPLIFICATION CHECKLIST.

"1. Are my criteria or definitions too general to give me adequate guidance? Must I be more specific?

2. Are there internal conflicts in my criteria? Are the things I want contradictory?

3. Do I have too few criteria by which to judge my alternatives?

4. Do I have too many criteria so that I am confused by all the demands?

5. Are my criteria and/or the alternatives to be decided upon unrelated or incompatible?

6. Are my criteria and alternatives too much alike and thus do they defy comparison?

7. Are my alternatives so similar that they provide no real choice?

8. Do I have too many alternatives to realistically deal with them? Should they grouped, classified and decided on in batches?

9. Do I have too few alternatives from which to choose?

10. Are my ideas too general to decide on them?

11. Do I need to muster more maturity to be able to leave the rest behind as I make my decision for one of the alternatives?

12. Can I find a way to combine all the viable alternatives into one decision choice without losing the identity of those being joined?

"When my behavior is systematically planned, there is no further struggle with not knowing where to go from here. I am always amazed when others express confusion about not knowing what to do next. What a waste of life to spend the majority of it bouncing back and forth between personal indecision or the decisions and purposes of others when for only a short investment in time and energy we can consciously determine our own course while still considering the interests of others.

"I often look back to my own days as a VALUES TECH student: thinking how important these lessons have been to my career; calculating the many ways in which the Universal Life Process has entered my personal life; remembering how often I succeed in achieving my intentions by being conscious of what I was doing and by seeing how those dreams fit into the larger social-environmental spectrum.

"VALUES TECH has provided me with the tools I needed to clarify my life's purposes. It gave me the power to see I could achieve any dream that I could realistically set for myself as a goal. And now you have those same tools to use as you go forth to become the physical expressions of your own dreams. I cheer you on and again wish you well in the wonderful years which lie ahead. May all our dreams and constructive efforts be compatible with nature and the dreams of others.

"Thank you."

"Farewell"

"Graduation from VALUES TECH marks but another point in the process of a lifetime of learning. Although our curriculum is now finished, it remains for each of you to continue by following a curriculum of your own design. Other teachers and new lessons will appear as you need them. The source of your learning is within you. You are your own best counsel; the truths you seek are already a part of you, waiting to be expressed via the people, places and events of your future experience. As you discover the value relationship between those parts of your experience and your purposes in life your learning will be enhanced. For learning is no more than discovering the truth for yourselves. Experience merely provides the potential for discovery. It is not an education in itself.

"Your heads must spin with the apparent possibility of all that is left to learn. Yet I know that your experiences here will allow you to take all of those new responsibilities in due course with a coolness and an awareness of planning coupled with the enjoyment of being accountable for all that you strive to accomplish.

"Making better decisions takes both knowledge and skill as you now well know. Will power is not enough. That is but the motivation in process . . . your basic "acceptance plan." The knowledge required includes the many techniques and methods for comparing what you need or what you plan to accomplish with the resources and potential alternatives available to you. The skill comes with practice in making those decisions. Your training at VALUES TECH should have helped you to discover for yourself that evaluative thinking and an awareness of your own values and beliefs is the all-important key to the doorway to better decisions. You should now realize that a consciousness of your own values can improve your entire self-management program; that knowing more of what you are and what you plan to accomplish will help you to be ever more evaluative in the future.

"Your needs are now open to you and can be fulfilled in a far more satisfying way. You no longer need to be the victim of your own lack of awareness.

It has been my pleasure to facilitate your search for a more inquiring mind. But your quest is not yet over (just as my role as facilitator continues on to the new students now entering our enrollment office). You have much more of your life processes to live, minute by minute as far as you can stretch them out. And although you now know how boring it would be to know exactly how your lives might turn out in the end, you also know how comfortable and yet exciting it is to be in control of the parts of your lives as they unravel before you.

"Good luck! May you all live with the satisfaction that your futures can truly be what you want them to become; the fullfillment of your own desires within a framework of responsibility."

President Brandywine

the
POLYTECHNIC SCHOOL of VALUES

BE IT KNOWN THAT THE TRUSTEES OF THE POLYTECHNIC SCHOOL OF VALUES ON RECOMMENDATION OF THE FACULTY HAVE CONFERRED UPON

_____

A HIGHER DEGREE OF SELF-AWARENESS

WITH ALL RIGHTS AND PRIVILEGES THEREUNTO APPERTAINING

Given under the Seal of the School this date _____

Matthew B. Brandywinett
President of the School

Elizabeth D. Evans
Associate Dean

Faculty

Faculty

the LIBRARY

Adams, James. *Conceptual Blockbusting*
  The Portable Stanford Series, Palo Alto, CA., 1974.

Alderfer, C.P. *An Empirical Test of a New Theory of Human Needs.*
  Organizational Behavior and Human Performance, 4(2), 142-174. 1969.

Anderson, W. *Politics and the New Humanism.*
  Goodyear, Pacific Palisades, CA., 1973.

Anthony, Daniel S. *Is Graphology Valid?*, p.343ff.
  Reading in Psychology Today, CRM Books, Del Mar, CA., 1967.

Assagioli, Roberto. *Psychosynthesis.*
  A Viking Compass Book (C323), N.Y., 1965.

Barden, G. & McShane, P. *Towards Self-Meaning.*
  Herder & Herder, N.Y., 1969.

Barrett, Donald N. (ED). *Values in America.*
  Univ. of Notre Dame Press, Notre Dame, Ind., 1961.

Beardsley, Monroe C. *Thinking Straight.*
  Prentice-Hall, Englewood Cliffs, N.J., 1956-1965.

Berne, Eric. *Transactional Analysis in Psychotherapy.*
  Grove Press, N.Y., 1961.

Blofeld, John. (Tr. & Ed.) *I Ching, The Book of Change.*
  Dutton, N.Y., 1965.

Bloom, B.S. (Et Al). *Handbook on Formative and Summative Evaluation of Student Learning.*
  McGraw-Hill, N.Y., 1971.

Bluhm, Wm. T. *Ideologies and Attitudes.*
  Prentice-Hall, Inc. Englewood Cliffs, N.J., 1974.

Brautigan, Richard. *Trout Fishing in America; a novel.*
  City Lights Books, San Francisco, 1967.

Brautigan, Richard. *The Pill Versus the Springhill Mine Disaster.*
  City Lights Books, San Francisco, 1968.

Brim, Orville G., Glass, David C., Lavin, David E. & Goodman, Norman.
  Personality and Decision Processes.
  Stanford Univ. Press., Palo Alto, CA., 1962.

Bradley, Margaret E. *Be Yourself.*
  Robt. B. Luce Inc., Washington, D.C., 1972.

Bronowski, J. *The Identity of Man.* (Revised)
  Doubleday (Amer. Mus. of Nat. Hist.), Garden City, N.J., 1971.

Buber, Martin. *The Way of Man.*
  Wilcox & Follett, Chicago, 1951.

Campbell, Joseph. *Myths to Live By.*
  Bantam, N.Y., 1973.

Cannel, Ward & Macklin, June.
  The Human Nature Industry.
  Anchor (Doubleday), Garden City, N.Y., 1974.

Chase, Stuart. *Goals for America.*
  The Twentieth Century Fund, N.Y., 1942.

Churchman, C.W. (Et Al).
  Introduction to Operations Research.
  Wiley, N.Y., 1957.

Churchman, C.W. *Prediction and Optional Decision.*
  Prentice-Hall, N.Y., 1964.

Clark, Charles H. *Brainstorming.*
  Doubleday, N.Y., 1958.

Copi, Irving M. *Introduction to Logic.*
  Macmillan, N.Y., 1972.

Crowell, F.R. *Values in Human Society.*
  P.Sargent, Boston, 1970.

Crystal, John C. & Bolles, Richard N.
  *Where Do I Go From Here With My Life?:
  A Workbook for Career-Seekers
  and Career Changers.*
  Seabury Press, N.Y., 1974.

Dalkey, N.C. *Delphi.* (p. 3704)
  The Rand Corporation, Oct., 1967.

Darden, Bill R. & Lucas, Wm H.
  The Decision-Making Game.
  Appleton-Century-Crofts, N.Y., 1969.

David, H.A. *The Method of Paired Comparisons.*
  Chas. Griffin, London, 1963.

Dewey, John. *Theory of Valuation.*
  Univ. of Chicago Press, Chicago, 1939 (1944).

Edel, A. *The Evaluation of Ideals.*
  Journal of Philos., XLII, 11, 1945.

Edwards, A. *Techniques of Attitude Construction*.
Appleton-Century-Crofts, Ind., 1957.

Faraday, Ann. *Dream Power*.
Berkeley Medallion (D2294), N.Y., 1973.

Feibleman, James K. *Ontology*.
Greenwood Press, N.Y., 1968.

Fendrock, John T. *Goals in Conflict*.
Amer. Management Assoc., N.Y., 1969.

Festinger, Leon. *Conflict, Decision and Dissonance*.
Stanford Univ. Press, Palo Alto, CA., 1964.

Findley, J.N. *Values and Intentions*.
Macmillan, N.Y., 1961.

The Editors of Fortune. *Consumerism*.
Perennial (p-286) (Harper & Row), N.Y., 1972.

Freud, Sigmund. *The Interpretation of Dreams*.
(Trans. by James Strachey).
Basic Books, N.Y., 1955.

Fromm, Erich. *The Forgotten Language:
An Introduction to the Understanding of Dreams,
Fairy Tales & Myths*.
Holt, Rinehart & Winston, N.Y., 1970.

Gardner, John. *Self-Renewal*.
Harper & Row, N.Y., 1963.

Good, Victor & Elizabeth. *Ontology: A Study in
Metaphysical Calculus*.
Carlton Press, N.Y., 1966.

Goodman, Linda. *Sun Signs*.
Bantam (T 6719), N.Y., 1974.

Graves, Clare W. *Levels of Existence:
An Open System of Values*.
Journal of Humanistic Psych., Fall, 1970,
Vol. 10, No. 2, Pp. 13-154.

Gregg, Richard B. *What's It All About and What Am I?*
Grossman Publishers, N.Y., 1968.

Hall, Jay. *Decisions: [Group Problem-Solving]*.
University Books, N.Y., 1968.

Harre, R. *The Philosophies of Science:
An Introductory Survey*.
Oxford Univ. Press, London, N.Y., Oxford, 1972.

Harris, C.W. (Ed.) *Problems in Measuring Change*.
Univ. of Wisc. Press, Madison, Wisc., 1963.

Helmer, Olaf. *Analysis of the Future: The Delphi Method*.
(p 3558), The Rand Corporation, March 1967.

Hoffer, Eric. *The Ordeal of Change*.
Harper & Row, N.Y., 1963.

Hofstadter, A. *Principles of Philosophy
A Simplified Summary & Instant Reference*.
Data-Guide Quick Chart, Data-Guide, Inc.,
Flushing, N.Y., 1967.

Horney, Karen. *Our Inner Conflicts*.
Wm. Norton & Co., N.Y.., 1945.

Howard, Jane. *Please Touch*.
McGraw-Hill, N.Y., 1970.

Hughes, Ann J. & Grawiog, Dennis E.
*Linear Programming: An Emphasis on
Decision Making*.
Addison-Wesley Publishing Co., Menlo Park, CA., 1973.

Illich, Ivan. *Tools for Conviviality*.
Perennial (p 308), Harper & Row, N.Y., 1973.

Jackins, Harvey. *The Human Side of Human Beings:
The Theory of Re-Evaluation Counselling*.
Rational Island Publ., Seattle, Wash., 1965.

James, Muriel & Jongeward, Dorothy. *Born to Win:
Transactional Analysis with Gestalt Experiments*.
Addison-Wesley, Menlo Park, CA., 1971.

Janis, Irving L. *Group Think*.
Psych. Today, Nov. 71, P. 43 ff.

Jenkins, I. *The Process of Evaluation*.
Review of Metaphysics, Vol. 6., 1952.

Jourard, Sidney M. *Self-Disclosure: An Experimental
Analysis of the Transparent Self*.
John Wiley & Sons, N.Y., 1971.

Kaufmann, A. *The Science of Decision-Making*.
McGraw-Hill, N.Y., 1968.

Keen, Sam and Fox, A.V. *Telling Your Story:
A Guide to Who You Are and Who You Can Be*.
Signet, N.Y., 1973.

Kirschenbaum, H., Napier, R., & Simon, S. B.
*Wad-Ja-Get? The Grading Game in American
Education*.
Hart Publ. Co., N.Y., 1971.

Krishna Murti, Jiddu. *Freedom from the Known*.
Harper and Row, N.Y., 1969.

Koberg, Don & Bagnall, Jim. *The Universal Traveler:
A Soft Systems Guide to: Creativity, Problem
Solving and the Process of Reaching Goals*.
Wm. Kaufmann, Inc., Los Altos, CA., 1973.

Lakein, Alan. *How to Get Control of Your Time and
Your Life*.
Signet (W 5931), N.Y., 1973.

_____, *Toward the One*.
Lama Foundation, Box 444, San Cristobal,
New Mexico, 1973.

Land, Geo. T. Lock. *Grow or Die*.
Random House, N.Y., 1973.

Lau, James. *Behavior in Organizations*.
Richard D. Irwin, Inc., Homewood, Ill., 1975.

Lewis, C.S. *The Abolition of Man*.
Macmillan, N.Y., (1947), 1973.

Lindheim, Roslyn. *On Human Needs*.
(Paper presented before the Amer. Assoc. of the
Advancement of Science, Feb. 25, 1974, S.F.)
Journal of Arch. Educ., Vol XXVI, No. 2, 3.

Luscher, Max. *The Luscher Color Test*.
(Trans. by Ian Scott)
Pocket Books, N.Y., 1971.

Mager, Robert. *Goal Analysis*.
    Fearon, Belmont, CA., 1972.

Mailer, Norman, *Advertisements for Myself*.
    Putnam, N.Y., 1959.

Malott, Richard. (Et Al). *Contingency Management in Education, or I've Got Blisters on my Soul and other Equally Exciting Places*.
    Behaviordelia, Inc., P.O. Box 1044, Kalamazoo, Mich., 49005.

Maslow, A.H. *Motivation and Personality*.
    Harper, N.Y., 1954.

Maslow, A. (Ed.) *New Knowledge in Human Values*.
    Harper, N.Y., 1959.

Maslow, A. *A Theory of Metamotivation: The Biological Rooting of the Value-Life*.
    Journ. of Humanistic Psych., (1967) 2:109-110.

May, Rollo. *Man's Search for Himself*.
    Delta (Dell), N.Y., 1953.

McMahon, Frank B. Jr. *Psychological Testing — A Smoke Screen Against Logic*.
    Readings in Psych. Today, CRM Books, Del Mar, CA., 1969.

Miles, Lawrence D. *Techniques of Value Analysis and Engineering, 2nd Edition*.
    McGraw-Hill, N.Y., 1972.

Moreland, Frank. *Dialectic Methods in Forecasting*.
    The Futurist, Aug., 1971.

Morris, C. *Varieties of Human Value*.
    Univ. of Chicago Press, Chicago, Ill., 1956.

Moustakas, Clark E. *The Self; Exploration in Personal Growth*.
    Harper, N.Y., 1956.

Mueller, Conrad G. *Sensory Psychology*.
    Foundations of Modern Psych. Series, Prentice-Hall, Englewood Cliffs, N.J., 1965.

Muir, John. *The Velvet Monkey Wrench*.
    John Muir Publ., Box 613, Santa Fe, N.M., 1973.

Mukerjee, R. *The Dimensions of Values: A Unified Theory*.
    Geo. Allen & Unwin Ltd., London, 1964.

Mumford, Lewis. *Values for Survival*.
    Harcourt-Brace & Co., N.Y., 1946.

Musgrave, Gerald L. & Elster, Richard S.
Management by Objectives and Goal Setting.
    Bibliography No. 577, Grad. Fac. of Admin. Sc. Naval Postgrad. Sch., Monterey, CA., 1974.

O'Neill, George & Nena. *Shifting Gears: Finding Security in a Changing World*.
    M. Evans, N.Y., 1974.

Osgood, C.E., Suci, G.J. & Tannenbaum, P.H.
The Measurement of Meaning.
    Univ. of Ill. Press, Urbana, Ill., 1957.

Otto, Herbert A. *Guide to Developing Your Potential*.
    Wilshire Book Co., N. Hollywood, CA., 1973.

Otto, Herbert A. *Ways of Growth*.
    Grossman, N.Y., 1968.

Parnes, Sidney and Harding, Harold.
A Sourcebook for Creative Think.
    Scribners, N.Y., 1962.

Perin, Constance. *With Man in Mind*.
    MIT Press, Cambridge, Mass., 1970.

Perls, Frederick. *Gestalt Therapy Verbatim*.
    Bantam, N.Y., 1972.

Perry, R.B. *Realms of Value*.
    Harvard Univ. Press, Cambridge, Mass., 1954.

Plutchik, Robert. *The Emotions*.
    Random House, N.Y., 1962.

Polanyi, Michael. *Personal Knowledge — Towards a Post-Critical Philosophy*.
    Harper & Row, N.Y., 1958.

Popham, W.J. & Baker, Eva L.
Establishing Instructional Goals.
    Prentice-Hall, Englewood Cliffs, N.J., 1970.

Raths, Louis E., Hermin, Merrill, & Simon, Sidney B.
Values and Teaching.
    C.E.Merrill, Columbus, OH., 1966.

Raw, Isaias; Bromley, Anita; Vournakis, John; Pariser, Ray et al. *What People Eat*.
    William Kaufmann, Inc. Los Altos, CA. 1975.

Rein, Irving J. Rudy's Red Wagon:
Communication Strategies in Contemporary Society.
    Scott, Forsman & Co., Glenview, Ill., 1972.

Richards, Howard. *Life on a Small Planet: A Philosophy of Value*.
    Philosophical Library, N.Y., 1966.

Riesman, David. (Collab. with Revel Denney & Nathan Glazer). *The Lonely Crowd*.
    Yale Univ. Press, New Haven, Conn., 1950.

Rockefeller Foundation. *Values in Contemporary Society*.
    Working Paper, March, 1974.

Rogers, Carl R. *On Becoming a Person*.
    Houghton Mifflin Co., Boston, 1961.

Rokeach, Milton. *The Nature of Human Values*.
    The Free Press, N.Y., 1973.

Rokeach, Milton. *The Open and Closed Mind*.
    Basic Books, N.Y., 1960.

Royce, Joseph R. *The Encapsulated Man*.
    D. Van Nostrand, Princeton, N.J., 1964.

Ruby, Lionel. *The Art of Making Sense: A Guide to Logical Thinking*.
    J.B.Lippincott Co., Phila., 1954-1968.

Runes, Dagobert D. *The Art of Thinking*.
    Wisdom (Philosophical) Library, N.Y., 1961.

Russell, Bertrand. *The Conquest of Happiness.*
　Avon (G-1095), N.Y., 1930.

Rutstein, David D., M.D. *Lifetime Health Record.*
　Harvard, Cambridge, Mass., 1973.

Saint-Germain, Comte C de. *The Practice of Palmistry.*
　Sam Weiser, N.Y., 1970.

Samson, Richard. *The Mind Builder: A Self-Teaching
　Guide to Creative Thinking and Analysis.*
　E.P. Dutton & Co., N.Y., 1965.

Samuels, Mike, M.D. & Bennett, Hal.
The Well Body Book.
　Random House, N.Y., 1973.

Satir, Virginia. *People Making.*
　Science & Behavior Books, Palo Alto, CA, 1972.

Scheerer, M. *Problem-Solving.*
　Scientific American, Vol. 208, (1963), Pp. 118-128.

Schoonmaker, Alan N. *A Students' Survival Manual or
　How To Get An Education Despite It All.*
　Harper & Row, N.Y., 1971.

Schutz, William C. *Joy.*
　Grove Press, N.Y., 1967.

Sears, Robert R. & Feldman, S.S. (Editors).
The Seven Ages of Man.
　William Kaufmann, Inc., Los Altos, CA., 1973.

Sheldon, Wm. H. (Collab. with C.W. Dupertius &
　E. McDermott). *Atlas of Men.*
　Harper & Bros., N.Y., 1954.

Sheldon, Wm. H. (Collab. with Stevens, S.S. &
　Tucker, W.B.) *The Varieties of Human Physique.*
　Harper & Bros., N.Y., 1940.

Sheldon, Wm. H. (Collab. with Stevens, S.S.)
The Varieties of Temperament.
　Harper & Bros., N.Y., 1942.

Shoemaker, Sydney. *Self-Knowledge and Self-Identity.*
　Cornell Univ. Press, Ithaca, N.Y., 1963.

Shostrum, Everett L. *Man, the Manipulator.*
　Bantam N3409, N.Y., 1968.

Simon, Herbert A. *Models of Man.*
　Wiley, N.Y., 1957.

Simon, Sidney B. *Values Clarification: A Handbook.*
　Hart, N.Y., 1972.

Skinner, B.F. *Beyond Freedom and Dignity.*
　Alfred P. Knopf, N.Y., 1971.

Solzhenitsyn, Aleksandr. *Truth and the World's Values.*
　From Nobel Prize for Literature Acceptance Speech.
　Excerpts, The Wall Street Journal, Sept. 6, 1972.

Stanford University. *A Stanford Education.*
　Stanford Univ. Press, Palo Alto, CA., 1973.

Stonehouse, Dr. Bernard. *The Way Your Body Works.*
　Crown, N.Y., 1974.

Stringer, Lorene A. *A Sense of Self.*
　Temple Univ. Press, Phila., 1971.

Taylor, G. C. *The "Who Am I?"
　Techniques in Psychotherapy.*
　Psychosynthesis Research Foundation,
　40 East 49th St., N.Y., 1968.

Taylor, Gordon R. *The Conditions of Happiness.*
　Houghton-Mifflin, N.Y., 1950.

Taylor, Gordon R. *Rethink.*
　E.F.Dutton, N.Y., 1973.

Thurstone, Louis L. *Multiple-Factor Analysis.*
　Univ. of Chicago Press, Chicago, 1947.

Toffler, Alvin A. *Future Shock.*
　Bantam, N.Y., 1971.

Toffler, Alvin A. *Learning For Tomorrow.*
　Random House, N.Y., 1974.

U.S. Environmental Protection Agency.
*The Quality of Life Concept A Potential New Tool
　For Decision-Makers.*
　Office of Research & Monitoring, Envir. Studies Div.
　Washington, 1973.

U.S. President's Commission on Nat'l Goals.
Goals for Americans.
　Prentice-Hall, Englewood Cliffs, N.J., 1960.

Vickers, Geoffrey, *Freedom in a Rocking Boat.*
　Pelican (A 1205), Baltimore, 1971.

Watt, Bernice K. and Merrill, Annabel L.
Composition of Foods.
　Agriculture Handbook No. 8, USDA, Washington,
　D.C., 1963.
　Supt. of Documents, U.S. Govt. Printing Office,
　Wash., D.C. 20402.

Watts, Alan. *Does It Matter?*
　Vintage, N.Y., 1971.

Watts, Alan. *The Book; on the taboo against knowing
　who you are.*
　Pantheon, N.Y., 1966.

Weaver, Major Carl A, Jr. *Biorhythms:
　The Question of Ups and Downs.*
　U.S. Army Aviation Digest, Jan. 1974, P☐. 13-17.

Werkmeister, W.H. *Man and His Values.*
　Univ. of Nebr. Press, Lincoln, Nebr., 1967.

Whitehead, Alfred N. *Process and Reality.*
　Macmillan, N.Y., 1929.

Wilcox, Jarrod W. *A Method for Measuring
　Decision Assumptions.*
　MIT Press, Cambridge, Mass., 1972.

Wilson, John. *Thinking with Concepts.*
　Cambridge Univ. Press, London, 1963.

Wittmer, Joe & Myrick, Robert D. *Facilitative Teaching.*
　Goodyear Publishing Co., Pacific Pallisades,
　CA., 1974.

Wittrock, M.C. & Wiley, D. E. *The Evaluation of
　Instruction.*
　Holt, Rinehart & Winston, N.Y., 1970.

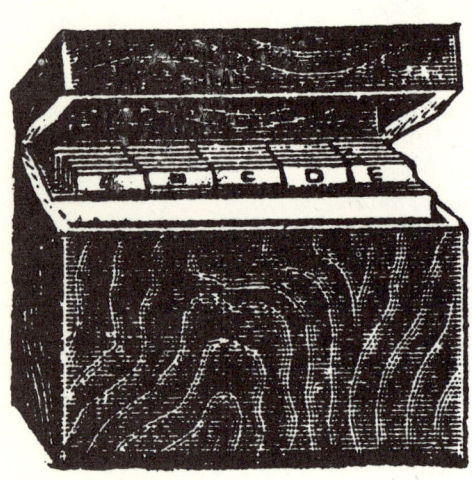

the School Secretary's File

Acceptance. . . 54,56,58,230
Accountability. 147
Acting. 35,38,195
Adjectives. 76
Advanced Level. 11
Adversity. 39,40-41
Advertising. 112ff
Aim. 7,135
Algorithm. 66
American Goals. . . .137-139
Ambivalence. 110
Analogy. 21,75
Analysis. 38,54,136
Anger. 37,38
Anxiety. 50,173,222
Application. 3
Architect. 149
Argument. 109,153
Arrowhead. 82
Art. 56
Artifacts. 84
Assertive. 12
Assistance, Importance of...
. 155,169-170,176
Attitudes. 1
Automobile. 128
Awareness. 7,9,10
Balance. . . .12,101,106,120
173,196,214
Bargains. 183-186
Behavior. . . .1,36,40,60,72
75,90,116,195
Belief. 10,178
Benefits. . .8,9,134,179-180
Biorhythm. 36
Bird-Dogging. 20
Body. 32
Budgeting Resources. . . 178
Brainstorming 24,172
By-Products. 171-172
Captions. 38,77
Cards. 42

Change. 3,9,19,134
181,211,215
Choice, Choosing. . .1,3,7,8
46,56,60,68,143,197
Christmas. 82
Classical. 8
Classification. 21-22
Classics. 78
Classroom. 8,9
Color. 38
Combinations. 62
Commitment. 14
Common Denominator. . . .211
Communication..112ff,149,227
Companion. 8,25
Comparative. 8
Comparing. 1,61-63
Competition. . . 103,126,160
Concentration. . .50,179-180
222,223
Concepts. 84
Conclusions. 18,19
Conflicts. . 77,99,103,105ff
120,173,228
Conscious,-ness. . .1,9,12
97,100,143,166
Consequences. . . .3,64,70
Consumer. 177
Contingency. . .14,158-159
173-176
Contrast. 106
Control. 3
Convenience. 129
Cooking. 124
Costume. 202
Creativity. . .10,56,147,165
Criteria,-ion. . . . 1,59,64
74-75,76,123,125,143,144
147-152,154,159,164,228
Cultural Needs. 90
Curriculum. . . .1,3,8,11,25
55,143,230

236

Death. 130
Deciding. 1
Decision. . . .3,7,11,12,56-57
      162-163,230
Decision-Making. . . .1,7,11
   56-59,66-67,68ff,228-229
Deductive Thinking. 20-21,33
Defer. 24,163
Definition. 54,75-76
Details. 19,82
Difference. 157,163
Differentiation. 223
Directions. 10
Discovering. 3,7.9,27
Diversion. 51
Dogmatic. 117
Dollar. 114,119ff
Drawing. . . 15,33,44,77,124
      170,174,210
Dreams. . . 3,7,8,10,15,36
      135,225
Dues. 1,8,9,177,196

Economics. 121-122
Ego. 29
Emotions. 33,51,68
Energy. . . .8,13,15,91,173
Enhancing. . . .9,190,212ff
Enrollment Form. 15
Environment, Physical.201-203
Error. 11
Ethics. 72,88
Evaluation. . .3,13,55,153ff
Evaluation Techniques. . . .
      13,157ff
Evaluation; Classifications
      155
Exam. 11,25
Expectation. . . . 13,178-179
Experience. . . .1,65,155,227
Experiment. 8
Extrinsic Values. . . . 156

Facilitator. 8,171,230
Family. 15,31,32
Famous Persons. 44
Fatigue. 51
Faust. 130
Fear. 27,50,51
Financial Statement. . .30-31
Flag. 140
Food. 34,127,150
Forces. . . 104,120,135,153
Formula. 224
Fortunes. 115-116
Frankenstein. 220
Friends. 30,42,219
Future. 9,63,77,85-86
      187,206
General Studies. 153ff

Goals. 9,10,135-137
      144-147,166,224
Good and Bad. . . 100-101,224
Grading. 13,14,164-168
Grouping. . . .23,60-61,63,66
Groups. 68,136
Growth. . . . 35,88,211,221
Guarantee. 86
Guidebook. 8
Habit,-ual. 56-57,173
Hamburger. 124-125
Harmony. 188-189,214
Health. . . . 90,91,118,136
Heroes. 222
Hidden Costs. 183-186
Histogram. 36-37,79
History. 76,78,81ff
Home. 32
Honesty. 76
Horoscope. 32
Humor. 40,111

Ice Cream. 60
Id. 29
Idealization. 190
Ideas. 54,56
Identification. 223
Identity. 191,228
Imagination. 3,50,197
      219,223,224
Imbalance. 51
Implementation. 55-56
Importance. 63
Incremental Evaluation. . . .
      166-171
Incubation. 20
Independence. 190
Individual. 8,9
Individuality. 78
Inductive Thinking. . . 19-20
      33,57
Instinctual Needs. 90
Intentions. 1,3,13,142
Interdependency. 7
Interlacing. 20
Intermediate Level. 11
Interrelation. . . . 23,188ff
Intrinsic Values. 156
Introductory Level. 11
Intuition. 66,118
Invitation. 3
Janus. 2
Journal. 25
Knowledge. 1,7
Laboratory Experiments. . . 1
Lakein, Alan. 16,109
Language. 3,45
Leader. 70,147-148
Learning. 23,166,169
Learning, barriers. 51

Legal Decisions. 67
Lewin, Kurt et al 69
Library. 8
Life. . . . 1,3,75-76,130,154
Life-Process. 7
Lifestyle. 148,194ff
Links. 188-190
Lists. 24,148,149
Logic. 20,23,66
Margins. 25
Marriage. . . . 144-145,177
Maslow, Abraham. . . 90,218
Matrix. 62,63,141
Meaning. 1
Measuring. 151
Memory. 79,216
Method,-s. . . 1,7,18,19,28ff
59ff,213ff
Mind-Control. 59
Mirror. 32,169
Mistakes. 17,21
Model. 47-48,99,120
131,159,222,223
Money. 16,43
Motivation. 113
Name 15,32,144
Nature; natural. . 3,26,51,67
88,91,98,119,181,189,205,214
Needs. . . 12,43,89ff,110,120
136,140,157,177,230
Newspaper. 39,40
Notebook. . .10,13,25,129,141
Nudity. 41
Numbers. 34

Objectives. . . . 144-147,169
177,224
Objectivity. 48,51
Observation. 7.48
Occupation. 15
Open-Mind. . . .18,28,98,99
134,165,191
Opinion. 59,70,162,169
Opportunity. 7
Options. 1,9,13
Osborn. Alex. 24
Osgood, Suci and Tannenbaum
64,77
Oxbow Incident. 69

Paper Dolls. 31
Participation. 8
Past. 9
Pattern. 8,12,20,47,82
173,188-189,213
Penny 124
Pepper, Stephen. 87,97
Perception. 18,118
Personality. 44-45
200-201,212

Philosophy. . . 44,47,75-76
78,100,111
Photograph. . . .15,31,79,129
Planning. 187ff,192
196,211,212
Population. 82-83
Potentials. 3,9,224
Power. 51,52
Pragmatic. 21
Preference. 59,62-63
Prayer. 142
Prerequisites. . .11,17,24,26
Pride. 9
Priorities. 141
Problem Solving. . . 10,42,58
Procedure. . 1,11-12,24,47,58
70,79,106-107,207,213
Process. . . . 10,12,21-22,25
54-55,58,70,82
84,120,154,166
Product. 12,25,82,84
Purpose. 10,12,13,47
75-76,154
Pyramid Matrix. 63
Quality. . 64,151-152,156,182
Quantity. . . .24,151-152,155
Questions, value of. . . . 75
Ranking. . .61,63,160-162,164
Realization. 223
Reasonable Thinking..51-52,56
Reasoning. 17,21-23
Record-Keeping. . 25,32,34,35
129,166-167,170-171,199
Reinforcement. . . 13,173,176
Relaxation. . . 28,50,132,223
Reliability. 67-68
Religion. 40,84
Responsibility. . 11,13,68,72
227,230
Responsive. 56-57
Risk. 15
Rock and Roll. 161
Role. .8,40,188,197ff,203-205
St. Ignatius. 218
Satisfaction. . . . 90-91,157
179,230
Science. 52,56
Secret Ballot. 70
Security. 67
Selecting. 1,46,55,60
Self. 3,26,211,224
Self-Control. . . . 3,7,25,89
174,194
Self-Evaluation. . .166-168
Self-Finding. . . . 26,29ff
Self-Fulfillment. . . .88,212
Self-Inventory. 27ff
Self-Love. 26
Self-Regulating. 8

Selfish. 27
Semantic Differential. .64,77
Seminar. 8
Senses. 215
Shakespeare. 35
Sin. 37,160
Skills. 1,33,46,154
Society. 3,82-84
Speculation. 223
Standards. 12,13,14
Strategy. 28
Student   8,27,134,229
Sub-Problems. 64
Subverting. 20
Success. 224
Sucker. 185
Sugar. 127
Sun. 128
Superego. 29
Supermarket. . . .127,128,196
Supplies. 10
Survival. 88,153,227
Swap Meet. 219-220
Symbolism. . . .114,116,140
System,-atic . . .16,20,56,57
                60,63,229
Teacher. 8,13,30,111
                141,171,204
Teaching. 20
Technique. 7
Telephone Book. 128
Television Rating. . .161-162
Ten Commandments. 37
Testing. 48
Theory. 7
Thinking. 17,155,204
Thinking Methods. . . . 18-22
Thinking Process. 22
Time. 9,16,35
Tips. . .18-19,28-29,50,67-68
          175,209-210,216
Tools. 7,10,17,47,55
            82,215,229
Transfixing. 20
Travel. 30
Tutors. 9
Twelve Angry Men. 68
Universal Life Process. .7,16
       54-55,131,153,221,229
Universal Traveler, The. . 10
Vade Mecum. 25,77,212
Values. 3,7,26,37,72ff
Values: Chain. 94-95
Values: Encyclopedia. . . 95
Values: Increasing. . .177ff
Values: Personal Values. . 1
Values: The Polytechnic School
  of Values. 1,7,54,227
Values, Pyramid. 94
Values: Qualifiers. . .95-96
Values Study: Subdivisions..
                    96-97
Values: Theories. . .120-121
Values: True Values. . . . 9
Van Gennep, Arnold. . . . 221
Weakness. 27
Weigh. 15,61,160-162
Will-Power. . . 174,223-224
Wishes. 39,179
Words to the Wise. . 50-52,59
          67,134-135,224-225
Workshops. 1,102ff
Writing. . . 28,33,38,39,41
              196,206-207
You. 7,15

A LETTER FROM THE OFFICE OF THE ALUMNI ASSOCIATION

Dear Alumnus:

The organization of graduates of the Polytechnic School of Values exists solely for the purpose of feedback. We have awarded our diplomas with the intent that the curriculum which it symbolizes is of high value and potentially beneficial for all life consumers. Our school's famous Universal Life Process of systematic problem solving provides each of you with the security of knowing that all energy spent in the process of evaluation is fully refundable and that the returns on all of your conscious decision-making efforts normally amount to far more than the investment.

If for any reason you are not completely satisfied with the lessons and experiments you have chosen here to improve yourself, the Alumni Association staff will reply to your complaints promptly with a full measure of understanding and concern.

If you are pleased with the return on your investment, we would also be grateful to receive your testimonial.

> Stafford Library
> Columbia College
> 10th and Rodgers
> Columbia, MO 65216

Don Koberg and Jim Bagnall, Chairpersons
Values Tech Alumni Assn.
c/o School of Architecture and Environmental Design
California Polytechnic State University
San Luis Obispo, CA 93407